Global Business Etiquette

GLOBAL BUSINESS ETIQUETTE

A Guide to International Communication and Customs

SECOND EDITION

Jeanette S. Martin and Lillian H. Chaney

 PRAEGER

AN IMPRINT OF ABC-CLIO, LLC
Santa Barbara, California • Denver, Colorado • Oxford, England

Library of Congress Cataloging-in-Publication Data

Martin, Jeanette S.
    Global business etiquette : a guide to international communication and customs / Jeanette S. Martin and Lillian H. Chaney. — 2nd ed.
        p. cm.
    Includes bibliographical references and index.
    ISBN 978–0–313–39717–2 (hard copy : alk. paper) — ISBN 978–0–313–39718–9 (ebook)
1. Business etiquette. 2. Intercultural communication. 3. Business communication. I. Chaney, Lillian H. II. Title.
HF5389.M375   2012
395.5′2—dc23   2011039312

ISBN: 978–0–313–39717–2
EISBN: 978–0–313–39718–9

16 15 14 13 12   1 2 3 4 5

This book is also available on the World Wide Web as an eBook.
Visit www.abc-clio.com for details.

Praeger
An Imprint of ABC-CLIO, LLC

ABC-CLIO, LLC
130 Cremona Drive, P.O. Box 1911
Santa Barbara, California 93116-1911

This book is printed on acid-free paper ∞

Manufactured in the United States of America

CONTENTS

PREFACE AND ACKNOWLEDGMENTS

Global business relationships are not always easy to establish or maintain. In addition to the usual issues with language and nonverbal communication, cultural differences in rules of proper behavior can create barriers to successful interactions with people of other cultures. During international encounters, knowing the correct thing to do or say in business and social situations is preferable to attempting to correct social blunders after they have been made.

Growing concern over the lack of good manners by people of the United States is evidenced by requests from companies that universities integrate civility and good manners into selected college courses, by increased sales of books on etiquette, and by corporate requests for in-house seminars on etiquette. In recent years, behavior at sports and political events, as well as behavior while driving on U.S. highways, has resulted in the conclusion by many that U.S. manners have become problematic. Two surveys conducted in 2010 point clearly to the fact that U.S. Americans are very aware of the lack of manners in their country.[1] This fact is of special concern to those who interact with people of other cultures because in many countries, good manners are essential to building and maintaining successful business relationships.

This second edition of *Global Business Etiquette* includes the addition of chapters on Etiquette for International Businesswomen and International Negotiation Etiquette. Other additions include three topics to the chapter on Gestures and Other Nonverbal Communicators as well as additional sidebars to chapters in the first edition. Country-specific information at the end of each chapter was updated, resulting in the replacement of the Netherlands by Brazil in the list of top 10 countries with which the United States conducts business. Also, the United States was added to the list of countries at the end of each chapter. Information from recent journal articles and books was incorporated to update information in the first edition.

We appreciate the support of our families and friends in preparing this second edition of *Global Business Etiquette*. We wish to thank Nicholas Philipson, who was helpful in publishing the first edition, and Brian Romer, our editor on this second edition.

Jeanette S. Martin and Lillian H. Chaney

INTRODUCTION

Successful interactions with people of other cultures involve knowledge of rules of global etiquette to avoid inadvertently offending them during intercultural encounters. With the increased globalization of business and the multiethnic composition of the U.S. workforce, such encounters are becoming more frequent. In addition, travel to other countries is on the rise resulting in more cross-cultural interactions.

Knowledge of global business etiquette is especially important to people of the United States because of the negative impressions people from other cultures have formed of U.S. Americans. In an article entitled "Overseas, We're Seen as Ugly Americans," Burris reported results of his research which found that in many countries U.S. Americans are viewed as arrogant, self-absorbed, unwilling to listen, exploiters, ignorant, and lacking an interest in other cultures. A former international marketing executive who was interviewed for the article expressed concern that too many U.S. travelers have little knowledge of the cultures they visit and, in fact, have little regard for the norms of the cultures they encounter. Becoming knowledgeable about other countries and how U.S. Americans are perceived abroad is becoming increasingly important because, as this marketing executive pointed out, "In this global world, we need all the friends we can get."[1]

Lack of knowledge of proper global business etiquette can be costly when U.S. executives host business executives from other countries or when U.S. Americans visit other countries as the following incidents demonstrate:

- A Chinese delegation of a potential business partner arrived at the U.S. offices and was not greeted in the lobby by a senior executive. The non-verbal message conveyed was that the Chinese visitors were not sufficiently important to warrant being greeted by a senior executive. This type of mistake, though unintentional, can delay or even destroy a deal.[2]

- A Silicon Valley company almost lost a business deal when a top executive of a French company arrived in California on a 7:30 p.m. flight and was met by a limo and driver sent by the U.S. firm; the driver took the Frenchman to his hotel. U.S. executives assumed their guest would want to relax after a long flight and planned to pick him up the next morning. The Frenchman was offended because no top official met him at the airport. In addition, he expected to be taken out to dinner since the French eat dinner late. This faux pas nearly cost the company the deal.[3]

- President Bush used an expletive when conversing with the British Prime Minister Tony Blair during a meeting in Germany in 2006. Since the summit was a formal occasion, many Europeans felt that President Bush's actions were demeaning.[4]

U.S. Americans should learn the etiquette of the countries they visit and with whom they conduct business. As Powell points out, "Manners and correct behavior are learned; we aren't born with them. What is polite in some cultures may be downright insulting in others."[5] Learning correct behavior in other countries is important to avoid personal and professional embarrassment as well as unintentionally offending people during international encounters.

Is there any such thing as international etiquette? Perhaps there is not. However, Leaptrott has identified some guidelines for universal etiquette that apply around the world. In the areas of greetings and introductions, she recommends shaking hands moderately, erring on the side of formality, and avoiding the use of given names unless invited to do so. Dining suggestions include waiting for the host to begin and reciprocating hospitality when possible. Recommendations in the areas of oral and nonverbal communication include the following: avoid telling jokes; avoid initiating discussions about politics, crime, religion, or personal topics; keep your hands out of your pockets; avoid touching others; gesture with your full hand only; keep your mouth closed when not speaking; keep both feet on the ground; and be punctual for business meetings (follow local customs for being prompt for social events). Additional suggestions include dressing conservatively; showing respect for the elderly; avoiding colors and negative connotations in certain countries; and avoiding gifts of roses, lilies, and chrysanthemums. In addition, gifts of flowers should be given in an odd number, except 13.[6]

The first edition of *Global Business Etiquette* covered the following topics: Travel Customs and Tips; Language, Greetings, Introductions, and Business Cards; Socializing; Gestures and Other Nonverbal Communicators; Dress and Appearance; Cultural Attitudes and Behaviors; Dining and Tipping Customs; Conversational Customs and Manners; and Oral and Written Customs and Etiquette. Based on feedback from reviewers and readers of the first edition, chapters on Etiquette for International Businesswomen and International Negotiation Etiquette were added to the second edition. Other additions included three topics (clothing and physical appearance, objects, and symbols) to the chapter on Gestures and Other Nonverbal Communicators as well as sidebars to existing chapters. In addition, country-specific information at the end of each chapter was updated; Brazil replaced the Netherlands in the list of the top 10 countries with which the U.S. currently trades. The United States was added to the list of countries at the end of each chapter to make comparisons between the United States and other countries easier. Information from new books and journal articles, as well as from revised editions of books cited in the first edition, has been incorporated into the second edition.

Take time to research proper etiquette of the country you plan to visit or the home country of the international visitor you are hosting; the time spent will be worth the effort and will pay dividends in the international business arena.[7] This second edition of *Global Business Etiquette* will provide much useful information in your quest to enlighten yourself about the customs, conduct, and manners of people in other countries. Armed with your knowledge of global business etiquette, you will then feel confident that your international encounters will be successful and that impressions you make on people from other cultures will be positive.

Chapter 1

TRAVEL CUSTOMS AND TIPS

Building global business relationships depends on the innate ability to learn about other cultures and proper training to help a person adjust once he or she is in another culture. Whether one is traveling for business or pleasure, new cultures are generally part of the process. Although there are many differences between cultures in the world, there are also similarities. The similarities do not get us into trouble, but the differences can destroy a business deal or a pleasure trip. Learning some facts and some of the patterns of other cultures, as well as various travel customs and tips, can help you be successful. Preparation, support, and training before venturing abroad can help you meet the challenges of an intercultural assignment or trip. Employees who work globally should be trained in technical knowledge, such as import and export laws of other countries, comparative management styles, and business protocol, etiquette, and ethics. Regardless of how much you learn about another country, always remember you are dealing with individuals who may or may not possess the aspects of the culture that you have learned. Stereotypes are as dangerous as ethnocentrism. We are all individuals, and when traveling abroad you must learn to handle every individual separately.

Posters in Heathrow advertising HSBC make a good point about cultural differences concerning how the grasshopper is viewed: "U.S.A.—Pest, China—Pet, and Northern Thailand—Appetizer." Even though taxonomists define a grasshopper as an Acrididae, culture determines how the insect will be perceived.[1]

Memorizing facts about a new culture is helpful; however, the real goal to cultural sensitivity is to be able to recognize and determine cultural differences, learn about those cultural differences, and respond appropriately in a new setting. To be culturally sensitive, one must monitor internal and external cues.[2] The more cultural and emotional intelligence individuals have, the easier it will be for them to acculturate and assimilate in a new culture and build relationships.

PREPARING FOR DEPARTURE

First you need a passport. If you do not have one, it can take from 8 to 12 weeks for the government to process a request in the United States. To obtain a passport, you will need proof of U.S. citizenship (certified birth certificate or naturalization certificate), proof of identity (driver's license, state or military ID, or student ID), and two passport photographs. Once you have a passport, make copies of it, place the copies in various pieces of luggage, and leave one with a person at home. If you lose your passport, it is much easier to have it replaced if you have a copy.

Visas are required to travel to many countries. To obtain a visa application, contact that country's embassy or consulate. You can find most of these by searching the country name on the Internet. Many times there is a fee, and a photo is required. Be sure to allow sufficient time for the processing of your request before your departure date, as it normally takes anywhere from two to eight weeks to obtain a visa.

Because most of the world is on the metric system, it is nice to know how you can convert distances from miles to kilometers. The conversion is done by multiplying the miles by 1.6 (10 miles × 1.6 = 16 kilometers), or convert kilometers to miles by multiplying the kilometers by 0.62 (10 kilometers × 0.62 = 6.2 miles). Similarly, converting Celsius temperature to Fahrenheit is done by multiplying the Celsius temperature by 1.8 and adding 32 (25°C × 1.8 = 45; 45 + 32 = 77°F). To convert a Fahrenheit temperature to Celsius, subtract 32 from the Fahrenheit temperature and divide the remainder by 1.8 (77°F − 32 = 45; 45 ÷ 1.8 = 25°C).

Some hints for packing and traveling are to start packing in advance, pack materials that do not wrinkle easily, use suitcases and garment bags with rollers, check baggage and weight restrictions with the airlines, consider the weather where you are traveling, remember voltage adapters for electrical hair dryers and shavers, and pack a portable iron for remote cities. Be sure to take a folding tote bag, comfortable shoes for the flight, earplugs, a toothbrush and toothpaste, reading material, a travel alarm, and an umbrella.[3]

Make and use a travel checklist, such as the following one; be sure to add anything to the list that is germane to your trip.

___ Passport and visas	___ Other lists for the house and work	___ Contact lists
___ Government-issued picture ID	___ ATM card	___ Hygiene products
___ Plane tickets	___ Medicines	___ Glasses or contacts
___ Lodging info	___ Credit cards	___ Alarm clock
___ Car rental info	___ Money	___ Electric current adapter
___ Insurance cards	___ Clothing	___ Raincoat
___ Business cards	___ Umbrella	___ Camera

Some things you can do to reduce jet lag are to exercise regularly before departure, get a good night's sleep prior to your flight, change your watch to the time at your destination when you board the plane, and start acting as if you are in the arrival time zone. Also, avoid alcoholic and caffeinated beverages, heavy meals, smoking, unnecessary medications, and drink plenty of water. Upon arrival, stay awake until it is time to go to bed in the destination country. If you are going to arrive at your destination in the morning, then taking a mild sedative to help you sleep on the plane will be helpful. Likewise, if you are going to arrive in the early evening, you will want to stay awake on the plane so you can go to sleep at your destination. See "Dressing for Travel" in Chapter 5 for appropriate travel attire suggestions.

When traveling by airplane, remember to practice airplane etiquette. Checking your manners with your baggage is not the way to have a pleasant flight. Cheapflights.com surveyed 2,000 travelers to find out what they consider the most offensive airplane etiquette infractions. As shown in the following survey results, the incessant talker topped the poll.

- Incessant talker: 23 percent
- Rapid recliner: 20 percent
- Armrest hog: 12 percent
- Carry-on champ—bashes bags against everyone: 12 percent
- Seat back grabber when getting up: 11 percent[4]

Next, you need to read about the new culture and be trained to respond appropriately in the new culture. Although some people do this instinctively, most of us need to have some training if we are to be successful.

If you are successful in your own culture, that success is not a guarantee that you will be successful in another culture.

CONSIDERING YOUR HEALTH

If you are near a modern city, most over-the-counter medical supplies can be purchased as they are in the United States. It is always a good idea to have a first-aid kit for emergencies, however. Some items to include in the kit include sleeping pills, aspirin, motion sickness medication, diarrhea and constipation medication, adhesive bandages, antiseptic, antibiotic cream, and medications for any condition you may have. It is a good idea to carry a short medical record with your passport that includes any medical conditions you have, your blood type, medications you take, allergic reactions to medications that you have, your doctor's information, your insurance information, and an emergency contact.[5]

If you are traveling to an area where medical care is not readily available, it is important to talk with a travel physician concerning immunizations you may need or, if you have special conditions, whether it is safe for you to travel to the location. A doctor's certificate stating the medications you take may be helpful when clearing customs; also carry medication in its original prescription bottle. In case a flight is delayed or you have to extend your trip, be sure to take extra medication, and always carry your medication with you in your carry-on luggage rather than in your checked luggage.[6]

Traveling in crowded airplanes, buses, and trains with recirculated air is conducive to getting sick; however, if you are well at the beginning of your flight and have taken precautions, hopefully you will stay well. Take a pillow for your back and neck, walk around the plane during the flight, and drink plenty of water to prevent dehydration. Be cautious of the water you drink when abroad; the safest thing to do is to drink bottled water from a sealed bottle.[7]

If you get sick, you need to realize that your health coverage may not make payments outside of the country, and Medicare does not make payments outside of the United States. If you travel outside of the United States on a regular basis, you may want to get medical insurance for travelers. International SOS Assistance provides emergency health-care assistance and may be reached at 800-523-8930.[8]

CHOOSING ACCOMMODATIONS

When traveling to other countries, do not take for granted that what you regard in the United States as first class will be the same abroad. Explain to the person making your reservations at the location exactly what you would like. For example, explain that you want a bathroom in your room that includes a Western-style toilet and shower, double bed, and access to the room via elevator. Any amenities that you are interested in should be checked out in advance to be sure the hotel or inn can accommodate you.[9]

Bathrooms can be a big concern for people. Many parts of the world have communal bathrooms, some of which are unisex. Then you have the toilets that are flat on the floor, that are simply a hole in the floor, or that you must straddle without a seat. If these differences are important to you, discuss them with the person making your reservations. Except for remote areas, you can usually find Western-style bathrooms if you check.

Many accommodations in Europe include certain meals with your room. If you have a continental breakfast, lunch, and dinner, it is considered *pension complete*; breakfast and one other meal is *demipension*; an American breakfast, lunch, and dinner is called the *American plan*; and *modified American plan* is breakfast only.[10]

Choosing hotel accommodations that offer concierge services can be particularly helpful. A concierge can generally help with transportation, event and entertainment suggestions, sightseeing, restaurants, and appropriate customs and gifts. Most concierges can also help make business services arrangements for you, including translators, computers, and international cell phones.

ARRIVING AT YOUR DESTINATION

Be sure not to bring any plants, fruits, weapons, scissors, or other sharp instruments with you as these items can make going through customs and security very difficult; the items will be confiscated.

Once you arrive at your destination, you will need to exchange dollars for the local currency. Because it is easy to use ATM machines abroad, do not take much cash with you. When you need additional cash, simply use your bank card or credit card to obtain more cash. Do check ahead of time to be sure this is an option; be sure you know your PINs. Normally, you can exchange currency using your ATM cards in the airport or at banks. In some countries, such as France, the banks do not exchange currency except through their ATM machines. There is normally a nominal exchange charge for this service. Hotels can normally exchange currencies for you as well. Although traveler's checks are welcomed in some countries, they can be difficult to use in other countries. Even if traveler's checks are welcomed, the cost for converting to the local currency may be exorbitant, such as a $7 charge to exchange a $20 traveler's check (in Barcelona, Spain)! Be sure to check this out before you arrive at your destination.

If you have not had time to learn the language, you should take the time to learn some common phrases in order to use the transportation system and to get to your hotel, words for different food items so that you can order from a restaurant menu, and the proper words and behavior to use when greeting people.

Some safety tips to follow include using your business address rather than a home address on your luggage, arriving at the airport early to accommodate the screening process, securing a strap of your luggage under a chair leg when waiting at an airport, putting valuables in the hotel safe or your room safe, and double-locking your hotel room door.[11]

CONSIDERING LEGALITY AND ETHICALITY OF CULTURAL PRACTICES

Because cultural diversity is part of the world, it is necessary to consider that an ethical behavior in one culture may be seen as unethical in another culture. It is important to be cautious and understand the differences between ethics-based judgments and judgments based on concern and practicality.[12] Although it may seem that the easiest thing to do is duplicate successful ethics from the home country to the host country, this type of duplication can be disrespectful of the host country's culture.

Standards of moral behavior—what is right or wrong—are the bases of ethical judgments. If a judgment is based on what is easiest, best, or most effective to achieve an objective, then it is based on practical ethics. Subjective judgments measure by degrees rather than by absolutes what is ethical or unethical in a society. People generally disagree as to the exact difference between ethical and unethical acts.[13]

Currently, many global business managers are trying to use hypernorms, which are norms that are forming transnationally by which all cultures can live. The hypernorm would say that bribery is wrong. Although it is true that every major religion considers bribery to be wrong, bribery still exists in many parts of the world. Political participation (democracy) and efficiency strategies both would argue that bribery is wrong; however, democracy does not exist throughout the world. Many economies are not developed to the point of being efficient, hence bribery makes inefficiencies economical. In 30 years, hypernorms may be followed more than they are today as we work toward transnational norms.[14]

Four approaches to dealing with ethical differences include the foreign country approach, empire approach, interconnection approach, and global approach. According to the foreign country approach, you conform to the local customs. The empire approach applies the home-based ethics to the new host situation. The interconnection approach does not consider either home or host country as having the ethical answers, but the needs of the companies that are interacting. The global approach looks at what is good for the world rather than the local ethical customs.[15]

The different approaches to dealing with ethical differences have shortcomings. The foreign-country approach has no oversight or restraints on the host-country's ethics. Both the empire and the global approaches maintain that what your culture (home country) believes is correct and that the other culture should accept your ethics, leaving no room for movement by the host culture. The interconnection approach looks at both cultures and tries to balance the ethical requirements. The bottom line is that multinational companies should be helpful to a host country rather than harmful.

In the business world, four motivations for unethical conduct exist: profits, competition, justice, and advertising. The three dimensions of negotiation ethics are means/ends, relativism/absolutism, and truth telling. The means/ends question is measured by utility. The moral value and worth of an act are judged by what is produced—the utility. The players in the negotiation game and the environment in which the negotiators are operating help determine whether the negotiators can justify being exploitative, manipulative, or devious. The relative/absolute question considers two extremes: Either everything is relative, or everything is without deviation from the rule. Although most people are somewhere between the extremes of relative and absolute, they debate which point between the two extremes is correct. Of course, it is a matter of judgment or culture as to what particular point on the continuum is correct.[16]

Truth telling considers whether concealing information, conscious misstatements, exaggeration, or bluffing during negotiations is dishonest. Judging how honest and candid one can be in negotiations and not be vulnerable is difficult. Intercultural negotiators have the added problem of different business methods, different cultures, and different negotiation protocols. Although the decision to be "unethical" may be made to increase power and control, it is important whether the decision was made quickly, casually, after careful evaluation, or on the basis of cultural values.[17]

Bribery in particular has undergone close international scrutiny in the past few years. Bribery is influencing others by giving them something. In Mexico, bribes are known as *mordida*; in Southeast Asia, *kumshaw*; and in the Middle East, *baksheesh*. Although bribery unofficially is part of doing business in many parts of the world, bribery is not approved of officially in any country. While the practice is not officially approved, it is considered neither unethical nor immoral in a number of countries practicing the art of "greasing the palm." Examples include paying the customs agent in Nigeria in order to leave the airport or giving a tip to the driver's license bureau agent in Thailand and Indonesia in order to get a driver's license.[18]

Vivek Paul of Wipro tells of not being able to get a local telephone line between his office and factory unless he paid a bribe. Since he would not pay the bribe, he had to figure out another way to communicate. He communicated through his mainframe computer fiber-optic lease line, which did not require a bribe, rather than the one in town, which did require a bribe.[19]

Bribery is considered wrong in the United States. The Foreign Corrupt Practices Act of 1977 requires U.S. companies to account for and report international transactions accurately and prohibits bribes. The act states that companies found guilty of paying bribes to foreign officials can be fined up to $1 million and individual employees may be fined up to $10,000.[20] Not only can U.S. competitors in Italy, Germany, and Japan use bribery in international transactions, but they may deduct the amount of the bribe on their taxes as a business expense.

Some examples of such payoffs include an Italian oil company paying $130 million to agents for an oil contract in Saudi Arabia; a German firm paying an intermediary in order to sell submarines to the Indian government; and Siemens paying an official in order to obtain the contract to build an Indonesian steel plant.

Bribes generally are in the form of gifts or entertainment. When a company receives something in return, they have engaged in bribery. For example, a U.S. firm's giving a Russian utility official money for the Russian's personal use to get an electric line brought in to a new construction site is an example of bribery. The Foreign Corrupt Practices Act of 1977 often puts U.S. firms at a disadvantage when trying to compete with companies from cultures that have no problem with the practice of "gift giving," which U.S. persons would call a bribe. To protect the company and their employees, many U.S. companies do not allow bribery. Bill Pomeranz, an employee with Hughes Space and Communications Company, says that only two contracts have been lost over the years because Hughes failed to pay bribes. It is important to note that Hughes is the market leader in their field and has more to offer than those who might make payoffs. He responded as follows when asked about bribery: "It's illegal. Whether it's the way somebody would want to do business or not, it's illegal—and the company has a rigid code of ethics that prohibits unlawful conduct." Many Fortune 500 companies have rules concerning bribery that they expect their employees to follow.[21]

Expediting business transactions in some countries can be done with the help of consultants who make sure that roadblocks are cleared. It is bribery for employees of U.S. firms to be directly involved in paying these commissions; however, by having a consultant, distributor, or joint-venture partner take care of the fees, the U.S. firm is not directly involved and probably should not ask about or have knowledge of the practice.[22]

Export Administration Regulations subscription is available by going to http://bookstore.gpo.gov/index.html or http://www.access.gpo.gov/bis/ear/ear_data.html and is helpful to those involved in international business. The U.S. Department of Commerce's 1993 booklet *International Business Practices*, although out of print, is an excellent source of information (available at http://bookstore.gpo.gov/index.html or Federal Depository libraries), lists foreign laws by country, and offers the following guidance on distributor agreements:

- Check legal differences between the countries.
- Check translations for correct meanings.
- State the jurisdiction for handling disagreements.
- Identify arbitrators to settle disagreements if needed.
- State foreign laws that are to be waived in contracts.
- State the benefits to both parties.
- Put the agreement in writing.

Because laws are different and companies are responsible for both the home- and host-country laws, the Doctrine of Sovereign Compliance was designed as a defense in your home country for work carried out in a host country when the two countries' legal positions are different. For example, a U.S. manager working in Mexico may have to trade with Cuba even though it is illegal to do so in the United States. The manager could use the Doctrine of Sovereign Compliance as a defense. If a U.S. citizen is held to the U.S. law outside of the U.S. borders, it is called extraterritorial.

Joint-venture trading companies, which are normally not allowed in the United States due to antitrust, are allowed through the Export Trading Act of 1982.[23] An example of this act would include Exxon and BP's development of a joint venture to drill for oil.

Building global business relationships is affected by the laws of the countries in which companies do business and the growing body of international law. Laws tend to develop when the normal cultural beliefs, values, and assumptions no longer are sufficient. Because managers in the United States are faced with situations in other countries that are considered illegal in the United States, they must be aware that different perceptions exist internationally concerning gifts. Bribery is culturally conditioned, and one country's tip is another country's bribe.[24] Examples of bribes given to clients include box seats at sporting events or lavish entertainment.[25]

To be sure you do not break the law in other countries, follow these tips:[26]

1. Because of political unrest in the world, register with the U.S. embassy or consulate when you arrive in a foreign country.

2. If you have any kind of trouble, turn to the embassy or consulate for legal, medical, or financial problems.

3. If you are taken to jail, understand that the U.S. consul can visit you in jail, give you a list of attorneys, notify family, and protest any mistreatment; however, the consul cannot get you released or provide for bonds or fines.

4. While you are in another country, remember that you are subject to the laws of the country.

5. If you stay for a prolonged time period, register with the local authorities. You may be requested to leave your passport overnight or to complete certain forms.

6. While in another country, use only authorized outlets for cashing checks and buying airline tickets; avoid the black market or street moneychangers that you will see in many countries.

7. Before you take a photograph, ask for permission.

8. In many countries, notary publics have broader powers than in the United States.

9. Avoid infractions of the law in other countries, including trying to take historic artifacts or antiquities out of the country, customs violations, immigration violations, drunk and disorderly conduct, and business fraud.

10. If you need to drive, obtain an international driver's license. Travel agents can assist with this. Many countries require proof of insurance while driving. Your U.S. insurance is generally not recognized in other countries.

11. Although dealing in drugs is a serious offense in all countries, the penalties can be much more serious than in the United States and may include the death penalty.

12. In order to protect your credit card numbers and traveler's check numbers, keep a list of the numbers in a safe place.

13. Obtain a copy of the U.S. State Department's *Safe Trip Abroad*, available through http://bookstore.gpo.gov.

14. Telephone numbers and addresses that may be beneficial include the following:

    • The U.S. State Department, 2201 C Street NW, Washington, DC 20520, 202-647-4000, http://www.state.gov.

    • Amnesty International USA, 5 Penn Plaza, 14th Floor, New York, NY 10001, 212-807-8400, http://www.amnestyusa.org.

    • International Legal Defense Counsel, 1429 Walnut Street, Philadelphia, PA 19102, 215-977-9982.

15. Your health could be a major concern. Obtain a copy of the *Health Information for International Travel* by the Centers for Disease Control and Prevention at 888-232-3299 or from http://www.cdc.gov. This will offer disease and immunization advice and health risks for countries. Health precautions may include the need to take a series of inoculations before you leave. International SOS Assistance is a health provider that will work through the red tape of language, insurance, travel, or anything else you may need. They can also provide travel health insurance. They may be reached at 800-523-8930 or 215-244-1500.

ANTICIPATING CULTURAL SHOCK

Cultural shock is experienced when you enter a culture different from your home culture. Cultural shock involves the frustration of not understanding verbal and nonverbal communication, customs, and the value system of a new culture.[27] Common frustrations include lack of common foods, less than adequate standards of cleanliness, bathroom facilities that are unusual, and fear for one's safety. The English saying, "That song is best esteemed with which our ears are most acquainted," states the fact simply: We like things as we are accustomed to having them. If you anticipate some of the differences in advance, some of the shock will be removed. Jack London, in his story "In a Far Country" published in 1900, stressed that a visitor to another culture should acquire new customs and abandon what feels comfortable. It is amazing that we are still dealing with cultural shock and the unfamiliar more than 100 years later.

An example of cultural shock is finding that women are not allowed to drive in Saudi Arabia. As annoying as this is to the women, it is even more confusing to an eight-year-old who has never seen his mother drive until they return home to the United States from Saudi Arabia.[28]

Cultural shock may have five stages: initial euphoria, crisis, adjustment, acceptance, and reentry. If you look at the letter U, you would find at the top-left side of the U the positive euphoric beginning, crisis would start as you move down the left side to the base of the U, adjustment starts at the base of the curve, acceptance moves up the right side of the U, and reentry to the home culture starts at the top-right side of the U. Because reentry shock starts another U cycle, this would become the first stage on the left side of the U for reentry shock in the home culture.[29]

The first stage can last a few days or several months and is excitement and fascination with everything new. You will find the food and the people interesting and different. Sometimes this stage is referred to as the "honeymoon" stage, during which your enthusiasm for the new culture causes you to overlook minor problems, such as having to drink bottled water and the absence of central heating or air conditioning.[30]

During the second stage, the honeymoon is over and the crisis or disenchantment period begins. Excitement turns to disappointment as you encounter all the differences between your own culture and the new culture. Problems with people who do not speak English, transportation, and unfamiliar foods are exasperating. Bargaining over the purchase price of everything, which was initially fun, is irritating. Emotions of homesickness, irritation, anger, confusion, resentment, helplessness, and depression occur during the second stage. You may feel like fighting back by making disparaging remarks about the culture or by leaving, either physically, emotionally, or psychologically. Other characteristics include withdrawal from people in the culture, refusing to learn the language, and developing coping behaviors such as excessive drinking or drug use. Other individuals deny differences and will speak in glowing terms of the new culture. The second stage can last a few weeks or several months.[31]

You begin to accept the new culture by the adjustment phase. You begin to adjust to foods, make adjustments to accommodate the shopping lines, and to accept other inconveniences. You are able to laugh at situations and realize you have to change your attitude toward the host culture.[32]

In the fourth phase, you feel at home and have entered the acceptance or adaptation phase. By becoming involved in activities, cultivating new friendships, and feeling comfortable in social situations with people from the host culture, you learn to adjust. You learn the language and may adopt the host culture's way of doing things. You may learn to enjoy customs such as afternoon tea or the midday siesta and miss them when you return to your home country.[33]

Reentry shock starts the U curve again; it can be almost as traumatic as the initial adjustment to a new culture if you have had an extended stay abroad. Feeling the same emotional, psychological, and physical reactions as when you entered the new culture can be very surprising. Reentry shock is experienced on returning to the home country and may follow the stages identified earlier: initial euphoria, crisis or disenchantment, adjustment, and acceptance or adaptation. You would have an initial euphoria about being home, and then become disenchanted as your friends show no interest in hearing about your experiences abroad, your standard of living changes, and skills such as a foreign language or bargaining in the market are not useful. Moving into the adjustment stage, you become familiar and appreciative of new technology, the variety of foods and clothing, and the improved cleanliness standards. With the reacceptance of the mores of the home culture, you move into the acceptance stage, feeling comfortable with your earlier views and behaviors.[34] College students who had traveled abroad experienced four types of reentry shock that were statistically significant: readjusting to lifestyle, change in social life, change in standard of living, and reestablishing friendships.[35] The longer you are separated from your home culture, the more severe the stages may be.

A former student from the United Arab Emirates called his U.S. professor to ask for information on purchasing property on the North Carolina coast. He went on to explain that he was homesick for the United States and had decided to bring his family here every summer. After spending 15 years in the United States earning his bachelor's, MBA, and PhD degrees with only occasional visits back to his home country, he was experiencing reentry shock. He made the readjustment and did not buy the North Carolina property.[36]

Train and interact with people from the culture if you can find them locally. Learn as much of the language as possible before you go. Learn about the new culture, particularly time differences, communication, conflict resolution, climate, power, standard of living, transportation, ethical practices, holidays, superstitions, taboos, technology, language, and cultural shock items for the culture to which you are traveling. One of the challenges is overcoming ecoshock. *Ecoshock* is the result of a person's "physiological and psychological reaction to a new, diverse, or changed ecology."[37] Items that are included in ecoshock include the similarities, differences, and tasks of the position or trip and how these are acted upon by communication, new people, complex travel, new location, organization, duration of the travel, cosmopolitan versus provincial location, giving versus exchanging versus getting role, technologies, less support, less structure, and more time needed. An example of one of these is travel dysrhythmia, or jet lag, when our biological clock has problems synchronizing with the local time. This time difference can affect the circadian rhythms of the body, including eating times, sleeping, body temperature, and kidney and liver functions. Additionally, you have to physiologically adjust to the temperature, humidity, altitude, food, and so forth.[38]

The following strategies may be used for coping with the new culture during short visits. Do not accept the host culture and continue to act as you would have in the home culture. Make no effort to learn the language or customs of the host country. Some people will substitute host-culture behaviors for their home culture's customs. Some people will add behaviors of the host culture when with host-country people but will maintain the home culture when with home-culture people. Synthesis is used by many and is a way of integrating the two cultures. The fifth strategy is resynthesis and is an integration of ideas not found in either culture but choosing items from a third culture.[39]

RESPECTING HOLIDAYS, SUPERSTITIONS, AND TABOOS

It is important to know the holidays, superstitions, and taboos of the country you are visiting. Lack of knowledge can be insulting to your host, cause you to lose business, or fail to build positive global relationships.

Superstitions, although inconsistent with the known laws of science, can hold a great deal of weight in some societies. Examples of superstitions include a belief that special charms, omens, or rituals have supernatural powers. Superstitions are not the same around the world. In many Southeast Asian countries, spiritualists are highly regarded, and it is not unusual that they are consulted in making business decisions. An example of a superstition is a hotel that was built in Taiwan over a cemetery. The people told the government they would not stay there, and workers currently will not work there except during the day. This has caused all the food to be cooked off the premises, and only foreigners will stay at the hotel. When doing business with persons who take business advice from seers, it is best to respect these beliefs.

Numbers are associated with bad luck and even death in many countries. Curiously, it tends to be different numbers for different cultures. People of the United States, for example, think that 13 is an unlucky number. Most U.S. hotels do not have a 13th floor, and even a hotel number ending in 13 may be refused. Friday the 13th is perceived as an unlucky day, causing people to not schedule important events on this day. The Chinese feel that four is the most negative number because it sounds like the word for death. Hotels in China, Hong Kong, and Taiwan often have no fourth floor, and some Asian airports have no Gate 4. Numbers also have positive meanings in China. For example, the number six represents happiness, and nine represents long life. For many Chinese, having an uneven number of people in a photograph will bring bad luck, such as that the middle person in a photo of three people will die.[40] Number superstitions can be very important when building global relationships. Additional superstitions regarding numbers and gift giving are covered in Chapters 3 and 8.

Practices or verbal expressions considered by a culture as improper or unacceptable are called taboos. Taboos are rooted in the beliefs of the people of a specific region or culture and are passed down from generation to generation. They can have a very strong hold on a society. Common business taboos include asking an Arab about the health of his wife or writing in red ink in Taiwan, because this has death connotations.[41]

Pointing with one's index finger is taboo in Malaysia, but the thumb is okay. In Indonesia, it is taboo to touch the head because it is considered sacred. Patting young children on the head would be cause for great concern in Indonesia. Placing one's head in a higher position than the head of a senior person is taboo. The Russian Federation has a number of taboos: No whistling in the street, no coats worn indoors, and no lunches on park lawns. Madagascar has some very unusual taboos: Pregnant women are forbidden to eat brains or sit in doorways, women may not wash their brothers' clothes, and children are not permitted to say their father's name or make reference to any part of his body.[42]

If you want to build global relationships, you must take into consideration the holidays and holy days observed by the people in the culture. All countries have holidays and holy days that you must be aware of before scheduling telephone calls and making business trips. Holidays generally celebrate a prominent person's birthday, commemorate a historic event, or pay homage to a group. Holy days are religious observances. More information on religion is included in Chapter 6. Knowing the days that businesses do not operate is essential when working abroad.

Knowing when to distribute promotional items can be very important, as a cereal company discovered after delivering two sample boxes of cereal with the Sunday edition of the newspaper. Jewish customers were incensed due to the fact it was the first day of Passover and they are required to keep their homes free of all bread and grain products for the weeklong celebration.

People who travel to the United States would need to know that business is not conducted on Christmas Day, Thanksgiving, or the Fourth of July. Most businesses, with the exception of retail establishments, are closed on Sunday, which is the Sabbath for many religions. The Jewish Sabbath is observed on Saturday, whereas the Muslims observe the Sabbath on Friday.

Although some holidays across the world are similar to those celebrated in the United States, there are also a number of differences. Many Catholic countries, such as Germany, have a carnival season (similar to New Orleans' Mardi Gras), which is not a good time to conduct business. Although many countries celebrate the New Year, the time of year varies and the calendar that is followed to determine the New Year is different. In China, for example, the Chinese New Year follows a different calendar from that used in the West.

Because holidays are so important to developing global relationships, the holidays of the 10 countries with which the United States conducts most of its international business are listed here. (An asterisk [*] indicates holidays for which dates vary and may be found online or on a calendar of the country.)

Brazil[43] has many holidays. Carnaval is a five-day festival preceding Ash Wednesday. Tiradentes Day (April 21), Festas Juninas (June Festivals) are celebrated during the feasts of St. John and St. Peter, Easter, Labor Day (May 1), Independence Day (September 7), Memorial Day (November 2), Republic Day (November 15), Christmas Eve and Christmas Day, and New Year's Eve.

Canada[44] celebrates many of the same days as the United States, including New Year's Day (January 1), Easter Sunday and Monday*, and Labor Day (May 1). Other Canadian holidays include Victoria Day (third Monday in May), Canada Day (July 1), Thanksgiving Day (second Monday in October), All Saints' Day (November 1), Remembrance Day (November 11), Christmas (December 25), and Boxing Day (December 26). Quebec has two additional holidays: the Carnival de Quebec (February) and St. Jean Baptiste Day (June 24).

China[45] has numerous holidays that are very different from the West, including Chinese Lunar New Year and Spring Festival*, International Working Woman's Day (March 8), Youth Day (May 4), Children's Day (June 1), People's Liberation Army Day (August 1), and National Day (October 1).

France[46] celebrates a number of holidays, many of which have religious significance, including New Year's Day (January 1), Mardi Gras (Shrove Tuesday)*, Easter Sunday and Monday*, Labor Day (May 1), Liberation Day (May 8), Ascension Day*, Whit Monday*, Bastille Day (July 14), Pentecost*, Assumption of the Virgin Mary (August 15), All Saints' Day (November 1), World War I Armistice Day*, and Christmas (December 25).

Germany[47] celebrates the following holidays: New Year's Day (January 1), Good Friday*, Easter Sunday and Monday*, Labor Day (May 1), Ascension Day*, Whit Monday*, Day of German Unity (October 3), All Saints' Day

(November 1), Day of Prayer and Repentance*, and Christmas (December 25).

Japan[48] celebrates a number of days during the year; however, they are not religiously oriented and include the following: New Year's Day (January 1), Coming of Age Day (January 15), National Foundation Day (February 11), Vernal Equinox (March 21), Greenery Day (April 29), Constitution Day (May 3), Children's Day (May 5), Bon Festival (August 15), Respect for the Aged Day (September 15), Autumnal Equinox (September 23), Sports Day (October 10), Culture Day (November 3), Labor Thanksgiving Day (November 23), and Emperor Akihito's Birthday (December 23).

Mexico[49] has numerous holidays, and because it is one of the top trading partners of the United States, you will want to know the following holidays: New Year's Day (January 1), St. Anthony's Day (January 17), Constitution Day (February 5), Carnival Week*, Birthday of Benito Juarez (March 21), Easter*, Labor Day (May 1), Cinco de Mayo (May 5), Corpus Christi*, Assumption of the Virgin Mary (August 15), President's Annual Message (September 1), Independence Day (September 16), Columbus Day (October 12), All Saints' Day (November 1), All Souls' Day (November 2), Revolution Day (November 20), Day of the Virgin Guadalupe (December 12), and Christmas (December 25).

South Korea[50] has a number of holidays that are similar to U.S. holidays and some that are new to people in the West: The New Year (January 1–3), the Lunar New Year (January or February*), Independence Day (March 1), Buddha's Birthday (April or May*), Memorial Day (June 6), Constitution Day (July 17), Liberation Day (August 15), Ch'usok, Harvest Moon Festival (September or October*), National Foundation Day (October 3), and Christmas (December 25).

Taiwanese[51] holidays are as follows: Founding Day (January 1), Chinese Lunar New Year (January or February*), Birthday of Confucius (September 28), Double Ten National Day (October 10), Taiwan Restoration Day (October 25), and Constitution Day (December 25).

The United Kingdom[52] probably celebrates fewer holidays than any other European country. The holidays include New Year's Day (January 1), Good Friday*, May Day*, Easter Sunday and Monday*, Spring Bank Holiday*, Late Summer Holiday*, Christmas (December 25), and Boxing Day (December 26). Northern Ireland also observes St. Patrick's Day (March 17) and Battle of the Boyne (July 12). The Welsh also include Patron Saints Day, or St. David's Day (March 1). The Scottish honor poet Robert Burns (January 25), Remembrance Day (the Sunday closest to November 11), and other local holidays.

In addition, business is not usually conducted during certain other times of the year. For example, August is the vacation month in Europe, and many corporations are closed. During Ramadan, the Islamic fasting month, Arabs conduct less business. Various holidays and birthdays are celebrated in Japan from April 29 to May 5, and businesses close.

COUNTRY-SPECIFIC INFORMATION

Before you travel to a foreign country, find out what documents are needed, what hotel accommodations and modes of transportation are available, what laws affect behavior (such as the legal drinking age), and other pertinent information to ensure personal safety and comfort so that your sojourn is a pleasant one. There are many country-specific books and Websites to consult to gain knowledge of a particular country. Because space does not permit an extensive examination of numerous countries, the following travel tips are limited to the top 10 countries with which the United States conducts most of its international trade.

Brazil

- Passports are required and should be valid for six months from the date of entry.
- Check for recommended immunizations for cholera, typhoid, and yellow fever if travels are planned outside urban areas.
- Hotel accommodations vary; check the hotel's rating, which ranges from one to five stars. Confirm amenities, such as air conditioning and TV. Motels should be avoided; they are often rented hourly by lovers.
- Public transportation includes taxis and buses that travel between cities. Avoid city buses. Subways are available in larger cities; trains between São Paulo and Rio de Janeiro are comfortable and inexpensive.
- More information on traveling in Brazil is available from the Embassy of Brazil, 202-238-2700, http://www.brasilemb.org, or from the Brazilian Tourism Office, 800-727-2945, www.braziltourism.org.[53]

Canada

- Passports are required.
- Visas are not required for visits of up to 180 days.
- Hotel accommodations in the large cities are Western style.
- Voltage connectors and plug adapters are not needed.
- Public transportation systems exist in Montreal and Quebec City. Domestic air transportation or cars are used elsewhere in the country. Radar detectors are illegal.

- Additional information about traveling in Canada can be obtained from the Canadian Consulate General, 212-596-1759, http://www.canada-ny.org, or the Embassy of Canada, 202-682-1740, http://www.canadianembassy.org.

China

- Passports are required and should be good for at least six months beyond the visit period.
- Visas are required.
- Hotel accommodations may or may not be Western style.
- Public transportation systems include a subway system, buses, taxis, and railroads. Bicycles are still the main mode of transportation.
- Intellectual property right infringements have made trade with China contentious.[54]
- More information about China can be found through the Embassy of China, 202-328-2500, http://www.china-embassy.org, or the China National Tourist Office, 888-760-8218, http://www.cnto.org.

France

- Passports are required.
- Hotel accommodations may be U.S. style or with a bath down the hall and no air conditioning. Generally, a breakfast is included.
- Electrical converters are necessary for small appliances.
- Public transportation in France includes the Metro (subway), buses, taxis, and the TGV (*train à grande vitesse*, a high-speed train connecting 36 European cities). Keep your TGV tickets until the end of the ride. Use official taxis. If driving in France, do not honk your horn as this is illegal.
- Additional information about traveling in France is available from the French Government Tourist Office, 410-286-8310, http://www.us.franceguide .com, or the Embassy of France, 202-944-6000, http://www.ambafrance-us.org.

Germany

- Passports are required.
- Hotel accommodations generally include a continental breakfast; however, heat may be an extra charge. If you want private bath facilities, inquire when making your reservations.
- Electrical converters are needed to use small appliances in hotels.
- Public transportation includes buses, streetcars, subways, trains, and taxis. Mass transit tickets should be purchased in advance. Keep your tickets until the end of the ride.
- An international driver's license is required for driving in Germany.
- Crosswalks are the only place to legally cross streets.

- Tap water in towns along the Rhine may contain dangerous chemicals, so drink bottled water.
- More information on traveling in Germany is available from the Embassy of Germany, 202-298-4000, http://germany.usembassy.gov/acs/ or German National Tourist Office, 212-661-7200, http://www.germany .travel/en/index.html.

Japan

- Passports are required.
- Hotel accommodations include Western-style hotels in the large cities. The accommodations may be somewhat different from those to which you are accustomed.
- Public toilets are often for both genders and quite different from those that people of the United States are accustomed to using.
- Electrical converters are not needed for small appliances.
- Public transportation includes trains, subways, taxis, and buses. The bullet train, which runs between major cities, offers regular and first-class service.
- Additional information about travel in Japan is available from the Japan National Tourist Organization, 212-757-5640, http://www.jnto.go.jp, or the Embassy of Japan, 202-238-6700, http://www.us.emb-japan.go.jp.

Mexico

- Passports are usually required to return to the United States.
- Vaccinations may be necessary in remote areas.
- Hotel accommodations are generally Western style. Because Christmas and Easter are important vacation times in Mexico, hotel reservations must be made in advance for these time periods.
- Public transportation includes the subway of Mexico City, buses, trains, and taxis. Driving a car in many parts of Mexico is not advisable.
- Additional information about traveling in Mexico is available from the Mexican Government Tourist Office, 212-755-7261, http://www.visitmexico .com, or the Embassy of Mexico, 202-728-1600, http://www.sre.gob.mx/eua/.

South Korea

- Passports are required and must be good for six months after the anticipated return date.
- Visas are required for visits of more than 30 days.
- Hotel accommodations include Western-style hotels or the Korean-style *yogwan* inns. Because many amenities are different, discuss this with the person making your reservations.

- Public transportation includes rail, subways, buses, taxis, and private cars. South Korea's first bullet train was tested in 2004 and cuts in half the travel time between Pusan and Seoul.

- For more information about travel in South Korea, contact the Embassy of the Republic of Korea, 202-939-5600, http://www.koreaembassyusa.org, or Korea National Tourism Organization, 201-585-0909, http://www.knto.or.kr.

Taiwan

- Passports are required.

- Visas are required for stays longer than 30 days.

- Hotel accommodations tend to be Western in style and often include meeting facilities, fitness centers, and such. During the month of October, book well in advance.

- Public transportation includes buses, taxis, and subways.

- For information about traveling to Taiwan, contact the Taipei Economic and Cultural Representative Office, 202-895-1800, http://www.taipei.org, or Taiwan Visitors Association, 212-867-1632, http://www.roc-taiwan.org.

United Kingdom (England, Scotland, Wales, and Northern Ireland)

- Passports are required.

- Hotel accommodations may include early-morning tea delivered to your room. Larger hotels may include a continental breakfast in the room price.

- Electrical converters and plug adapters are needed to use small U.S. appliances.

- Public transportation includes subways, trains, buses, and taxis. If you choose to drive, be aware that in the UK, people drive on the left side of the road. They also walk on the left side of the sidewalk or stairs.

- More information on traveling in the UK is available from the Tourist Information UK, http://www.tourist-information-uk.com, or the United Kingdom Embassy, 202-588-6500, http://ukinusa.fco.gov.uk/en/

United States of America

- Passports are required and must be valid for a minimum of six months from the date of entering the United States; visas are required for longer stays.

- Hotel accommodations are considered spacious by European standards and include central air conditioning and private baths. Other amenities, such as hair dryers, safes, and irons and ironing boards, are provided in most rooms.

- Public transportation is available in large cities; rental cars are widely available. When driving keep your driver's license and vehicle registration with you. Wearing a seat belt is mandatory.

- Additional travel information may be obtained from the U.S. Department of State, 202-647-6575, http://www.state.gov.

When in other countries, learn about their local laws and obey them, be courteous, learn the common phrases in their language, and speak positively about the country. If you do not speak their language, realize that you may feel frustrated at times if they do not speak English. However, if they speak English, even poorly, be thankful, and go the extra mile to understand them and help them understand you.

Chapter 2

LANGUAGE, GREETINGS, INTRODUCTIONS, AND BUSINESS CARDS

Building a business relationship has a lot to do with the first impression you make. That first impression could be your use of a language (yours or theirs), how you greet people in another country, how you make introductions, how you shake hands, or how you exchange business cards. In this chapter we will look at the importance of these items in building a business relationship.

LANGUAGE

Meeting, speaking, and being understood are necessary if you are to build global business relationships. Therefore it is necessary that you learn the basic history and culture of the country you are visiting and a few phrases in their language. Although English may be the international language of business, it is not spoken by everyone, everywhere. Even if it were, their English is probably not the same as yours. Learning key phrases, such as "Do you speak English," "Yes," "No," "Good day," "Good night," "Excuse me," "Where is the restroom?" "Thank you," "Please," and "Help" can be very useful. Everyone appreciates someone who tries to speak their language, even if it is only a few phrases. Research has shown that proficiency in the host language reduces cultural shock due to the ability to effectively communicate, whereas a lack of knowledge inhibits adjustment to a new culture.[1]

Politeness or building rapport is done through the use of language. An element of language that Westerners tend to give less attention to is that of saving face. Anything that happens during discourse to cause one of the members to lose face can be devastating to the relationship in many cultures in the world. Building a relationship or establishing rapport with a business colleague is the only way to do business in many parts of the world. Rapport has five domains: the act of speaking, the discourse content, inclusion or exclusion of people present, stylistic aspects, and the nonverbal domain.[2] Understanding how the host culture's members speak to one another, what the proper discussion topics are, who to speak to or include in comments, what style to use, and what nonverbal actions to use can be very important in making a positive first impression and building a good business relationship. Host-country language knowledge increases the opportunities for social and daily interactions with host nationals. Being able to speak the language allows you to have in-depth conversations with the people with whom you are working, neighbors, and store personnel. The more you speak the language and learn the meaning of nonverbal cues, the greater the opportunity you have to be included in social interactions. Many aspects of these domains will be discussed in Chapters 4, 6, 7, 8, and 9.

GREETING BEHAVIORS

Customary greetings vary from culture to culture but are very important for building relationships in all cultures. Persons from other cultures are surprised by the informality of U.S. Americans who often say "Hi!" to complete strangers. In most countries of the world, saying "Hi" to strangers is uncommon. Also, U.S. citizens are often perceived as insincere when they use the standard greeting of "Hi, how are you?" because it does not mean that they are actually inquiring about the state of the other person's health. Because U.S. citizens are in reality private and slow to form friendships, this outward show of friendliness is often misleading. The use of "Hello, I'm pleased to meet you" is a more appropriate greeting to use.

An Asian colleague working in the United States was asked on Monday morning, "What did you do over the weekend?" He began on Friday evening and listed every event that took place over the past two days. It was far more information than his polite U.S. colleague wanted, and she spread the word around the office: "Never ask what he did on his time off!"[3]

When greeting someone for the first time, be sure to know how they should be greeted. Should you use their first name, last name, or title? Is it okay to be familiar and use common greetings of the area, such as

"G'day, mate," which is used in Australia? Generally, it is going to be a good idea to stay with the formal Mr. Young and Mrs. Connor until you are invited to use their first names. If someone has a title, it is proper to use that title, such as President Obama or Dr. Chan. For both business and social situations, you should arrive on time; however, the ending time is fluid. After the initial introductions and greetings, you may be given a beverage to share before the business meeting begins. It is very important that you accept whatever you are offered, unlike in the United States, where it is acceptable to decline the offer of refreshments.[4]

Many international guests in the United States find the question "How are you?" to be insincere. As one Israeli woman observed, "No matter if your children are on drugs, your spouse is leaving you, and you have just declared bankruptcy, you are expected to smile and say, 'Everything is great!' Why do Americans ask if they don't really want to know?" Americans do not mean to be insincere. The question "How are you?" is simply a pleasantry and an example of the greeting rituals typical of people in the United States.[5]

MAKING INTRODUCTIONS

Because a first impression is very difficult to change, you will want to understand how to make introductions properly when you meet people from another country for the first time. One universal is both men and women stand when they are being introduced to each other. Because women in all cultures do not shake the hands of men, women should extend their hand first to indicate it is all right to shake hands. In the United States, the person of highest rank initiates the handshake. When making introductions, the name of the person of the highest rank is mentioned first. An example is "Vice President Biden, may I present Senator Dianne Feinstein." Although age and gender were considerations at one time when making introductions, this is no longer true.

One important procedural difference between cultures is the use of titles and first or last names when making formal introductions. Because this use of titles and names is not consistent around the world, you must ask what is correct before you attempt an introduction. In the United States, first names are used very quickly. In such cultures as Germany, Italy, and Mexico, titles are used when introducing people because they indicate the person's professional or educational level. As mentioned previously, you always use a title when addressing someone in Germany, such as "Herr Guenther" or "Frau Kurr" until you are told it is okay to use first names. Be careful of surnames, because they are reversed in many Far Eastern cultures, including China and Japan. You address Ching Lo Chang as Mr. Ching.

President Clinton, in a meeting in Korea, addressed South Korean President Kim Young Sam's wife, Mrs. Sohn Myong-suk, as Mrs. Kim. He should have addressed her as Mrs. Sohn, since in Korea it is the custom for women to maintain their maiden name when they marry. President Clinton made a common error in assuming that Koreans used the same naming tradition as the United States.[6]

In Latin American countries, people add their mother's maiden name to their surname, such as Maria Gomez Sanchez. When addressing Maria, you would say Señorita Gomez. When Maria marries, she will drop her mother's surname and add her father-in-law's surname. In Portuguese-speaking countries, however, the mother and father's names are reversed. In some cases, the French form of address will be used for women, for example, Madame Susan. In Iraq and in India, titles such as professor and doctor, used with the last name, are used as part of the introduction. In African countries, such as Nigeria and Kenya, titles are used with last names until you get to know the people well and they ask you to call them by their first name.[7] Because of such widely diverse customs in the use of titles, it is wise to research the customs of the particular culture involved.

Family titles can also be confusing. In Hong Kong, India, and other countries, they often call relatives by their family relationships rather than by their first name. Thus, if you are invited to a home, you would greet Paul's sister as "Sister" rather than by her first name of Sally. Many cultures also call cousins sisters and brothers.[8]

HANDSHAKE CUSTOMS

Introductions are accompanied by a handshake, embrace, air kiss, real kiss, or a bow, depending on the culture. Hugging or embracing when being introduced is considered inappropriate in business situations in the United States but is common in many South American countries, Middle Eastern countries, some African countries, and parts of Europe. The bow, common in China and Japan, is uncommon in many other cultures.

The handshake is acceptable as a greeting in many parts of the world, including Nigeria, Kenya, Saudi Arabia, Egypt, Finland, and others. Many Far Eastern countries, such as Japan and China, use the bow instead of the handshake as their greeting. Handshakes between the genders, however, have different customs around the world. In India and Saudi Arabia, for example, the handshake is only between men. In other countries, such as Germany, you would want to wait to see if the woman extended her hand for the handshake rather than assume that all women shake hands. The duration, number of pumps, and vigorousness of the handshake also can be different. In countries such as Saudi Arabia, you will find the handshake is often done, and they will hold your lower arm while shaking hands. In Finland, however, it is customary to greet women before men with a firm handshake. The U.S. handshake is moderately firm in comparison to the light, quick grasp of the French; the soft or gentle grasp of the British; the Latin American moderate grasp; and the firm grasp of the Germans.

Another form of greeting used in place of or with the handshake is the kiss or hug. Although a kiss or hug is generally not appropriate as a greeting in the United States, in some countries it is customary. Middle Eastern men will shake hands and kiss on both cheeks as they hug. Russians are famous for their bear hug, which will be followed by a strong, firm handshake between male friends. Scandinavians prefer to have no body contact with strangers and do not hug or kiss. Latin Americans, Mediterranean people, and many Africans embrace, often accompanying the embrace with a slap on the back.[9] Latin American, Mediterranean, and African women who are close friends often hug or kiss each other as part of their greeting. Both men and women in France will hold each other's shoulders lightly and give an air kiss first on one cheek and then on the other cheek.

As you can see, greetings vary around the world. Asians, Northern Europeans, and most Canadians and U.S. people are uncomfortable with touching and hugging. Some countries have multiple ways of greeting each other, such as the Greeks who may shake hands, embrace, and/or kiss a person at the first meeting or at every meeting. Although bowing is the customary form of greeting in Japan and China, the handshake is becoming much more acceptable with the Japanese who work internationally.

You will often find when conducting business with the people of Japan or China that the handshake is often combined with a bow so that each culture shows the other proper respect.[10] In India, the traditional greeting is the *Namaste*, which one says while pressing palms together with fingers up and placing the hands below the chin. A slight bow accompanies this gesture when greeting supervisors or others to whom you wish to show respect. Because greeting customs vary so widely, be sure to check out this first-impression maker before arriving at your destination.

EXCHANGING BUSINESS CARDS

The importance of the business card exchange should never be underestimated. In the United States, businesspeople carry business cards, and they are exchanged if there is a reason to do so. Since knowing a person's rank, title, and profession are necessary in other cultures, be sure to include your position, titles, degrees, all phone numbers with international codes (fax number, mobile number, and office number), and e-mail address on your business cards. Because of the problems concerning the meaning of colors, avoid colored type and paper. By choosing white paper with black ink, you will have a dignified, acceptable business card. Paper quality can be very important in some cultures, so use a good-quality card stock. The size of the card may need to be changed so that it fits the client's card filing system. In non-English-speaking countries, have the information on your card printed in English on one side and in the local language on the other side of the card. Be sure to have a competent translator, as many slogans or bylines do not retain their original meaning when translated. It may be necessary to rethink part of what is written on your card.

In some cases, in order for the titles to fit the country, it may be advisable to give international executives multiple sets of business cards—one for the United States and one for each country in which they are traveling and working. In many countries, the title has to do with the reporting level and importance of the person within the company.[11] An exchange of business cards is an expected part of business introductions in most countries of the world. Because the business card plays such an important role in relationship building, it would be wise to have cards for every country translated into the country's first language.

Although it is permissible in the United States to glance at a business card just received and place it in a pocket, this practice is not acceptable around the world. In fact, such abruptness is seen as rude by many other people in the world. In countries like Japan, the examination of the business card is carried out with deliberateness. The Japanese will make a comment, study the card for clues to social protocol and hierarchy within the firm, then they will place the card where they can refer to it during the meeting, such as on the top of the meeting table. When meeting with people of such cultures, you should examine the card carefully, looking at both the front and back of the card. Nodding your head as you read the information on the card indicates that you understand the information on the card. Like your counterpart, it is proper to make a comment or ask a question about something on the card. If you are not sure about how to correctly pronounce a name or what titles to use, ask your contact for assistance. Do not put the card away until a reasonable amount of time has passed. You will use both hands when presenting your card in Japan or South Korea, positioning the card so that the person can read it.

In the Middle East, Southeast Asia, and African cultures (with the exception of Israel), however, you will only use your right hand to present and take business cards, as the left hand is reserved for taking care of bodily functions.[12] Be sure to call the other person by their last name (noting that in Japan, China, and Korea, their last name will be printed first), until you are requested to call them by their first name. Because Scandinavians are respectful of age, it is advisable to include your company's date of establishment on your business cards if the company's history is a long one.[13] Australian businesspersons do not usually carry business cards; thus, when you offer them your card, you may not receive one in return. In Latin American countries, business titles are important on business cards.[14]

COUNTRY-SPECIFIC INFORMATION

Country-specific information on language, greetings, introductions, and business cards for the countries with which the United States conducts most of its international business is provided in the sections following.

Brazil

- The handshake is the typical business greeting. Personal greetings between women include one to four air kisses to each cheek during the handshake; married women usually kiss twice, while single women kiss three times. Personal greetings between men do not involve kissing. Men do, however, pat each other on the back while shaking hands.[15]
- Use of appropriate titles during introductions is recommended. The title *Doutor* or *Doutoro* (Doctor) is often used to show respect, particularly with older persons, even though the person may be neither an MD nor a PhD.
- Business card exchange is important; having business cards printed in English on one side and in Portuguese on the reverse side is recommended.[16]

Canada

- Conservative social and business etiquette is more prevalent in Canada than in the United States.
- Province differences are very important for businesspeople. In Quebec, close male or female friends may embrace lightly, and females will add a light kiss to the cheek when greeting. In the Western and Atlantic provinces, the greeting is a handshake for the men; women may or may not shake hands but instead will say "hello" and nod their heads.[17]
- Handshakes are firm, with direct eye contact, when meeting associates and upon departure.
- Canadians do not want to be referred to as "American" or "Yankee," meaning the same as U.S. American. Canadians feel closer to England than to the United States.[18]

- Business cards should be printed in English on one side and French on the other side of the card. Legally, everything must be labeled in both languages in Canada.

China

- The Chinese greet the most senior person first. Also, you will hear the surname spoken first, followed by the first name. Titles should be used with the name, such as President Yuan Li.[19]
- Chinese bow or nod when greeting but have generally learned to offer a gentle handshake to Westerners.
- Agents are used to introduce you to those with whom you want to do business.[20]
- Business cards should be printed in English and Mandarin Chinese in black ink.

France

- The handshake is light and quick upon greeting and when saying goodbye. People who work together shake hands upon arriving and leaving work. Women typically wait for a man to initiate the handshake. Women are kissed on both cheeks as part of the greeting; however, men only kiss each other on the cheeks when they are good friends or relatives.
- Business cards are exchanged at initial meetings; they are presented first to the person of higher rank to show respect.
- Business cards should be printed in English and French.
- Introductions should be done by someone who knows the person to whom you wish to be introduced, as this gives you legitimacy.[21]

Germany

- Handshakes are firm and used upon meeting and departing.
- Status is recognized, and men allow people of higher status or women to precede them when entering a door or elevator.
- Titles and the family name are used when speaking or writing to someone until you are asked to use their first name. First names are rarely used by most Germans.
- Business cards should be printed in English and German, and titles and degrees should be included.

Japan

- Greeting form is a bow rather than a handshake; however, many Japanese who regularly associate with persons of other cultures may use both a bow and a soft handshake. Follow the lead of your Japanese host.

- Business card exchange is considered an important ritual, so be sure you have a good supply. These should be printed on one side in English and the other side in Japanese. Remember to address your Japanese host by his last name; only family members and close friends use the first name.[22]

Mexico

- The usual greeting in Mexico is to shake hands using a moderate grasp and repeating the pumping action numerous times. People also shake hands when saying goodbye. It is not unusual for men to give each other an *abrazo* (hug); this is to be considered a compliment and a sign of acceptance. When introduced to a woman, a man will bow slightly and will shake hands if the woman initiates it.

- Address the person by his or her last name, as first names are not used during initial encounters.

- Business cards are exchanged at a first meeting; remember to include the Spanish translation on your cards. Indicate your position with your company and your university degrees. Deference is shown to someone whose age, social status, or position warrants it.

South Korea

- A greeting between men is a bow, accompanied by a moderate handshake. To show respect, the left hand is placed below the right forearm while shaking hands. The junior person should initiate the greeting and be the first to bow. Women do not shake hands as frequently as men. Be punctual for meetings. Matching rank of individuals for meetings is important.[23]

- Business cards should be in English and Korean.

- Business cards are exchanged between professionals during initial encounters; the cards are presented and received with both hands. Both age and social standing are taken into consideration when greeting someone.[24]

- The honorific term that you add to a South Korean family name is "*ssi*," for men and women.[25]

Taiwan

- Bowing is a common form of greeting in many Asian countries; however, in Taiwan it is more common to use a gentle handshake. Rank is important, so be sure to acknowledge and shake hands with the person of higher rank first.

- Handshakes are light and precede the business card exchange. Because business cards are exchanged frequently in Taiwan, you will want to carry an ample supply with you. Not presenting your business card to your Taiwanese associates would be viewed as unprofessional. Having a translation of the information on your cards printed in Mandarin on the back of the card is recommended. Because the business card presentation is important to the Taiwanese, the card should be presented with both hands with the card turned so the recipient can read it.

- Introductions by local contacts to set up initial meetings are extremely important, and the U.S. Commerce Department or an international bank can help you with this.[26]

United Kingdom (England, Scotland, Wales, and Northern Ireland)

- Handshakes are soft and accompanied by "How do you do?"
- Conversations that are loud are considered unacceptable in public.[27]
- Business cards are printed in English and should include titles.

United States of America

- Greetings are rather informal; people often say "Hi" when greeting others. Greeting behavior is highly ritualistic; the expected response to the typical greeting of "Hello, how are you?" is "Fine" or "Very well, thanks." "Goodbye" or "Have a nice day" are typically said when leaving; some people will say "See you later" (even if they do not plan to see you again) or—especially in the South—"Y'all come to see us" (even though this is not meant as an invitation). These expressions are simply rituals.

- Greetings are accompanied by a firm handshake. In business settings, both men and women are expected to rise and shake hands when being introduced to someone. A woman is no longer expected to initiate the handshake. Eye contact is expected when shaking hands.

- First names are often used in both business and social situations. However, when greeting someone for the first time or when meeting international visitors, using a title and last name is recommended.

- Business cards are exchanged when there is some reason to contact the person later. There is no set ritual for the business card exchange.

Chapter 3

SOCIALIZING

Socialization is what makes life worth living. Socialization is how we interact with the world or culture around us. Although we learn these skills in our own culture from the time we are born, when we switch cultures, what has become automatic in our home cultures may no longer work socially in intercultural situations. As we assimilate into a culture, we also learn how to properly socialize within that culture. This chapter will discuss forming friendships, gift giving, punctuality and time, relationship building between males and females, and country-specific information on these topics.

FRIENDSHIPS

What is considered a friendship has a great deal of variation around the world. To the U.S. businessperson, a personal relationship can be separated from business; a friendship is formed quickly and dissolved quickly. Many view the U.S. relationship as shallow and short-term oriented. In many other cultures, such as China, relationships are viewed as lifetime commitments.[1]

Some people have an innate ability to adjust to a new culture and build the necessary friendships. You must very quickly learn where relationships develop, such as at meetings of professional societies, clubs, churches, and so forth. People who are extroverts tend to form more social ties with people in the new culture than do people who are not extroverts.[2] Unfortunately, what one has learned in his or her native culture is probably not going to work in a new culture, as these settings change from culture to culture. Once the contacts are made, then you need the skills to maintain and build the relationship. If this relationship is not maintained properly, it can be very difficult for the person taking over the assignment later. Just as important for the new person taking the position is the ability of the former person to say goodbye in a culturally acceptable manner.[3]

The smile is one of the most universal signs of friendship and will help you build relationships almost anywhere in the world. Be careful about the smile's meaning, however. In some cultures, people also smile when they are embarrassed as well as when they are happy. Also, people of some cultures smile more easily than others, so you would not want your smile seen as insincere. Generally, however, the smile will be one of your best means of communication in most cultures.

PUNCTUALITY AND TIME

Perceptions and the concept of time vary widely from culture to culture. What is considered punctual may change from country to country. People who work internationally must have many definitions of time. The word *mañana*, used in Latin American countries, and the word *bukra*, used in the Middle East, have a similar attitudinal meaning. The expressions mean that what cannot be done today will be done tomorrow. Time for these cultures is a mixture of past, present, and future, rather than a separation of time segments as is true in the United States and in many Northern European countries.[4] Do the people in a culture look at time as formal and task-oriented, or do they look at time as an opportunity to spend time and develop an interpersonal relationship? Is the task driving the clock, or is the clock driving the task?[5] Time allows workers to know what time is theirs and what time the employer is paying them to work.[6] How time is used is culturally learned, including the concept of time itself, the compartmentalizing of time, and the perception of time.

Although people in the United States believe the time of an appointment should be kept (task-oriented time), in another culture, it is acceptable to be an hour late because time is flexible (event time).[7] In some cultures, superiors make subordinates wait for their appointments to show the superiors' importance and higher rank. Power and dignity are shown by arriving late; this is a tactic used in Middle Eastern countries.[8] In such areas of the world as Latin America, Africa, and the Middle East, time is not important. Being late for an appointment in these areas is normally not considered offensive behavior.[9] In many countries, it is expected that you will be late to dinner or parties; in fact, if you arrived on time they may not be ready for you.

In some international situations, the name of a country will be inserted after the meeting time to indicate if one is to assume task time or event time. The insertion of a country name allows all participants from different cultural backgrounds to understand if the time is fixed or fluid. An example of this practice would be, "The meeting will be at 9:00 a.m., Malaysian time" for event timing, or "The meeting will be at 9:00 a.m., U.S. time" for task-oriented time. The task and event time concepts carry over to how much of the workday is given to company tasks and how much time is given to socializing. In the United States, the division is typically 80 percent task and 20 percent social. In Latin American countries, it is typically 50 percent task and 50 percent social. If you are in a culture in which relationships are important, such as collectivistic societies, then you need to adjust how you view time. Using time properly is important to relationship development in many cultures.[10]

In addition to the task/event component of time, you also have the mono-chronic/polychronic component of time. Monochronic time involves the ability to do one thing at a time, and polychronic time involves the ability to do multiple tasks simultaneously. On a scale of 1 to 5, the United States ranks 3.18, meaning U.S. people are in the middle of the monochronic/ polychronic continuum. There are also many differences within a society. In the United States, you may find a CEO who is aggressive and task-oriented, who eats, drives, and talks on his cell phone all at the same time; then you will find CEOs who prefer to do one thing at a time. People in the United States are moving toward polychronic time use when engaged in multiple activities at the same time in order to "save time." U.S. people may refer to this practice as multitasking. They refrain from engaging in this behavior in the presence of others, however, as this is viewed as rude. Traditional Asians will be ranked four on the five-point scale toward polychronic time. Although Asians can do more things at once, it is not proper in their culture to do multiple tasks. Modern, industrialized Asians, however, are ranked three on the monochronic/polychronic scale. These differences are not unusual within a society.[11] Globalization of business is probably influencing how the concept of time is viewed around the world, particularly at the individual level more than at the country level.

Part of the view of time is whether you "work to live" or "live to work." Although most Europeans work hard, they also play hard, enjoying some of the longest vacation times in the world. When working with Europeans, it is necessary to know when their vacation times are, as it is not customary for them to interrupt their vacations for business. The United States and Japan have the least vacation time.[12] Work time and personal time are separated from one another in a monochronic culture, but not clearly separated in a polychronic culture. An example of how time is viewed differently in the United States and Tahiti is illustrated by the following story.

A woman from Chicago, Illinois, on vacation in Tahiti, was riding a bus from the business area back to her hotel. As they neared the hotel, she got up to get off at her stop as she would have done on the subway or a bus in Chicago. The bus driver in Tahiti stopped the bus in the middle of the street. When she indicated she wanted to get off at the next stop, the bus driver very nicely told her that they had all day, that she was to sit down, and that he could wait for her to walk to the door after he stopped the bus.

Pace-of-life studies have three ways of assigning countries: "walking speed on urban sidewalks, how quickly postal clerks fulfill a request for a common stamp, and the accuracy of public clocks." Based on these three variables, Switzerland, Ireland, Germany, Japan, and Italy are the fastest-paced countries; Syria, El Salvador, Brazil, Indonesia, and Mexico are the five slowest-paced countries; and the United States places 16th, near the middle of the 31 countries ranked.[13] Africans consider time to be two-dimensional, with a long past, a present, and very little future. For much of Africa, time is a series of events that is experienced, and because the future has not been experienced, it has very little meaning.[14] For the Middle East, time is seen as in God's control and the term *inshallah*, "if God wills it," is used often. Middle Easterners are very patient and deliberate in how they do business; however, plans can change quickly, particularly if a family member is involved.

In Saudi Arabia, time is marked by the lunar cycle. This means a Saudi may actually wear two wristwatches: one with Greenwich-based time and the other with Saudi lunar time. Because of their casual regard for time, one oil company executive quipped:

"Arabs have clocks, two of them in fact, but it often seems to a Westerner that neither clock has hands."[15]

Other parts of time are the linear and nonlinear aspects of language that involve thought patterns. The thought processes indicate how people think and communicate. With linear language, there is a beginning and an end that is object-oriented. English is a linear language that looks at time as a continuum of present, past, and future. Linear languages lead to the business practice of short-range planning. Nonlinear language is circular, tradition-oriented, and subjective. In nonlinear languages, everything is cyclical with repeating patterns. People who speak nonlinear languages are people who tend to be more long term in their business planning. Japanese and Chinese are nonlinear languages.

An example of a problem that can arise out of this aspect of language follows. In the United States, a linear explanation would be expected and the "why there was a problem" question would be answered; a Japanese person, on the other hand, would answer with what happened. "The parts are defective" is a why answer; "The parts were attached as normal, then the stress test was done on 20 vehicles, and that determined the parts were defective," is a nonlinear answer. People living in a present-oriented culture live for today and usually have short-term perspectives. Wasting time is seen as undesirable because time is a scarce commodity. Many Middle Eastern countries tend to have a past-oriented view of time. According to this view of time, because things have worked well for a thousand years, there should be no rush to change things now. Europeans and many Asian countries are also very loyal to tradition and the past; however, the loyalty to the past does not prevent them from being very future-oriented. The future-oriented person is going to take longer to explain a new idea, versus the present-oriented person who will get to the point immediately. The present-oriented people look at the past for guidance but are rushing into the future; past-oriented people look at the past as the roots of their existence, and the past is viewed more positively than the present. Globalization is testing this past orientation, and globally we seem to be moving to more of a present orientation.[16]

Time-style dimensions involve how one plans and include analytic time, or accounting for every minute of the day, to holistic time, which is more spontaneous but looks at time in larger chunks. The Western orientation is more analytical in its time-planning orientation and creates small, exclusive appointments for 15- to 30-minute intervals. Eastern countries tend to be more holistic in time planning, look at broad, overlapping categories, and have fewer but longer meetings.[17] Although a U.S. businessperson may have many short meetings and keep a very tight schedule, an Asian businessperson will have fewer, longer meetings and leave room in his or her schedule for the unexpected. A problem that can happen when strict deadlines are maintained is that quality is compromised. Many long-term, value-oriented Asian countries have tried to adopt the speed of Western cultures but have found problems with the resulting quality of the product being produced. Likewise, multicultural work teams need more time to achieve their tasks and to build group cohesiveness; however, this time is well spent, as many times they are more effective once they get to know each other.[18] In a business meeting, all the participants will experience the same presentation; however, different cultures will feel differently about the passing of time during the presentation.[19]

Understanding personal time and business time and being aware of your own and others' views of time will help in communicating with people of other cultures. Hall's description of time as a silent language of intercultural communication is one of the hardest value differences to accept.[20]

GIFT GIVING

Gift-giving practices and seasons vary around the world. In religiously oriented countries, gift giving is done during religious celebrations; in nonreligious countries, specific times of the year are devoted to gift giving. Certain events, such as the conclusion of a business contract, may also necessitate gift giving. Because gift giving is an integral part of building global relationships, you need to understand the subtleties of the gift-giving art. Some of the important considerations include the laws surrounding gift giving, gifts that are appropriate or not appropriate, the wrapping of the gift, and knowing when to reciprocate.

Due to tax regulations and laws, business gifts in the United States are limited to $25. If you are visiting someone's home, flowers or chocolates (except in many Asian countries where people are lactose intolerant) are nice. Always ask your hotel concierge what type of gift or flowers would be appropriate. If flowers are appropriate, find out how they should be presented. Otherwise, something that is unique to the United States, such as pins, pens, small china or crystal items, key chains, or other accessories, are appreciated. In Saudi Arabia and China, the eagle symbol signifies bad luck, so you would not want to give something with an eagle on it even though the eagle is the U.S. national bird.

It is important to find out when and to whom gifts are given when working with an international firm. In the United States, we observe many office holidays, such as Secretaries' Day, with a lunch or flowers. It would be inappropriate to give gifts of cologne or lingerie to a member of the opposite gender, however. Gift certificates to restaurants or specialty shops are always appreciated. Supervisors tend to set the tone of gift giving, but when you are new, it is wise to ask what is acceptable for this office, particularly when you are in another country. In the United States, it is not unusual for gifts to take the form of cash for custodians or contributions to food banks or other nonprofit organizations during the Christmas season. Other countries have celebration times when they also help the poor and nonprofit organizations.

When people of the United States select business gifts for people in other countries, they should remember that the gifts should be made in the United States, be utilitarian, and have conversational value. Good choices include things that are representative of the United States, such as Native American art or jewelry, DVDs of U.S. movies, U.S.-made sports equipment, or food that is unique to the United States, such as candy, nuts, and California wines. Avoid gag gifts; people of some cultures do not appreciate them.[21]

A Japanese American, whose firm conducted business in Japan, told how he once averted a near disaster in U.S.-Japanese relations. His company selected and addressed 500 Christmas cards to its Japanese joint-venture partner. The cards were red (in Japan, funeral notices are red). The Japanese American manager stopped the mail just in time. He said, "We almost sent 500 funeral cards to our Japanese partner!"[22]

In many parts of the world, such as Japan, Taiwan, Hong Kong, and South Korea, gifts are not opened in front of the giver as they are in the United States; you would also accept the gifts with both hands. In countries where you do not open the gift immediately, you would admire the gift and verbally express appreciation. Thank you notes are written upon returning home or to your office unless the gift has a company logo. Communal gifts that are sent to the office should be shared with office colleagues and not taken home. It is the manager's responsibility to write a note of thanks to the company that sent the gift and express appreciation from the entire staff. In many countries, such as Mexico and Germany, it is appropriate to open the gift when it is presented. Another twist is that in Middle Eastern countries, you present the gift in front of others to show that it is not a bribe.[23]

Although flowers make appropriate gifts, there are many cultural taboos related to color, variety, and number. Red roses are only given by lovers or spouses in some cultures. White is the color of mourning in China; and because white gladioli are often used in funeral sprays, they would not be an appropriate gift. In Brazil, purple flowers are associated with death by the lower class. Carnations are used to decorate cemeteries in France and Germany, as chrysanthemums are in Belgium, Japan, and Italy; therefore, in these countries you would want to avoid these inappropriate flowers as gifts. To Mexicans, yellow, red, or white flowers have specific significance including romance and death, so flowers in these three colors should be avoided as gifts. The number of flowers being given has significance in many cultures.[24] An uneven number of flowers is given on happy occasions by Armenians and an even number of flowers for funerals. Because three is a lucky number in Thailand and Hong Kong, giving gifts in threes in these countries would be considered lucky.[25] Your hotel concierge or a local flower shop in the host country can help you follow local traditions concerning flowers.

Because gift giving is an art in many parts of the world, the following tips could be helpful:

- Pick the perfect gift, perhaps for a hobby or collection the person has.
- Buy your gifts in the United States; they should be U.S. made.
- Be aware of superstitions and taboos related to gifts.
- Check the significance of numbers in gift giving for the country.
- Due to politeness, expect a gift to be declined at least once in some Asian countries; they will then accept. You are expected to do the same.[26]
- Present gifts at the conclusion of contract negotiations in Latin American countries.
- Present your gift upon arrival at Western European homes.
- Avoid giving a knife, as it is interpreted as wanting to end a relationship, or a handkerchief, as it is associated with tears in South American countries as well as in other parts of the world.
- Avoid gifts of liquor or wine in all Islamic cultures, as it is forbidden by their religion.
- Avoid gifts of cowhide in India, because the cow is sacred.
- Exercise restraint in admiring personal possessions in the Middle East; Middle Easterners may feel obligated to give the item to you.[27]

RELATIONSHIP BUILDING

Relationship building begins with communication. When you add different cultural orientations, communication becomes more difficult. Some truisms of communication are that communication cannot be avoided, what is communicated may or may not be understood, communication is irreversible, communication occurs in context, and communication is dynamic.[28] Most importantly, communication is the basis for building a relationship.

Although males and females are equally successful in global assignments on the three criteria of retention, adjustment, and supervisor-rated performance, it is interesting, but not surprising, that women are less cross-culturally adjusted than men in countries with a low number of female managers and low female workforce participation.[29] One of the cultural constraints between male and female business-relationship building is the cultural norms toward such relationships in the host national culture. Of course, the language skills and personality types of the males and females involved will constrain or promote business-relationship building. Women tend to be more relationship-centered than men and can carry on a professional conversation with ease socially, which can help women in developing relationships if they know the language.[30]

Although there are many different norms for male and female expatriates, there are more limitations for females, particularly single females. Single women will tend to be isolated from social situations that involve family. Also, in certain countries, being single beyond a certain age has a negative connotation. Many expatriate women report being lonely and having limited dating opportunities.[31]

Due to the stigma of cross-gender friendships in many countries, women may find having a social relationship with a male host national to be difficult. If the woman has a high-status position within the organization, she may have problems having social relationships with host national females in cultures where hierarchy is important, because one does not befriend a senior manager whether he or she is male or female.[32]

If a culture gives women lower social status, it may undermine a female expatriate's authority both inside and outside of the organization. Gender stereotyping is still prevalent in some countries. It is interesting, however, that even some countries that have these gender stereotypes see Western female expatriates as professionals first and as women second. It is assumed that if the Western organization sent a female, then she must be very competent.[33]

The more men and women interact with the host nationals, the more they will increase their knowledge of the norms and behaviors that are appropriate. The interactions will consequently increase the expatriate's psychological well-being, assuming the interactions are positive. The more an expatriate is seen favorably, the more likely the host nationals will be socially supportive. Mentors and other expatriates are also good at providing social support and helping new expatriates adjust to the new culture.[34] Some attitudes and actions that facilitate interacting with host nationals include having a nurturing style, being more compromising than domineering, having a sensitivity to other's needs, being compassionate and understanding, being cooperative rather than competitive, engaging in rapport talk, having an inclusive leadership style, adopting a listening behavior, avoiding conflict by emphasizing harmony, and using more indirectness rather than directness in communications.[35] Developing relationships in a new culture is difficult, but building relationships between males and females is sometimes even more difficult due to cultural differences. The important thing to remember is that many women and men have done so very successfully. In some cases, because women in business are a curiosity factor, they have gained access to higher-level managers more easily than men.[36]

Males and females should both receive cultural-diversity training and cultural-awareness training for their host country. Training helps to shorten the cultural-learning curve; it looks at biases and stereotypes and addresses cultural shock and other differences the expatriate is going to face, including relationships between the genders. A recent study of 409 senior and middle managers found seven actions that were considered important and that all expatriates should know or do: select and choose the best cultural values of the home and the host country; conform and adapt to the norms of the host country as much as possible; do not keep a distance between yourself and the host-country nationals; conform to the corporate headquarters if there is an inconsistency with the host country; be open to the culture of the host country; be knowledgeable about the host-country's culture; and socialize with host-country nationals from similar cultural backgrounds.[37] When you sign a contract in Latin American or Asian cultures, you do not signal an end to a sale or negotiation, but a continuation of a relationship with obligations and duties in the future. Your word is more important than any document you may sign.[38]

COUNTRY-SPECIFIC INFORMATION

Information on socializing in the countries with which the United States conducts a majority of its international business follows.

Brazil

- Giving business gifts, though not required, is appreciated. Business gifts are not typically given at the first meeting; gifts at subsequent meetings may be CD players, iPods, wine, good-quality whisky, or mementos of your country. Gifts should be wrapped attractively and are opened in the presence of the giver.[39]

- Avoid gifts that are black or purple, as these colors suggest mourning. Also avoid gifts that are sharp, such as letter openers or knives, as this indicates a desire to sever the relationship. Likewise, handkerchiefs are not a good choice as they are associated with funerals.[40]

- Making business appointments at least two weeks in advance is recommended. Avoid making appointments in July (a school holiday month) and mid-December through the end of February (summer vacation period).[41]

- While punctuality is important in business, meetings may begin from 10 to 30 minutes late due to heavy traffic in large cities. Arriving about 15 minutes late for social events is customary.[42]

- Building a successful relationship is important to conducting business; this requires a number of meetings over a period of time.[43]

Canada

- Understanding the Anglo- and French-Canadian differences is very important. The French Canadians consider themselves French first and Canadian second and may speak French rather than English.

- Exchanging business gifts is generally done at Christmastime; they should not be expensive and could be an office-related item, wine, liquor, or dinner at a nice restaurant. A gift is also given at the end of negotiations when the contract is signed.
- Building relationships is not necessary for doing business in Canada; however, it is helpful to develop a personal relationship as the business relationship grows.
- Timing in the form of promptness is important.

China

- Cultivating long-term friendships is good for a business relationship. Face saving is important. Direct questioning is viewed as rude.[44]
- Being on time is expected; however, the pace of business is slower.[45]
- Giving gifts is a common practice except at a first meeting. It is important to remember their lunar New Year. Recommended gifts (wrapped in red) are pens of high quality or a paperweight. Gifts to avoid are clocks, white flowers, and handkerchiefs because of their association with death. In addition, knives and other cutlery should be avoided because they suggest a wish to sever ties. Always wrap gifts (no bows) and include an appropriate card. Although wrapping the gift in red paper (the color of luck) is appropriate, using red ink when addressing the card or writing the accompanying note is not; in China, red ink indicates a desire to sever a relationship forever. The number four is bad luck, so do not give anything in fours.
- Choosing small gifts for an individual or for the company is appropriate.
- Building a relationship is a must before doing business in China.[46]

France

- Exchanging business gifts is done only after a business relationship has been established. Appropriate gifts include flowers (except chrysanthemums, carnations, or red roses), books, DVDs, or gourmet food items. Avoid giving gifts to the French until a personal relationship has been developed.
- Giving products marked with company logos is common.
- Sending flowers when invited to someone's home is acceptable, but avoid red roses and chrysanthemums as well as perfume and wine.
- Building personal relationships is important. Employees are very loyal to their employers; however, they are not workaholics. It is expected that colleagues will be knowledgeable, appreciative of cultural events, and successful at their jobs.[47]

Germany

- At the beginning of negotiations, business gifts are seldom exchanged but may be given at their conclusion. Gifts to your German host should be something simple and rather inexpensive, as Germans consider expensive gifts to be in bad taste. Gifts to Germans should not be wrapped in black, brown, or white.

- Bring the hostess a gift of flowers (an odd number except 13, but no red roses) when invited to their home.
- In Germany, giving gifts marked with company logos is acceptable. If you are invited to someone's home, chocolates are always appreciated.
- Making appointments a minimum of two weeks in advance is expected.
- Arriving on time is essential; even two or three minutes late will be considered an insult.
- Developing a relationship is not important for doing business in Germany.

Japan

- Meetings are held punctually. Meetings continue until the business at hand is completed. If the Japanese delay in keeping an appointment, they may politely be saying they are not interested.[48]
- Giving gifts for business has two appointed times, Ochugen (July 15) and Oseibo (December). Gifts are given as expressions of appreciation for past and future business. Bonuses are given to employees at these two appointed times also.[49]
- Presenting your gift properly shows the importance of gift giving and is shown by the wrapping of the gift and the manner in which it is presented. The color of the wrapping matches the occasion: gold and white for happy events, black and purple or black and white for other occasions. Gifts are not opened in front of the giver. Avoid giving a gift when someone else is present.
- Surprising your Japanese host with a gift may be embarrassing, as it might cause the person to lose face. Your host will want to reciprocate in kind, so you should mention ahead of time what you have found to give to them. Name brand items of high quality are good gift ideas. Items manufactured in other parts of Asia should not be given as gifts.[50]
- Building relationships and friendships is a necessary prerequisite for doing business in Japan.
- Being punctual is important; however, decisions are communal and may take more time than you would expect.

Mexico

- Being introduced by a third party is very helpful in Mexico. It is also necessary to build a relationship with them so that they know they can trust you. They look at business relationships as long-term relationships.

- Meetings are expected to begin on time; however, it is acceptable to be a few minutes late. You may be kept waiting, however, if your host has not finished his last meeting. Mexicans allow as much time as necessary to finish the current activity before moving on to the next activity. The Mexican culture is people-oriented rather than task-oriented.

- Choosing an appropriate gift is important and could be one of the following items: a gold pen, art books, or a bottle of Scotch. Be careful about giving flowers as gifts, as there are many dos and don'ts. Ask a florist or your hotel concierge so that you do not make a mistake before selecting a gift of flowers.

South Korea

- Arriving on time is expected, although you may have to wait for an appointment.

- Developing relationships and hospitality is important. Although harmony is important, South Koreans are more direct and express emotion more so than other Far Easterners. South Koreans will laugh when embarrassed.[51]

- Knowing when to present the business gift is also important. In South Korea, business gifts are usually given at the beginning of formal negotiations. Give gifts with both hands. Expect the gift to be refused at first and then accepted, as this is good manners. The clock is considered good luck and would be an appropriate gift. Gifts should not be made in Japan nor should you discuss your business relationships with anyone in Japan.[52]

- Being introduced or having a letter of reference is required; without one you may not be able to get an appointment. It will be necessary to develop a relationship before you can begin to discuss business.[53]

Taiwan

- Getting down to business happens faster in Taiwan than most other Asian countries; you still need to engage in polite conversation before engaging in business conversation.

- Being punctual is appreciated, but being early or late by a few minutes is acceptable. You may also be kept waiting, or the Taiwanese businessperson might not show up at all for the meeting.

- Presenting business gifts is done with both hands. Visitors should remember that the Taiwanese will refuse a gift initially, so you should continue to offer it until it is accepted; gifts are opened in private. Avoid giving clocks, knives, or umbrellas. Good gift ideas include Scotch, ginseng, or desk accessories. Red is the preferred color for wrapping your gifts. Avoid the colors white, black, and blue.[54]

- Build relationships through evening business entertainment, which may last late into the evening. Although personal relationships must be established before business, this does not mean you are a personal friend. Business negotiations will take many trips and patience.[55]

United Kingdom (England, Scotland, Wales, and Northern Ireland)

- Purchasing a striped tie would not be an appropriate gift for the UK man; it may represent the UK regiment other than his own.
- Giving gifts is not important in the UK; however, if invited to a home, sending a gift after the visit is appreciated.
- Being on time is considered appropriate.
- Developing a friendship is not important for doing business in the UK.

United States of America

- People of the United States have few close friends. Perhaps the mobility of the population is a factor in the difficulty in forming long-lasting friendships.
- Punctuality is very important for both business and social appointments. Although being five minutes late for business appointments is acceptable, an apology is expected.
- While gifts are not expected when invited to a party or dinner at someone's house, a small gift of flowers, wine, or a fruit basket is appreciated.
- Developing a relationship before conducting business is unimportant in the United States.

Chapter 4

GESTURES AND OTHER NONVERBAL COMMUNICATORS

Gestures and other forms of nonverbal communication can help you send and interpret messages when interacting with people from other cultures. These nonverbal communicators are especially useful when different languages are involved and people must rely on alternative methods of communicating. In addition to gestures, messages may be sent through the use of color, eye contact, facial expressions, paralanguage, posture, silence, smell, space and touch, and nonverbal leakage. Many nonverbal communicators are culture specific. Because nonverbal signals are interpreted immediately when they occur, whether they are judged in a positive or a negative manner is very important. You will want to investigate the nonverbals and their meanings before doing business in another country.

You also must understand that your nonverbal communication may be ambiguous in other cultures and be detrimental to relationship building. In the United States, nonverbals become even more difficult for foreigners because we are made up of many cultures. For example, Native American children avoid direct eye contact as a sign of respect; however, you will not find this to be true of all Native Americans. Nonverbal signals are never completely reliable. As people are exposed to another culture, they tend to take on some of the nonverbal aspects of the culture; therefore, it becomes very difficult to interpret the nonverbal communicator's meaning unless you know the person fairly well. As Hall and Hall in *Understanding Cultural Differences* have stated, we learn nonverbal behavior in the context of growing up in a culture; it is invisible and omnipresent. We take it for granted and do not consciously think about it. As cultures interact through travel, television, and business, the nonverbal signals of a culture change because they are learned behaviors.[1]

GESTURES

Gestures perform an important function when people communicate nonverbally. They are useful in adding emphasis to what is said. When used at inappropriate times or with people of other cultures, however, they may cause confusion or misunderstanding. Thus, caution is advised when using gestures with persons of other cultures because what is perceived as positive in one culture may be viewed as negative or even obscene in another.

No gestures have universal meanings across cultures; meanings are culture specific. For example, the U.S. "V for Victory" gesture (the index and middle fingers held upright with palm and fingers faced outward) is recognized as positive in many countries. In England, however, the gesture has a crude connotation when the palm is turned inward.[2]

Another related gesture with a positive connotation is the thumbs-up signal. Although this gesture means "good going" or "everything is great" to people of most European countries and North America, it has a rude connotation in Australia and West Africa.

Likewise, the OK sign (thumb and forefinger joined to form a circle) is positive to U.S. persons but considered obscene in Brazil. In France and Belgium, the gesture should be avoided as it means "worthless" or "zero." The meaning of the gesture is completely different in Japan—it signifies money.

One example to illustrate problems that may result when gestures are used in intercultural interactions is the story of an American engineer who offended his German counterpart by giving the U.S. "OK" gesture (thumb and forefinger joined to form a circle) to indicate he had done a good job. After the German engineer walked off the job, the American engineer later learned why: the gesture meant "You asshole" to Germans.[3]

Using a beckoning gesture (palm facing the body with fingers upturned) is sometimes used (but not recommended in some sections of the United States) to get a server's attention in a restaurant. Filipinos, Vietnamese, and Mexicans find this gesture offensive as it is used to call people considered inferior, such as prostitutes, and animals in these cultures.

The vertical horns gesture, which is a raised fist with the index finger and little finger extended, has a positive connotation in the United States; it is associated with the University of Texas Longhorn football team. In Italy, however, it has an insulting connotation. In Brazil and Venezuela, it signifies good luck. This symbol should be used with discretion because it has various meanings in U.S. subcultures, including serving as a satanic cult recognition sign signifying the devil's horns.

Even shaking the head to mean "yes" or "no" differs according to the culture. Shaking the head from side to side in the United States means "no," but in Bulgaria the gesture signifies "yes."

People of the United States use moderate gesturing; they usually keep gestures fairly close to the body. The elbows do not go above shoulder level except when waving to someone. In addition, people of England, Germany, and Switzerland use few gestures. On the other hand, people of France, Italy, Spain, Greece, and the Middle Eastern countries, as well as people of most countries of Central and South America, are more effusive and expressive in their gesturing. Because most cultures have standard gestures used in their daily interactions, learning these gestures before visiting another culture is recommended.

During the Iraqi War in 2003, many U.S. people did not understand the significance of the Iraqi people's removing their shoes and using them to hit pictures and statues of Saddam Hussein. To the Iraqis, the greatest insult they could give him was to use their shoes, which cover the most unclean part of the body, to show their disdain for this leader.

Other gestures rarely used in the United States but that will be apparent when traveling to European countries include the fingertip kiss, nose thumb, eyelid pull, nose tap, and fingers cross. The meanings of these gestures, which were studied by nonverbal communication researcher Desmond Morris, vary somewhat based on the specific European country and the context in which they are used. The fingertip kiss, in which the tips of the thumb and fingers are kissed and quickly moved forward away from the face, is a sign of affection and may be used as a greeting in Sicily and Portugal. The fingertip kiss is not used often in Italy and the British Isles, but it is common in France, Germany, Greece, and Spain to signify praise. The nose thumb, formed by placing the thumb at the end of the nose and fingers forming a fanning motion, is an insult and is common in all European countries. The eyelid pull, formed by pulling down the lower lid of an open eye with the forefinger, signals boredom in Austria, but in many other European countries, including France, Germany, and Turkey, it signals alertness. The nose tap, in which one simply taps the side of the nose with the forefinger, is used to convey a request for confidentiality or secrecy in Sardinia and the British Isles. Tapping the front of the nose changes the message to a request to mind one's own business in Austria, the Netherlands, and the British Isles. The fingers cross, formed by twisting the first and middle fingers around each other and lowering the remaining fingers, has several meanings, including a desire to break a friendship in Turkey. In other European countries, it can be used to signify that something is good or as a gesture of protection. This gesture should be used with caution because its meanings are quite varied.[4]

COLOR

Color, or chromatics, can have both positive and negative connotations; color can also affect a person's emotions and mood. Blue, for example, may have a positive connotation when used to represent the peace and tranquility associated with the blue of the sky or the sea. In other situations, blue may have a negative connotation when used to suggest sadness or depression. People say "I'm blue" to express melancholia. Black is another color that may be viewed in a positive or negative manner. Black is associated with sophistication and with high technology, but black may also be considered funereal and thus evoke feelings of sadness. White suggests purity and innocence; thus, white has been used successfully in marketing soaps as well as bridal gowns. In countries such as China, however, white is funereal.[5]

Colors may be associated with a particular nationality, such as the association of green with people of Ireland and red, white, and blue with people of the United States. Color is also associated with certain religions. Thus, companies doing business in the British Isles must understand that green is associated with the Catholic religion (however, the Pope's colors are white and yellow) and orange with Protestants to avoid unintentionally offending potential customers by using these two colors in their advertising and product packaging.[6] In a ranking of consumer color preferences in selected countries, blue was ranked as the color preferred by most consumers in the United States, Austria, and China; it was ranked second (after white) in Brazil. Green and white were other preferred colors by consumers in these four countries located on different continents; the findings for these four countries were consistent with the other countries studied.[7]

Companies planning to market their products worldwide will want to become familiar with the special meanings of colors before entering a specific foreign market. A U.S. company marketing a product in China learned this lesson when it placed yellow markers on its product, signifying that the product had passed inspection. The company later learned that to the Chinese, the yellow marker signified that the product was defective.

Even after an explanation of the meaning of the yellow marker in the United States, the Chinese were still uncomfortable accepting the shipment. Yellow, despite its positive associations with sunshine and happiness, may not be the best choice for marketing products internationally because of the negative connotations of the color, including cowardice. People in certain countries might be aware of other negative uses of yellow: Jewish people were forced by Nazis to wear yellow stars, and traitors' doors were streaked with yellow paint in France.[8]

Another U.S. manufacturer, which tried to sell white kitchen appliances in Hong Kong, learned that because white is associated with death, the Chinese would not buy white appliances. The company was successful, however, with the sale of almond colored appliances.[9] Some firms have used color to attract the visual attention of consumers without giving much thought to the meanings conveyed by the colors. One such company was FedEx, who selected orange and purple for their logo, even though these colors clash and are rarely used together. Their apparent goal, immediate attention and recognition with every FedEx package delivered, was successful. Thus, sometimes it may be more important to create brand identity than to be concerned with the nonverbal message attached to the colors.[10]

An exhibitor at a trade show was giving green hats to those who visited the booth. When they tried to give a Chinese visitor one of their green hats, the gift was rejected. The Chinese visitor said, "I don't want to wear a green hat before I marry, and I don't want to wear one after I am married, either." The exhibitors later learned that the Chinese have an expression, "He wears a green hat," which implies infidelity by his wife or girlfriend. While green generally has a positive connotation for the Chinese, this is not true of green hats.[11]

Some companies who tried to market their products in other countries were unsuccessful because they chose the wrong color either for the product or for its package. Green, although it has a positive connotation in France and Sweden because it is associated with cosmetics, has a negative connotation in countries with green jungles because of its association with disease. Red should be used with caution when marketing products internationally. Although a red circle on products sold in Latin American countries was successful, using red for packaging is not very popular in some Asian countries because it brings to mind the Japanese flag.[12] Likewise, use of red for a product or its package would not be recommended in South Korea because of the implied association with communism—an unwanted association by most South Koreans.[13]

Caution should also be exercised when using pictures of flowers because of the negative messages conveyed by either the type of flower or its color. Yellow flowers, for example, are associated with infidelity in France and with death in Mexico. White lilies, used by people of Mexico to lift superstitious spells, are used for funerals in France. White flowers are associated with bad luck or death in many Asian countries; thus, white flowers should be avoided in advertising and packaging products.[14]

Color, in addition to its influence on international sales, is also important in selecting clothing. In most countries of the world, blue is viewed as a masculine color; however, in France and the United Kingdom, red is perceived as masculine. The use of color in clothing is covered in greater detail in Chapter 5, "Dress and Appearance."

EYE CONTACT

Eye contact, or oculesics, is given more emphasis in some cultures than in others. In the dominant U.S. culture, made up of people of European, Latin American, and Middle Eastern descent, that now represents almost three-fourths of the population, direct eye contact is important. U.S. people, however, do not appreciate a steady, unbroken gaze; they are uncomfortable with prolonged eye contact and may interpret this behavior as intrusive and aggressive. At the very minimum, they would consider staring at another person as rude. Staring between men and women in the United States may be interpreted as an indication of interest in the other person. Prolonged eye contact between U.S. men and women may be considered sexually suggestive. U.S. persons prefer that eye contact be maintained for a few seconds before one person glances away.

Nonverbal messages conveyed by eye contact in the U.S. dominant culture are attentiveness, respect, truthfulness, and self-confidence; messages conveyed by avoiding eye contact are insecurity, disrespect, inattentiveness, dishonesty, shyness, and lack of self-confidence. Failure to make eye contact in a culture that values it sends the message that the other person is insignificant and not worthy of recognition. Avoiding eye contact may also indicate arrogance and a condescending attitude.

Differences in the use of eye contact exist in U.S. cocultures. For example, African Americans make direct eye contact when they are speaking; however, they look away when listening, unlike a majority of people in the U.S. macroculture.[15] Within the Native American coculture, the Hopi and

Navajos are offended by direct eye contact. According to a Navajo myth, a person who stares is giving you the evil eye.

During an interview with Mu'ammar Gadhafi, Barbara Walters did not understand why he would not look her directly in the eyes. She found out later that Middle Eastern men show women respect by not looking them directly in the eyes.[16]

The duration of eye contact when two people are interacting varies with the culture. Greeks, for example, use more contact in public places and expect others to look at them as well. Failure to make eye contact makes people of Greece feel ignored. Middle Easterners, too, use a lot eye contact while both talking and listening. They do not like to talk to someone wearing dark glasses because they are unable to see the eyes. People from Sweden, on the other hand, do not give as much eye contact while conversing as other Europeans. They do, however, look at each other for longer periods of time.[17]

Unlike members of the dominant culture in the United States, people in many Asian countries are uncomfortable with direct eye contact. People of China and Japan, specifically, tend to look just below the chin during conversations. They feel that not looking into the other person's eyes during a conversation shows respect and would feel that continuing to look into the other person's eyes would be quite rude. Iraqis, likewise, avoid eye contact while conversing out of respect for their elders.

Prolonged eye contact, on the other hand, is typical of people from the Middle East, France, Germany, and some Latin American countries. (Certain Latin American and Caribbean cultures, however, show you respect by not having direct eye contact.) They associate this direct eye contact with interest, assertiveness, and self-confidence. Even in these countries, however, lengthy stares at a woman would be considered inappropriate.

In some cultures, eye contact is associated with status. Latin Americans, for example, avoid direct eye contact when conversing with their supervisors. In the United States, on the other hand, using direct eye contact with the supervisor is totally acceptable. Supervisors are more likely to hold eye contact for a longer period, however; subordinates will look away more often.

FACIAL EXPRESSIONS

Facial expressions can reveal such emotions as anger, fear, happiness, sadness, disgust, and surprise. The meanings of these universal facial expressions are dependent on the culture, the situation, and the context in which the emotions are used, however. Although all cultures have a way of indicating emotions through facial expressions, the same expression does not have the same meaning in all cultures.

Tears, for example, are a clue to a person's emotions; but they do not always signal that a person is sad. Knowing whether a person who is crying is happy or sad is difficult unless you know the culture and take into account the situation and the context. In Mediterranean and Middle Eastern cultures, you will see men crying in public; however, in the United States, white males would suppress such emotions, as would Japanese men. People of the United States cry to express sadness; crying is acceptable behavior at funerals, for example. In some cultures, however, crying is an expression of joy and is considered appropriate at such happy occasions as weddings.

In addition to tears, the eyes can reveal excitement by whether or not the pupils are dilated or constricted. The pupils widen when a person is interested or emotionally aroused and close when the person is displeased.

One of the most frequently used facial expressions is the smile. The meaning of the smile, though, varies with the culture. A smile can convey happiness or sadness; the smile may also serve as a mask to hide the person's true feelings. These false smiles may actually be a way of expressing contempt for the other person; the accompanying facial expression would involve tightening the corners of the lips. Experts have even offered guidelines for interpreting false smiles, such as a lack of involvement of the eye muscles when a person is pretending to be happy.

U.S. people associate the smile with happiness, but in other cultures the smile may have a different meaning. In some cultures, smiling (sometimes accompanied by a slight nod of the head) is used in conversations to acknowledge what the other person has said, even though the message was not really understood. The Japanese use the smile to convey a wide range of emotions, from happiness and agreement to sadness and disagreement. They are inclined to smile or laugh softly to conceal discomfort or embarrassment. Although Koreans rarely smile, people of Thailand smile a great deal. Koreans view people who smile a lot as shallow, whereas the Thais value laughter and a smiling attitude. In fact, Thailand is known as the Land of Smiles.

When Chinese people were preparing for the 2008 Olympics, they had problems turning Beijing into a "city of smiles." One man who attended a class on smiling commented that he first thought it would be difficult to smile when you are tired but later realized that if one does not consider smiling as work, it would probably be easy to smile all the time. (According to popular Chinese literature, people who smile often or without a reason are often viewed as either devious or silly.[18])

PARALANGUAGE

Paralanguage, a term related to nonverbal communication, refers to how something is said; it refers to the volume or rate of a person's speech that affects the meaning of the message. An increased volume of speech could mean the person is angry, whereas a lower volume indicates that a person is more sympathetic. An increased rate of speech could be an indication that the person is impatient or in a hurry, whereas a decreased rate could imply a reflective attitude.

Cultural differences in volume of speech are apparent when comparing Middle Easterners and Germans to Filipinos and the Japanese, for example. Middle Easterners speak loudly because they associate volume with strength and sincerity; speaking softly would convey the impression of weakness. Germans, too, feel that using a commanding tone when speaking is important; speaking with authority conveys self-confidence. Filipinos, on the other hand, speak softly; they associate speaking softly with education and good manners. The Japanese also associate using a soft voice with good manners; speaking in a loud voice suggests a person lacks self-control.[19]

Cultural differences in rate of speech are apparent when listening to the speaking rates of Italians and Arabs, which are much faster than speaking rates of U.S. Americans. In addition to cultural differences in speech rate, regional differences exist within the United States. People who live in the northern United States speak much faster than those who live in the southern United States. This difference in speech rate may cause problems with understanding the intended message; this appears to be especially true when people who speak slowly try to understand people who speak rapidly.[20]

Another aspect of paralanguage is accent. Accent is very important to the British; they are often able to determine educational background by the person's accent. A person's accent may be a factor in hiring decisions, especially in some sections of the United States. In one study, people who spoke what is often referred to as Standard English were found in supervisory positions more often than were persons who spoke with a pronounced accent.[21]

Paralanguage provides useful information about a person's emotional state as well as information on a person's cultural, regional, and educational background. This information, when combined with spoken words, can provide insight into understanding the intended meaning of a message.

POSTURE

Your posture, whether standing, sitting, or walking, can convey such nonverbal messages as agreement/disagreement, confidence/lack of confidence, interest/disinterest, and high/low status. People who share the same point of view will often reveal this by assuming similar postures, whereas those who disagree will assume different postures. Posture is associated with confidence or a lack of it. Self-confident people sit and stand erectly and move easily and with assurance, whereas those who lack confidence tend to walk with stooped shoulders and move cautiously. Posture can reveal interest or disinterest in what another person is saying: Leaning toward the person shows interest; leaning back in the chair or turning away from the person when standing indicates disinterest. Status is also a consideration; people are more likely to face a person of higher status during a conversation than if the person were of lower status.

Posture when we are seated can send unintentional messages. The seated posture of people of the United States is quite relaxed. U.S. men cross their legs by placing the ankle on the knee, a posture seen as offensive by Europeans. Asians and Middle Easterners would also view this crossing of the legs as inappropriate. Correct posture when seated is especially important in the Arab world. Crossing the legs would reveal the sole of the shoe and involve pointing the toe at someone. Because the foot is the lowest part of the body and considered unclean, these behaviors would be viewed as offensive. In assuming a relaxed seated posture, U.S. persons, especially men, sometimes stretch their legs in front of them; Iranians would consider this posture inappropriate. Because seated posture is very important to the Japanese, do not slouch when conversing with them and place both feet on the floor.

Perhaps the best advice when interacting with persons of other cultures is to follow their lead. Watch how they stand and sit and mirror the posture they assume.

SILENCE

Silence is one nonverbal communication form that is interpreted very differently around the world. Silence allows time to think, express emotions, consider a response, or think about something other than the subject at hand. Silence, much like smell and touch, transcends verbal communication. People of the U.S. dominant culture are uncomfortable with silence. They use it to show disapproval or, in some cases, to collect their thoughts before saying something they might later regret. U.S. persons fill the silence with comments on the weather or anything else to avoid remaining silent. In other cultures, particularly in Asia and Scandinavia, silence is considered an integral part of communication. The Japanese would consider someone who had no periods of silence as someone who is giving very little thought to what they are saying; they further believe that what the person is saying may lack focus. When the Japanese use silence after a presentation, for example, they are showing respect for what has been said. The Japanese have been given price concessions by U.S. businesspeople simply because the U.S. negotiators interpreted Japanese silence incorrectly, thinking it meant that they did not like the deal. The people of Finland actually buy books on how to develop everyday chitchat so that they can fit in better when dealing with people from countries that use small talk to fill periods of silence, such as in the United States. Middle Easterners, on the other hand, do not require periods of silence.

Because you may encounter silence used in many different ways in different cultures, you need to give some thought to what is being communicated to you via the silence. Is the person conveying respect, or is the person simply confused or giving further thought to what has been said? Perhaps the person is really saying no or does not understand your message. The hardest part will be to step back, relax, and remember that silence can be positive.

Countries that are considered low-context cultures, such as the United States, are uncomfortable with silence. Low-context cultures consider silence as an indication that something is wrong. High-context cultures, such as Japan and Germany, are very comfortable with silence. To people in high-context cultures, silence is used to dissect what was said and to truly understand the other person's comments.

To understand different cultures' views of silence, consider their proverbs or adages:

- China: "Believe not others' tales; others will lead thee far astray."
- Japan: "It is the duck that squawks that gets shot."
- U.S.: "The squeaky wheel gets the grease."
- Native American: "It does not require many words to speak the truth."

SMELL

Smell, or olfactics, is part of nonverbal communication. People will react positively or negatively to other people based on the way they smell. A person's smell remains in another person's memory long after he or she has left the room. You smell like you do because of hygiene, what you eat (particularly spices), and the scents you apply to your skin. If you are from the United States, you probably find body odors, bad breath, perspiration, or too much cologne to be offensive. In many countries, however, such as France, Saudi Arabia, and South Africa, you will find that the men wear heavier fragrances than women. As clean as U.S. people think they are, many cultures find their smell offensive. Because people of the United States eat a lot more meat than people in many other countries, their body odor is different from that of people from countries in which more vegetables and fish are consumed. Japanese and Filipinos are raised to be very conscious of different odors and often complain about the way U.S. Americans smell. Although U.S. persons tend to be uncomfortable with natural smells, Middle Easterners and Filipinos believe being able to smell a friend's breath is pleasing. Not knowing how a culture perceives odors and how you are expected to react to the odors has affected many business transactions.

A medical doctor from Saudi Arabia was completing a medical internship in a hospital in the southern United States. Problems arose when patients refused to have the Saudi doctor examine them. Interviews with patients revealed two problems: he "smelled bad," and he breathed on the patients. The doctor's orientation had apparently failed to include the incongruence between Saudi and U.S. American perceptions of smell.

To be accepted by persons of other cultures, you will want to adopt the hygiene practices of the country you are visiting or in which you are conducting business as much as possible.

SPACE AND TOUCH

Space, known as proxemics, and touch, or haptics, are two very important nonverbal communication modes you will want to investigate about the country to which you plan to travel. Touch is one of the earliest forms of nonverbal communication we learn. Touch has been shown to be so important that children denied touch develop biochemical or emotional problems. As we mature, our culture teaches us what types of touch are appropriate and the proper space expected in various situations.

In the African American coculture, people of both genders touch each other when greeting much more than do people of the dominant U.S. culture. Cultures that believe in restraining their emotions are less likely to touch than cultures that encourage affection. Men and men or women and women kiss each other when meeting in Eastern Europe, Spain, Italy,

Portugal, or the Middle East. This is not a typical behavior of persons of the dominant U.S. culture.

A U.S. firm recently acquired a plant in Italy. One of the things Italian men are known for is squeezing females' derrieres to indicate to the lady that she is attractive. The practice is very much accepted in Italy. The U.S. firm brought some of the Italians to the United States for training. When a young lady's derriere was squeezed, she was not happy about the situation. When they explained to the man that in the work situation this is considered sexual harassment, he was in disbelief that the young woman would not like the attention. The company men even joked about making an Armani three-second rule for touching a female working companion because otherwise you would be offending the lady.

The amount of space one considers personal differs significantly from one culture to another. When someone invades our space, we may back up, stand still (but get a bit uneasy), or react strongly. Space is closely tied to touch and our desire either to be touched or not to be touched, as well as our desire to smell or not to smell someone with whom we are conversing.

The number of feet or inches between people when they are having a conversation changes dramatically from one culture to another. In the United States, you would stand less than 18 inches from a close friend or someone with whom you are intimate. If you are giving instructions to someone in an office, you would probably stand from 18 inches to 4 feet, depending on the type of activity: Viewing the same report or computer screen, for example, would necessitate being closer to another person than would being seated at a conference table. Businesspeople enter the 18-inch space only briefly, such as when they shake hands. In social situations, people of the United States stand 4 to 12 feet apart, and this is generally an appropriate amount of space for impersonal business interactions. The cultural attitude toward space is reflected in our need for privacy. Therefore, you will find that people of cultures that value privacy also usually want more space between themselves and others with whom they are communicating.

A psychology professor at a southern university gave his students an assignment to test the use of space in such crowded places as an elevator. Students reported the usual U.S. behaviors of facing the front and watching the illuminated floor indicator, assuming the Fig Leaf Position (hands/purses/briefcases hanging down in front of the body), and positioning themselves in the corners or against the elevator walls. Then the professor added another assignment: students were to break the rules and get on the elevator, stand at the front facing the other occupants, and jump backward off the elevator just before the door closed. One of the elevator occupants was heard to whisper, "Call 911; we've got a real weirdo here."[22]

You will find that U.S. people tend to use more space than Greeks, Latin Americans, or Middle Easterners. If you find yourself backing away from a person while you are having a conversation, they are probably accustomed to standing much closer to someone with whom they are interacting. What you will inadvertently do is step back until you are comfortable with the space between you or back up until you reach an object and can go no farther. Cultures in which people stand even farther apart than U.S. people are the Japanese and Southeast Asian cultures.

Standing close to someone in the United States may give the impression that you are upset, pushy, overbearing, or that you are making sexual advances. These types of unwelcome, negative positions should be avoided in the United States. In other cultures in which people prefer to stand close, you need to understand that they are only doing what is normal in their culture. U.S. Americans who are older or of higher status may touch persons who are younger or of lower status.

Cultures that reveal how they feel through touch and close proximity to the individuals with whom they are communicating often feel that people who are not effective in their communication are holding back information and not revealing everything, that they are tense rather than relaxed, and that they are not as trustworthy. If you are to be a good communicator interculturally, you must adapt your communication style as much as possible to the culture with which you are dealing. If you are dealing with a culture that seems unresponsive, cold, emotionless, or disinterested, remember they may be showing you respect. Likewise, if you are dealing with a culture that is very emotionally demonstrative, you need to learn about their history, culture, and way of life so that you can participate in their enthusiasm for developing friendships so that you will be seen as a good working business partner. The two extremes are seen as either coldhearted or out of control.

During an intercultural training session at a Japanese plant located in the United States, Mr. Suzuki asked the instructor what it means when someone pats you on the back. The instructor explained that means you have done a good job. All the men started to laugh. In Japan it means you have not done a good job and that you are in trouble with the boss. At the end of the meeting, everyone went out of the room patting each other on the back.

The way in which businesspeople arrange desks, chairs, or conference table seating also communicates through the use of space. When you are conversing with U.S. people, they generally prefer to be face-to-face. Although you might prefer chairs arranged at right angles to one another, the Chinese, for example, prefer the side-by-side arrangement. They may prefer this arrangement because it allows them to avoid direct eye contact, which is one of the ways they show respect. You also convey authority and position by your selection and arrangement of furniture. A large wooden desk and desk chairs with arms convey power and authority. Placing the desk and chair in front of a window or an arrangement of pictures on the wall creates a throne-like effect that adds to the sense of power.

You also send nonverbal messages with aspects of office arrangement. Although in the United States, private offices and windows in offices give you more status than offices that are inside without windows, this is not true in all countries. In France, top-level executives locate themselves in the middle of an office area with subordinates around them. The Japanese are all at desks in neat rows regardless of their position. In addition to office size, in the United States, higher-ranking executives have their territory better protected than do lower-status employees; doors and secretaries are often used as barriers to access.

Office location within a building also conveys power and status or an absence of power and status. In both the United States and Germany, top-level executives generally occupy the higher floors of an office building.

CLOTHING AND PHYSICAL APPEARANCE

Clothing, accessories, hair style, and jewelry are used to communicate status, feelings, respect, and social awareness and are factors in first impressions. In addition, physical appearance can be a factor in first impressions and in subsequent communication between people of the same culture as well as between people of different cultures.

As mentioned in Chapter 5, dressing conservatively in business attire is usually recommended for business functions. Most international businesspersons will find that wearing a dark, well-tailored business suit with conservative accessories and simple jewelry will be a safe choice of attire when conducting business in major cities around the world. In addition to a conservative suit, women conducting business abroad may wear businesslike dresses with hose and closed dress shoes with little or no detail and a minimum of jewelry.[23] Accessories should be of high quality; hairstyles should be fashionable, yet conservative.

Clothing is associated with showing respect, as two U.S. tourists learned when they tried to enter Vatican City wearing shorts.

The Vatican has strict dress codes; shorts are not permitted. One of the men indicated that he was a minister and had looked forward to visiting the Vatican for years. He said: "I don't see what the big deal is. If God can accept me wearing shorts, why can't you? Just wait until Judgment Day. You'll pay for this." The veiled threat fell on deaf ears. The tourists did not get into Vatican City.[24]

Clothing is also associated with credibility. Medical professionals are expected to wear appropriate medical attire. According to research, this attire includes a white doctor's coat worn over dress pants or khakis for men and a dark-colored skirt below the knee for women.[25]

A patient in a doctor's examining room, accompanied by her interpreter, had just arrived from Russia. A woman who was casually dressed entered the room, smiled, and said: "Hi, nice to meet you. I'm the nurse practitioner. How are you today?" the Russian patient scowled and asked the interpreter, "Who is this fool?" People from authoritarian countries who visit a doctor's office expect to see someone dressed professionally in medical attire. Immigrant patients also expect someone in a position of power and status to act formally.[26]

Clothing reflects the values of a culture. People of England, for example, dress conservatively in somber colors, as this is associated with social status. Upper-class Arabs dress carefully since dress is associated with self-respect, social standing, and wealth. Clothing and appearance are likewise important in Africa. Because of the importance people in some cultures place on clothing, it is best to remember that what might be inappropriate or excessively formal in one culture may reflect the culture's values and be appropriate in that culture. Showing tolerance toward differences in attire when interacting with people of other cultures is recommended.[27]

Physical appearance includes attractiveness, body weight, and physical fitness. Physical appearance is important in making a positive first impression. While the definition of attractiveness may vary according to the culture, it seems to be true that people who are physically attractive, as defined by their culture, have higher self-esteem than those who are perceived by their culture as unattractive.

Joyce had tried numerous diets in an attempt to lose weight without success and had become very sensitive about her appearance. One day as she walked across a U.S. university campus, she encountered a former male classmate from Iran who greeted her with the comment: "Joyce, you look good. You gained weight!" Joyce was very unhappy to have someone comment on her weight gain; she did not know that the student from Iran was complimenting her on her appearance. In the Middle East, women who are well proportioned and amply endowed are considered beautiful.[28]

OBJECTS

Nonverbal messages are sent by impersonal objects, such as a car, works of art, or office furnishings. A man may drive an expensive car to give the impression of wealth. This impression may be important to his professional and personal image, especially if he conducts business with wealthy international clients. Since research shows that aesthetic objects, such as wall hangings and works of art, have a positive impact on visitors and convey favorable interpersonal skills, these objects may be intentionally selected to give that impression. In offices where an impression of affluence is appropriate, the office décor would be opulent, including the display of antiques and artwork of substantial monetary value.

Displaying several clocks, each labeled with the name of a different city of the world, such as Rome, Tokyo, and Paris, can imply that the business is international in scope when displayed in the lobby of the firm or that the executive has international interests or contacts. Globes and framed pictures of the world convey a similar message.

Some professionals display framed credentials, such as university degrees or professional certification documents, to enhance their credibility. When certificates and awards are job-related, they imply to visitors that the person is competent and experienced and has received recognition for exceptional performance. Research into their effectiveness has revealed mixed results in U.S. surveys but may impress visitors from other countries who place great importance on professional credentials.

Some debate exists about the appropriateness of displaying framed family photographs in the office. Though such displays are not recommended in U.S. offices, except for medical doctors specializing in family practice and CEOs of organizations, displaying family photographs may be a good idea when entertaining visitors from countries that place a high importance on the family. In addition, displaying photographs of international clients taken during a game of golf with members of your organization on an earlier visit to their country would emphasize the importance of the business relationship.[29]

SYMBOLS

Symbols are emblems or signs used by all cultures to convey messages. One symbol for which the United States is well known is the Statue of Liberty, a gift to the United States from France in celebration of the United States' first 100 years as a nation. This statue symbolizes freedom throughout the world.

Some symbols are universally recognized. For example, a circle with a diagonal line through it symbolizes negation. If a circle contains a picture of a burning cigarette with a diagonal line through it, businesspeople from all countries recognize this symbol to mean "No smoking."

While the "No smoking" sign does not evoke an emotional response, the same cannot always be said of other universal symbols. Symbols of peace, though varied, are widely recognized. Some of the most well-known peace symbols are the olive branch, the red crowned crane, the peace flag, and the peace sign. The Greeks' traditional peace sign is the olive branch; in the Far East, the red crowned crane is a symbol of peace. To Italians, the peace symbol is the peace flag, consisting of seven rainbow stripes with *Pace* ("Peace" in Italian) printed in the center. The peace sign (a broken upside-down cross) was originally a symbol of the Campaign for Nuclear Disarmament; however, it is now widely recognized around the world as the symbol for peace. A country's flag is another symbol that may evoke an emotional response. Representatives of a country such as Bangladesh, for example, who are conducting business with an economic power such as Canada, might feel that Canadians who do not recognize the red circle on a green background, the Bangladeshi flag, consider Bangladesh as a small, unimportant country. The situation would be made even worse if the Bangladeshi recognizes the red maple leaf as an important symbol to Canadians.[30]

Other symbols are neither neutral nor emotional; corporate logos are typically an example of such symbols. Sometimes, however, these company logos may be perceived negatively in some parts of the world, as a company in India discovered.

The swastika symbol, long associated with the Nazis, has actually been used as a symbol of good luck in many countries for centuries. M.P. Been Products, Ltd., of India had used the swastika as a company logo on many of its packages. When the company decided to market a new German pilsner beer, they concluded that using a label containing a combination of the swastika with the name of the beer was not a good idea.[31]

When trying to establish a business relationship with a company, become familiar with the company's logo. If the significance of the logo is not apparent, asking for an explanation is advisable.

Symbols with religious or political meanings may be interpreted differently, depending upon the culture and the situation. Wearing a necklace featuring a cross, for example, is hardly noticed in many countries that are mainly Christian; however, when worn in Middle Eastern and North African countries, the cross would probably be noticed and might even be offensive.[32] An example of a political symbol is the Berlin Wall, a symbol of the Cold War's division of East and West Germany for 28 years between 1961 and 1989. The fall of the Berlin Wall symbolized the end of communism throughout Europe as communism fell in East Germany and in several other countries, including Czechoslovakia, Poland, and Romania.

When trying to interpret the meaning of certain symbols, it is important to avoid drawing conclusions about what such symbols mean as the following incident illustrates.

When Ann's next-door neighbor Sandy called out to her over the fence, "Happy Hanukkah, Ann," she replied with, "Happy Hanukkah to you, too, Sandy." When Sandy said, "But I'm not Jewish," Ann said, "Neither am I." Sandy then said, "But you always wear that six-pointed star around your neck." Ann explained: "That's because I work for the Sheriff's Department." (While the Star of David—the six-pointed star—has become a symbol of Judaism, the star's relationship to a sheriff's badge has quite a history dating back to a nineteenth-century Texas governor.)[33]

NONVERBAL LEAKAGE

Leakage occurs when people try unsuccessfully to control their nonverbal behavior and to conceal an attitude or information. Nonverbal leakage represents a person's actual feelings that lie beneath the social mask. Because people try harder to control facial expressions, and because facial expressions are easier to control, a lot of the nonverbal leakage occurs in the feet and legs as well as in the arms and hands. For example, people who are trying to deceive other people will often cross and uncross their legs or shuffle their feet. They will also use the hand shrug, which involves rotating the hands and exposing the palms. This gesture conveys helplessness; people using the hand shrug are attempting to elicit sympathy from others by implying that they are unable to help themselves. In addition, certain gestures occur more frequently with people engaging in deception.

These gestures include gripping arm rests, tapping fingers on a table, licking the lips, and touching an eye or the side of the nose.[34]

In one study, convicted muggers, who were interviewed separately, were shown videotapes of pedestrians in public places; they were able to identify the same people as potential victims. By examining nonverbal leakage, the muggers were able to spot behaviors that communicated the vulnerability of the pedestrians. Muggers, who must act quickly, become experts at nonverbal leakage.[35]

People who are untruthful engage in other nonverbal behaviors that may be obvious to people who have studied nonverbal communication. People who lie tend to avoid getting close to another person; they also tend to perspire, gulp, and play with a pencil or their glasses. Changes in pupil size as well as changes in skin color are examples of physiological changes that are not within a person's conscious control.[36]

In some cases, a person's body language contradicts what the person says. In these cases, body language is a better indicator of the truth than the verbal message.[37]

COUNTRY-SPECIFIC INFORMATION

The following countries are those with which the United States conducts a majority of its international business as well as those countries that are the destinations most frequently visited by U.S. travelers according to figures provided by the U.S. Department of Commerce, Office of Travel and Tourism Industries. Although Iraq and Saudi Arabia do not fall into either category, these countries are included as examples of Middle Eastern countries.

Brazil

- Brazilians use a lot of gestures. Flicking a finger beneath the chin means "I don't know" or "I don't understand." The "fig," which is formed by tucking the thumb between the index and middle finger, signifies good luck; the "thumbs up" gesture indicates approval; and the finger snap means to do it quickly.[38]
- Gestures to avoid include the U.S. "OK" sign, pointing the middle finger up, and punching the fist in an open palm; all are considered vulgar in Brazil. When in doubt, it is a good idea to ask for an interpretation of any unfamiliar gestures.[39]
- Eye contact is maintained during conversations with those of equal status; people who are younger or of lower status will look down to show

respect while conversing. Staring at people in public is common; women should not take offense when men stare at them.[40]

- Brazilians usually stand close together and touch each other during conversations. Stepping back should be avoided as this gives the impression of aloofness.[41]

Canada

- Most gestures used by U.S. persons are recognized in Canada.

- The beckoning signal, however, is a bit different: The palm of the hand is faced inward with the fingers up; the fingers are used to motion toward the body. This gesture, however, is not used to summon a waiter. To beckon a restaurant server, simply raise the hand above the head. Pointing with a single finger is rude. French Canadians tend to gesture more during conversations than do other Canadians.

- Direct eye contact is expected during greetings and when shaking hands as well as during conversations.

- Appropriate seated posture for men includes sitting with legs crossed at the knees or ankles or with an ankle crossed on the opposite knee.

- Canadians prefer to keep a distance of about a half-meter (1.7 feet) when interacting. Atlantic Canadians prefer more personal distance when conversing than do U.S. persons. Avoid casual touching; touching between close friends and relatives, though, is customary.

- The use of silence, smell, space, and touch is very similar to the United States.

China

- The thumbs-up gesture means everything is fine.

- Use the entire hand, rather than a single finger, to point.

- Use your downward facing palm with the fingers making a scratching motion to beckon.

- Direct eye contact should be avoided in public.

- Smiling is not common during introductions. In fact, the Chinese typically do not reveal their emotions by their facial expressions.

- Posture is important; sit erectly and avoid placing your feet on furniture.

- Silence is highly valued; it is equated with being polite and contemplative. Avoid interrupting someone during conversations.

- Standing close while conversing is common; the Chinese are accustomed to crowded environments.

- Body contact with strangers is inappropriate, as China is not a touch-oriented culture. Do not pat anyone on the head, back, or shoulder. Even placing your hand or arm on the back of a chair in which a

Chinese person is sitting is inappropriate. Embracing and kissing are not common greeting behaviors.

France

- The U.S. "OK" gesture means "worthless" or "good for nothing"; the French use the thumbs-up sign to signify that everything is going well.
- The "V for Victory" gesture may be done with palm in or out in France; the meaning is the same.
- Avoid using only the index finger for pointing; use the entire hand.
- Avoid snapping your fingers to get someone's attention; this is considered offensive.
- Do not stand with folded arms, as this is viewed as arrogant.
- To beckon a restaurant server, raise your hand slightly or try to make eye contact and nod your head, accompanied by "*s'il vous plait*" (if you please).
- Eye contact in France is quite intense; it exceeds the level of comfort of U.S. persons. Visitors to France should remember that this behavior is typical of the French and should not consider it rude. Avoiding direct eye contact in business or social situations would be viewed negatively.
- Smiling when passing people on the street is not common.
- Never chew gum in public.
- Posture while seated is important; sit erectly, either with knees together or with legs crossed at the ankle. Do not slouch, sit with legs apart, or sit with legs stretched in front of you.

Germany

- It is rude to have your hands in your pockets when talking with someone.
- Never point your index finger to your head.
- To wish someone good luck, squeeze your thumb by folding the fingers around the thumb.
- Direct eye contact is a sign of sincerity to the Germans.
- Germans rarely smile during business sessions with colleagues or visitors.
- Do not chew gum in public.
- Cross your legs at the knees.
- An upright posture is important to Germans; never place your feet on furniture.
- Leave the furniture as it is placed in an office; to move a chair is insulting.
- Stand farther from a German when talking than when talking to a U.S. businessperson.
- Privacy is important to Germans; doors are kept closed.

Iraq

- The left hand should not be used to eat, to hand something to someone, or to gesture.
- Never point the bottom of your feet toward someone.
- Direct eye contact is considered appropriate; however, young people will not maintain eye contact with their elders as a sign of respect nor will men and women maintain eye contact.
- Very demonstrative facial expressions are used to connote emotions.
- Touch members of the opposite gender only if they are related to you.
- Iraqis like to stand close, use touch, and body language in their conversation.
- Iraqi men often walk hand in hand. This is a sign of friendship only.

Italy

- Italians use more gestures than any other European country and are too numerous to list. Travelers may see Italian men kissing the fingertips, a gesture that signifies beauty or excellence; this gesture may be used to indicate that a woman is beautiful or that the food is excellent.
- Use of the "hand purse," fingertips together to signify a question, should be avoided; its use is confined to use by Italians.
- Gestures to avoid include putting your hand on your stomach (dislike of the person), pointing your index and little finger at a person (a wish for bad luck), and thumbing your nose (obscene).
- Rubbing the thumb and fingers together quickly means money.
- Eye contact is expected when shaking hands and should be maintained during conversations; failure to give eye contact suggests you have something to hide.
- Italians prefer to stand closer together than U.S. persons are comfortable with; avoid backing away, as this is viewed as an insult.
- Touching between Italian men is common; in fact, male friends often embrace. Italian women do not usually touch other women, however. Seeing people of the same gender walk down the street arm in arm is common.

Japan

- Wave all your fingers with the palm facing downward to get someone's attention.
- When referring to yourself, use your index finger and point to your nose.
- Gum chewing is not allowed in public.
- Indirect eye contact is used to show respect.
- Facial expressions are minimal; yawning in public is discourteous.

- The smile has numerous meanings, including pleasure, displeasure, and embarrassment.
- Politeness is a must, as the Japanese will seldom say "no."
- Sit straight with both feet on the floor. Men may cross their legs at the knees or the ankles.
- Young girls often walk hand in hand.
- Japanese use silence as respect, to cover embarrassment, to convey truthfulness, and to show defiance. The meaning depends on the situation and other events.
- Male-female touching in public is considered inappropriate.
- Refrain from backslapping and other forms of touching.

Mexico

- Mexicans use thumbs-up for approval, but thumbs-down should be avoided because it is considered vulgar.
- Placing your hands on your hips or in your pockets while standing and talking with someone would indicate that you are angry.
- Mexicans use their hands to gesture and exhibit many different facial expressions when conversing.
- Direct eye contact is used, except for Native Mexicans who tend to use indirect eye contact.
- Mexicans like to stand close and like to touch the person with whom they are conversing; pulling away or backing up would be considered unfriendly.

Saudi Arabia

- A finger or hand to point or beckon another person is not used.
- Avoid using your left hand to pass or receive items.
- Direct eye contact is considered sincere, except between genders, when males will use indirect eye contact to show respect.
- Do not point your feet at someone else.
- Cross your legs at the knees only.
- Stand close to your own gender when conducting business; however, you should keep your distance and not touch the opposite gender.
- To signal "no," tip the head back and click the tongue; to indicate "yes," simply nod your head up and down.

South Korea

- Avoid placing feet on chairs or desks.
- Wave the fingers together, palm down, to beckon someone; avoid beckoning with the index finger.

- Pass items with both hands.
- Maintain eye contact during conversations.
- Speak in a low voice; avoid loud laughter or speech.
- Avoid touching older people and persons of the opposite gender.
- Expect to see two people of the same gender holding hands while walking
- in public; it signifies friendship only.

Taiwan

- Use an open hand when pointing; do not use the index finger.
- Avoid winking; this is considered rude.
- Maintain a minimum of eye contact.
- Maintain a calm demeanor; avoid showing emotions.
- Pass items with both hands.
- Avoid placing an arm around another person's shoulder.
- Avoid loud behavior; avoid losing your temper.
- Do not place feet on a desk or table; do not use feet to touch or move
- objects.

United Kingdom (England, Scotland, Wales, and Northern Ireland)

- Gestures are kept to a minimum; people of the UK do not rely on gestures to add meaning to the spoken message.
- Eye contact is light; it is appropriate when greeting someone or when shaking hands, but prolonged eye contact and staring are not welcomed.
- Smiling when passing a stranger on the street is appropriate when accompanied by eye contact and a greeting such as "Good morning."
- Avoid showing emotions, including excessive enthusiasm or disappointment. Displaying emotions is not characteristic of the people of the UK.
- Do not stand too close while conversing; respecting another person's personal space (which is greater than that preferred in the United States) is expected.
- Touching is uncommon; however, it is acceptable for women to be kissed on the cheek by their male and female friends.

United States of America

- U.S. persons use moderate gesturing. Gestures are confined to below shoulder level, except when waving to someone. Some common gestures include the "V" sign (index and middle fingers form a V) to signify victory; the "OK" sign (thumb and forefinger joined to form a circle), which has a positive connotation; the thumbs-up sign indicating everything is great; and thumbs down showing disapproval.

- Avoid extending the middle finger alone as this is insulting.
- The posture of people of the United States is quite casual; they often sit in a relaxed manner with legs crossed.
- Direct eye contact, with short periods of glancing away, is important in both social and business situations. Lack of respect, inattentiveness, and disinterest are implied by failure to give eye contact.
- Smiling, even at complete strangers, is common. U.S. persons expect other people to return their smiles.
- U.S. Americans prefer a distance of about an arm's length when interacting. Standing closer causes discomfort and may result in a person's taking a step back.
- Little touching is normal behavior in the United States. In business settings, touching is usually limited to the handshake.

Chapter 5

DRESS AND APPEARANCE

Dress and appearance are aspects of nonverbal communication that convey impressions related to assurance, competence, credibility, and a concern and respect for other people. These first impressions, although not necessarily fair, are usually made within the first few seconds of meeting a person and are often lasting impressions.

First impressions often are as shallow as rain water on a leaky roof. Yet they are about as permanent as concrete, and if you're like most people, it would take at least a crowbar or an act of God to change them.[1]

Projecting a positive image by dressing appropriately is instrumental in developing trust and building rapport with others. Negative initial impressions can hamper effective communication and can impede the relationship-building process. People make assumptions about others quickly based on their first impressions. These assumptions often include a person's occupation, educational background, trustworthiness, and social and economic status. According to Seitz, "In social or business settings, clothing acts as a communicator of ourselves, our company, and our position; it is not hard to see why appearance constitutes 55 percent of the first impression we make on others."[2] In addition to dress, impressions are conveyed by one's overall appearance, which includes grooming, accessories, and jewelry. Research has shown, for example, that women whose grooming includes hair that is shorter, styled simply, and worn away from the face, together with moderate facial cosmetics and simple gold jewelry, are groomed consistent with a successful managerial style. Research has also shown that people of both genders who wear glasses are perceived as more successful, intelligent, and hardworking than those without glasses.[3] Shoes are also scrutinized; wearing inexpensive shoes is the ultimate negative impression, along with men who wear socks that expose skin when they cross their legs. Actually, the image of one's shoes remains in a person's mind longer than anything else; dirty shoes are a sign of weakness, regardless of the person's age or culture.[4]

Thompson and Kleiner sum up the importance of dress to projecting a positive image: "Successful people generally look successful. They wear clothes that look attractive on them, are well groomed, and hold themselves with confidence. The intended message is that they feel good about themselves and that others will feel good about them as well."[5]

DRESS AND CREDIBILITY

The link between attire and credibility is well documented. Initial credibility may be acquired by dressing in a manner that inspires trust and conveys competence. Suits, for both men and women, accompanied by simple, understated accessories, continue to convey messages of competence, authority, and trust, regardless of the culture. When your initial credibility is high, you are, in effect, establishing an account upon which you may draw. You then add other factors, such as expertise, rank, and building a personal relationship, to deal successfully with others, especially people from other cultures. Without this positive, initial credibility, you may not get an opportunity to show how competent or knowledgeable you are.

Larry, dressed in jeans, a T-shirt with a logo, and soiled sneakers, was informed by his supervisor that an important Japanese client had arrived unexpectedly to close a multimillion-dollar deal involving a project on which Larry had been working. When Larry's supervisor, upon seeing how he was dressed, asked another engineer to represent the department in the upcoming meeting, Larry was shocked and dismayed to learn that his attire had cost him an important career opportunity.[6]

Other evidence linking dress with credibility can be seen in the impression conveyed by a speaker who makes a presentation wearing a suit with buttons missing, a stained tie, and scuffed shoes. Regardless of how knowledgeable the speaker may be about the subject, the audience would tend to discount anything that was said because the speaker did not look like he or she knew the subject.

A couple's initial meeting with their mortgage broker was seriously affected by the broker's appearance: his clothes were too small, his shoes had run-down heels, and his hair was long and unkempt. The fact that the broker made a costly error did not actually surprise them; after all, his appearance had suggested incompetence. The couple made sure they warned other people to avoid doing business with him or his firm.[7]

Attention to grooming gives the impression of respect for self and others. People concerned with their credibility should make sure that hair is clean and styled conservatively. Because U.S. persons respond negatively to body and breath odors, odors of perspiration and offensive breath should be controlled or masked. Fragrances should be worn in moderation by both men and women. Hands and nails should be clean and well maintained; nails that are too long may damage credibility and may affect productivity. The effect of an expensive suit can be negated quickly by dirty nails; people will be so distracted by the unkempt nails that they will miss what the person is saying. Shoes should be shined and in good repair because shoes are one of the first things noticed about a person's appearance. Finally, everyone can enhance their appearance by being in good physical condition. Becoming physically fit will increase endurance, improve one's personality and posture, and make a person appear more confident.[8]

Credibility when conducting business with people of other countries is very important. Initial credibility is linked to wearing conservative business attire with a classic, traditional look (i.e., dark business suits for men and skirted suits or dresses for women) and to choosing conservative accessories of high quality. A woman's credibility when doing business abroad is enhanced by wearing skirt lengths that give good coverage; her credibility is damaged by wearing very casual attire or anything that is too revealing. Casual attire, when appropriate, should not be too casual. Men can adopt an informal look by removing their ties and jackets; women by removing their jackets.

BUSINESS PROFESSIONAL ATTIRE

According to U.S. researchers and image consultants, the suit is perceived as the most appropriate professional business attire for both men and women. The most professional suit for men is in medium or charcoal gray or navy blue with a white, pastel, or pinstripe long-sleeved cotton shirt. The most appropriate suit for women is in black, navy blue, or a medium shade of blue with a white blouse.[9]

Color is an important attribute of professional dress. Certain colors are associated with wealth, such as deep and dark colors. Other colors, such as neutral, basic colors, are considered safe for business attire. Generally speaking, darker colors convey authority, whereas lighter shades project an approachable image. (Darker colors have another positive aspect: they do not show wrinkles as much as lighter colors.) Meanings associated with various colors vary from dignity conveyed by blue, to white associated with cleanliness, and power conveyed by dark colors.[10] A consideration when selecting a suit in a particular color is what the color symbolizes. Green, for example, is an inappropriate color for a man's suit. Certain shades of green are associated with the uniforms of hotel and hospital staff members and, therefore, do not convey the status desired by business executives. Gray is a popular color; it conveys success and trustworthiness. Black can be used very effectively, especially by women. Women have long recognized the importance of having in their wardrobe a simple black dress of high quality that can be dressed down for the office and dressed up for social occasions. Women should build their business wardrobe around solid colors as this provides more opportunities to mix outfits; solids also make it easier for a woman to make a transition to attire appropriate for evening business events or when going straight to a party from work by simply changing jewelry or a blouse, adding a belt with a decorative buckle, and taking the small clutch purse she keeps in her briefcase. In addition, women are advised to use pastels to soften such basic colors as brown, black, and navy and to use jewel tones (emerald, sapphire, and amethyst), which convey confidence and energy, to brighten a solid-color basic suit.[11]

Certain colors have special meanings in other countries, so the color of one's attire should be selected carefully to avoid unintentionally offending people in the host country. Bright-colored shirts in wild patterns are inappropriate in any country. Wearing white in China should be avoided, as white is worn to funerals and is therefore associated with sadness. In fact, in about 80 percent of the world's cultures, white has a funereal connotation. In Ghana, though, red is associated with sadness. In China, red is associated with good luck, but it has the opposite meaning—bad luck— to many Koreans. Be cautious about wearing red in African countries because of its association with witchcraft and death in many countries there. In Brazil, avoid wearing green and yellow. These are the colors of the Brazilian flag, and people of Brazil do not wear them.[12]

Respect cultural, as well as corporate and professional, standards when choosing clothing colors. Consider the occasion, the season, the climate, and your skin and hair tones.

The fabric from which a garment is made conveys certain messages and is another consideration when selecting clothing. Pure, natural fibers, such as silk, cotton, linen, and wool, are associated with higher status, whereas synthetic fibers, such as polyester, are associated with clothing of the lower middle class. Although natural fabrics are preferred by those wishing to project a look of success, various blends are becoming more popular because blends of good quality have the look and comfort of the pure fibers but are easy to care for and are wrinkle-resistant. The preferred fabric for both men and women is 100 percent wool, followed by a wool blend that is at least 50 percent wool. Fabrics that are inappropriate for business wear include leather, suede, velvet, and satin.[13]

Regional differences exist in what is considered appropriate professional business attire. In Texas and some other Western states, for example, businessmen can wear well-polished cowboy boots with their business suits. Wearing cowboy boots with a suit outside that region, however, could be disastrous. Dress standards are more casual in California and Florida than in New York. Even within the state of Florida, dress is more conservative in Tampa than in Palm Beach. Generally speaking, business dress is more conservative on the East Coast than on the West Coast. Certain cities in the eastern part of the country are known to be especially conservative; they include Atlanta, Boston, Chicago, and Washington, D.C. Dress in the Pacific Northwest, on the other hand, tends to be rather casual. Regional differences also exist in what is considered proper footwear. The thin-soled leather slip-on shoes popular in Atlanta would be considered too informal in Boston, where a wing-tip leather shoe is considered more appropriate.[14] Of course, variations exist within these areas.

In additional to regional differences in dress, industry differences are also apparent. People who work in accounting firms, banks, law firms, government agencies, insurance, and other financial institutions are expected to dress more conservatively than those who work in an advertising agency, for example. Clients of legal firms expect the attorneys to look competent and authoritative; people who use financial institutions want to feel assured that the employees with whom they interact are responsible and stable in addition to being fashionable. Although people who work in creative jobs can dress to reflect their creativity, they would be wise to adopt a more conservative style when dealing with corporate clients.[15]

When doing business in other countries, it is generally considered safe to dress more conservatively and more formally than you would when conducting business in the United States. Men should wear suits of good quality that are styled conservatively and in solid, dark colors (except for brown). Ties and white shirts are the norm; however, in England, men would avoid striped ties because they symbolize certain schools. Black shoes that lace are usually considered more appropriate for business in Europe and Asia than loafers. When conducting business in European countries, men should avoid wearing white socks with dress shoes; they should wear only long-sleeved shirts, which should extend about a half inch below the sleeve of the jacket.[16]

Women who conduct business in foreign countries should wear a good-quality dress or skirted suit in a traditional business style and in a solid color. Pantsuits are inappropriate in some countries for women conducting business abroad. Very high heels or boots are inappropriate; jewelry and accessories should be of high quality and in good taste. Because women in Europe do not wear costume jewelry, businesswomen conducting business there should wear good jewelry. When conducting business in Japan, women would want to wear few accessories and conservative makeup. Fabric is important, especially in Asian countries, where the heat and humidity make wearing natural fabrics highly recommended. In Arab countries, women should wear long, loose-fitting dresses that cover the arms.[17]

Dressing guidelines for both men and women in various parts of the world include the following:

- In European countries, wear conservative attire; good grooming is very important. Shorts and jeans are inappropriate in main areas.
- In Africa, dress should be conservative; dress is somewhat formal in English-speaking countries and less formal in French-speaking countries.
- In Australia and New Zealand, business attire is executive casual, with dress more relaxed in summer.
- In many Asian countries, specifically in Japan, Hong Kong, and Korea, Western-style dark suits are the norm; women wear conservative dresses and suits in muted colors—no pantsuits. In addition, women should not wear tight, suggestive dresses; they should also avoid wearing shorts or tank tops except in resort areas. Because sitting on the floor is expected, women should avoid straight, tight skirts.
- Appropriate attire in South America is similar to that in the United States. Generally speaking, dress is more conservative on the western coast of South America than in countries along the eastern coast. Shoes and accessories should be of good quality. South Americans are fashion conscious and appreciate excellent quality in clothing, shoes, and accessories.[18]

BUSINESS CASUAL ATTIRE

Business casual attire, which was popular in the United States in the 1990s, is on the wane as companies become concerned that their employees project an unprofessional image. Employers found that as their employees dressed more casually, they were more casual in their work as well. Not only did casual attire damage the corporate image and encourage slacking off in work productivity, it brought an increase in jokes, comments, and flirtatious behavior, which created an environment conducive to sexual harassment.

In a survey of 1,000 companies conducted by a New York law firm, "employers were asked whether they had noticed an increase in absenteeism and tardiness after instituting a casual dress policy. Nearly half said *yes*, and 30 percent reported a rise in flirtatious behavior."[19]

Another problem with business casual dress was the lack of a clear definition of business casual attire. Some employees did not seem to know that sweatpants, shorts, cutoffs, and spandex were never considered acceptable business casual dress. Other employees felt it meant that they could dress like they dressed at home, including walking around without shoes. Still others came to work without proper undergarments. All in all, the environment became one that was not conducive to work.

The decade of business casual attire presented special problems for women, especially those who were trying to advance to managerial positions. They found it hard to be taken seriously when they dressed in casual attire. Molloy's research indicated that "when men dress casually and have to deal with relative strangers, they lose some of their authority; when women do the same, they lose most of theirs."[20] Based on his research, Molloy recommended that women purchase the most expensive business casual attire they could afford and stressed that their casual attire should be upper class, conservative, and traditional, including fabric, style, and color combinations. He further recommended that women select business casual clothing in such natural fibers as cotton, wool, and silk and that they choose colors and color combinations typically found in traditional men's sportswear, such as gray, navy, black, and khaki.

In some companies, such as financial institutions, business casual attire never worked. When people who worked in banks, for example, dressed casually, the subtextual message customers received was that employees would be casual in handling their money as well. A life insurance company, upon relaxing its dress code, found that during the summer months employees were coming to work in shorts and T-shirts; the impression conveyed was that this was a company picnic rather than a place of business. This impression was not what the company had in mind.[21]

The popularity of business casual in the decade of the 1990s was not limited to the United States. More than half of European countries also had casual dress policies. Sweden had the largest percentage of companies permitting casual dress, whereas England, a traditionally conservative country, had the lowest percentage of companies permitting business casual dress.[22]

DRESSING FOR TRAVEL

Travel attire, even with the more casual style of dressing that has become more common, should be neat and presentable. Wearing light-weight clothing made of a fabric with some stretch to it and comfortable shoes makes sense when you will be sitting in close quarters, either on an airplane or in an automobile, for several hours. The clothing should, of course, be clean, just as one's body and hair should be clean. Fragrances, if used at all, should be used sparingly, as some people are allergic to certain scents used in colognes and perfumes. Should you ever find yourself on an international flight seated next to a person with poor hygiene habits or whose fragrance is overpowering, you will quickly realize the importance of cleanliness and using fragrances in moderation.

Some business professionals recommend wearing business attire when traveling, particularly if you are making a short flight and have a business meeting the same day. In fact, some companies expect their employees to dress professionally when traveling on business; they feel that as representatives of the firm, their employees should convey a positive, professional image. Another point made by those who recommend dressing professionally for business travel is the possibility of meeting someone you may wish to impress during the flight or of being met at the airport by someone of importance.[23] Another benefit of wearing executive casual or a suit on the plane is that you will receive better treatment by airline personnel if you are well dressed; this better service may include being upgraded to business or first class without requesting the upgrade.[24] A frequent traveler who always dressed well en route reported that she had received numerous upgrades to first class. She has observed that when flights are overbooked, ticket agents look over the passengers in the waiting area carefully before deciding who to upgrade to first class. She is convinced that dress and appearance play a big role in their decision. In any case, whether you choose casual or professional dress for travel, certain attire is considered inappropriate. This inappropriate attire includes sweat suits, torn jeans, or anything that resembles sleepwear.[25]

One traveler who had an early Monday morning presentation took a Sunday night flight wearing jeans and sneakers. Since her luggage was sent to another destination, she had to give the presentation in her travel attire. Her confidence was shaken, and her credibility was lost.[26]

An important travel suggestion is that the clothing you bring should be appropriate for the activities you anticipate after your arrival. Women who plan to visit churches in other countries should remember to pack a scarf because in Islamic mosques and some Catholic churches women are required to cover their heads upon entering. In addition, women should remember that the upper arms should be covered in many churches and that shorts are not permitted. In fact, women may also be expected to cover their legs and feet as well. Because in many countries wearing good jewelry might attract the attention of criminals, women may wish to consider leaving expensive jewelry at home, unless they are traveling to Europe, where women wear good jewelry. In this case, you would wear the same items continuously. Wearing an inexpensive watch and costume jewelry (or jewelry that is a good imitation of the real thing) is recommended when traveling.[27] Women will also want to select one color scheme for travel wear so that everything goes with one set of basic accessories.

DRESSING FOR SOCIAL EVENTS

When invited to social events, it is important to wear what is considered proper for the occasion. Both propriety and appropriateness must be taken into consideration when deciding what to wear. Even though a woman may be tempted to wear a provocative black dress with a sheer top to a social event, chances are good that this attire would be inappropriate because she would be calling attention to herself in a negative way. Dressing modestly is good advice when dressing for international social events.

Sometimes the invitation will include a notation of the type of dress expected, such as *white tie, black tie, informal,* or *casual. White tie* is the most formal and is rarely required, except perhaps at state dinners. The black tailcoat is worn with a starched white shirtfront, white vest, and black patent shoes, sometimes with a black silk top hat. Women would wear a long ball gown with appropriate jewelry and long white gloves. *Black tie* usually means a black dinner jacket with a black tie and a plain shirt or one with a pleated front. This attire is not worn before 6:00 p.m. Appropriate attire for women would range from a full-length gown to a suit made from a dressy fabric, such as satin or velvet. *Informal* usually means a dark business suit for men, worn with a white shirt and subdued tie; women would wear a short cocktail dress or suit in a dressy fabric. For both black tie and informal events, shoes for men would be well-shined leather shoes or black patent leather; shoes for women should be made of fabric or good leather.[28] When conducting business in Europe, men should bring attire appropriate for black-tie dinners because conducting business in European countries often involves this type of attire. In addition, when doing business in Europe or in South America, women should be prepared for the formal, cultural events to which they may be invited by bringing along a black cocktail dress.

What is considered casual wear varies widely according to the section of the country in the United States and the international country you are visiting. When casual attire is indicated for the company picnic in the United States, for example, dress would depend upon whether the picnic is to be held at the CEO's country club or a public park as well as what activities are planned. If casual attire is indicated for a social event in a South American country, though, it is important to remember that their definition of casual attire is not the same as the standard U.S. definition. Women's casual attire, for example, often means long skirts with silk blouses; it does not include T-shirts, shorts, or tennis shoes.[29] When visiting the Mexican resort areas of Acapulco, Cancun, and Puerto Vallarta, remember that dress is more casual than in Mexico City.

If the type of dress expected is not included on the invitation, it is appropriate to call the host to ask. Another suggestion is to consult someone whose judgment you trust and who has attended these functions previously.[30]

CULTURAL CUSTOMS IN DRESS

The increased interaction with people of other countries has made it increasingly important to respect the customs of other cultures, including their dress customs. Wearing the native dress may be considered offensive. On some occasions, such as parties or special ceremonies, however, native dress may be considered acceptable. Thus, to avoid giving offense, people of the United States will want to wear their usual business suit or dress or ask whether native dress is acceptable for certain occasions.[31]

In Asian countries, do not attempt to dress in native attire. Unless you are sure of the proper way to wear such garments as a sarong or kimono, as well as the proper time and place to wear them, it is better to wear traditional U.S. business clothing.

An executive of a large U.S. firm, upon his arrival in Indonesia, visited a local shop and bought a *batik* shirt, which he wore with slacks to his first meeting with his prospective customers. To his embarrassment, the three men all wore dark suits and white shirts with French cuffs, and silk ties.[32]

In the Philippines, men wear the *barong*, which is a long embroidered shirt worn outside the trousers for both daytime and evening events. Filipino women wear a *terno*, which is a dress featuring a scoop neckline and large butterfly sleeves.

Certain types of attire typically worn in the United States should not be worn in Asian countries. Shorts or tank tops are not worn in cities, except at the beach or pool. In addition, brightly colored clothing should be avoided. Women should wear clothing that provides good coverage and that is not too tight or low cut. Visitors should remember that because shoes are removed in restaurants, homes, and temples, wearing shoes that slip on, rather than lace, is recommended.

Because Europeans are very conscious of dress and appearance, wearing appropriate attire is important to create a favorable impression. In Europe, dress is an indication of social status, so it is important to dress your best by selecting clothing made of quality fabrics with fine tailoring; accessories, too, should be of high quality and reflect good taste. Inappropriate attire in Europe includes sweat suits and tennis shoes (viewed as appropriate only for athletic activities), T-shirts, funny hats, and loud colors.[33]

In South American countries, people dress fashionably. When in doubt about what to wear for a specific occasion, it is better to dress in more formal attire. South Americans appreciate quality in clothing and accessories, including shoes. Before wearing traditional clothing of the various Indian groups in South America, it is best to know who is permitted to wear the items and under what situations they are typically worn.

Because Jane enjoyed Latin American handcrafts, she often wore her Peruvian hooded poncho, unaware that in the southern region of Peru, ponchos with hoods are worn only by men. When she wore it while shopping at a flea market in New Orleans, a Spanish-speaking woman approached her and expressed sympathy at the death of her husband. Jane, who had no husband, did not know that men and women wore different types of ponchos. Since they met at a flea market, the woman incorrectly assumed that Jane was wearing her husband's poncho because he had died and left her financially unable to afford her own poncho.[34]

In Southern Asia and in countries of the Middle East, styles of dress vary somewhat with the country. In India, attire varies with the region of the country and with the religion. Women wear a *sari*, which is a long piece of fabric draped in different ways to signify either a religious affiliation or their socioeconomic status. Western women should probably not attempt to wear them because they do not know the correct rules for placing and draping the material over the shoulder. Another type of attire is the Punjabi suit, loose pants with matching long blouse worn outside the pants. The *bindi*, a red dot worn on the forehead by Hindu women, signifies marital status and femininity. It is often worn in different colors to match the woman's clothing, however, and is considered an optional beauty mark. Although men of India often wear Western-style suits, they may wear such traditional clothing as the *dhoti*, which is a large section of cloth wrapped around the waist. In hot weather, men often wear the safari suit, a shirt jacket with short sleeves and matching pants, for official occasions. Turbans are worn by Sikhs.[35] In Saudi Arabia, women wear an *abaaya*, which is a black robe that covers the head and body. In some areas, women in public wear a veil to cover their faces. Men wear traditional Arab dress, which includes a *thobe*, an ankle-length shirt, usually in white, worn over long pants; and a *mishlah*, which is a cloak worn over the *thobe*. They also wear the *ghutra*, which is a cloth covering the head in white or red checkered cloth; the *igal*, a braided black cord, holds the *ghutra* in place.[36]

In the North African country of Egypt, Western-style clothing and traditional clothing may be seen. In rural areas, women cover themselves, except for the face and hands, in public. Indian women typically wear a *sari*. Men in rural areas often wear the *djellaba*, a long, loose garment. Men from the southern part of Egypt wear a head covering. Men wear either suits or shirts and trousers. Visitors should dress very modestly; they should not adopt native clothing because Egyptians find this offensive. In South Africa, Western-style clothing is worn, but women often include a scarf with a dress or blouse and skirt.[37]

When a U.S. woman wearing some beautiful Middle Eastern blue ceramic beads was laughed at by her Iranian brother-in-law, she could not understand what was so funny. Although she knew they were called "donkey beads," she did not know that Iranian peddlers actually decorated their donkeys with them. The young woman was quite literally "making a jackass of herself."[38]

COUNTRY-SPECIFIC INFORMATION

Suggestions for dressing appropriately when visiting the countries with which the United States conducts a majority of its international business follow.

Brazil

- Fashionable, conservative attire with stylish accessories is important to Brazilians.

- Grooming is also important. Nails should be clean and manicured; shoes should be polished.

- Business attire is conservative. Men should wear dark suits with shirts and ties; they should be aware that three-piece suits are worn by executives, while two-piece suits are worn by those holding lower positions. Women should wear suits and dresses that are conservative, yet elegant.

- Casual attire does not include jeans, which are worn only by young people. Shorts or tennis shoes are not worn in public.

- Avoid wearing yellow and green together as these are the colors of the Brazilian flag.[39]

Canada

- Dress is conservative: suit and tie for men and conservative business attire for women.

- Casual attire is seen less frequently in Canada than in the United States.

- Dress varies somewhat by region, from more casual attire in Vancouver to more formal attire in Toronto.

- Removing hats in buildings and removing sunglasses during conversations with others is good manners.

China

- Business professional attire is expected when conducting business in China; subdued colors are worn.

- Men should wear a dark suit, light shirt, and tie.

- Women should wear a skirted suit or business dress in neutral colors; dresses and blouses should have a high neckline; shoes should have low heels to avoid being taller than the hosts.

- Business casual attire is inappropriate in Chinese business meetings.

- Casual attire should be conservative; jeans are acceptable but not shorts, except for exercising.

France

- Fashionable attire and high-quality accessories are common in France; conservative, well-made clothing of high quality is expected.

- Men wear dark suits with shirts that are white, striped, or colored with complementary ties.

- Women wear suits or dresses; soft colors are compatible with their feminine style.
- Casual attire is somewhat formal by U.S. standards.
- Dress for the theater would include dark suits for men and dinner dresses for women.

Germany

- Business dress is conservative; Germans tend to follow European fashion trends.
- Men wear dark suits, white shirts, and coordinating ties; blue blazers with gray flannel slacks are also appropriate.
- Women dress in dark suits and white blouses; pantsuits are not customary.
- Casual attire is similar to that worn in the United States.
- Accessories should also be conservative for both men and women.

Japan

- Conservative attire in dark colors is expected.
- Men wear conservative suits with slip-on shoes.
- Women's attire is conservative; dresses and skirted suits are appropriate; pantsuits are inappropriate.
- Business casual is not the norm.
- Take quality accessories; a leather briefcase of high quality shows respect.

Mexico

- Business attire is conservative; Mexican business executives usually dress better than U.S. business executives, including high-quality accessories.
- Men wear dark, conservative suits and ties; shoes should be well maintained and polished.
- Women wear skirted suits or dresses; femininity is important, so women doing business in Mexico should bring high heels and hosiery.
- Casual wear is appropriate in some resort areas; however, shorts are not acceptable in Mexico City. Casual attire is more chic than the U.S. casual look.

South Korea

- Conservative business attire is expected. Dressing appropriately indicates respect.

- Men wear Western-style clothing: a dark suit, white shirt, and tie.
- Women wear dresses that are styled modestly; they do not wear tight, revealing clothing and rarely wear pants. Clothing selected should not be yellow or pink.
- Casual attire does not include shorts, sleeveless tops, halters, or short skirts.

Taiwan

- Dress is professional and conservative; modesty is important.
- Men wear dark, lightweight business suits.
- Women wear skirted business suits or dresses.
- Women should avoid pantsuits because these are considered business casual.
- Wearing clothing that is black, red, or white should be avoided.

United Kingdom (England, Scotland, Wales, and Northern Ireland)

- Conservative attire of excellent quality is important.
- Men should wear suits in dark colors; they should not wear shirts with pockets, striped ties, or loafers.
- Women should wear skirted suits or dresses with dress shoes; pantsuits are not usually worn.
- Men and women wear tweeds, slacks, and sweaters for casual wear.
- For theaters, concerts, or restaurants, men wear dark suits; women wear suits, dresses, or nice pantsuits.

United States of America

- Conservative attire is expected in many companies. While business casual attire is acceptable in some firms, business professional dress is recommended when conducting business with international clients or on occasions when making a favorable impression is important.
- Business suits in dark colors are recommended professional attire for men; skirted suits or dresses in dark or neutral basic colors and natural fibers are recommended for women.
- Pantsuits are sometimes worn by women; however, they often lack the credibility of skirted suits or dresses and are not recommended for occasions when a woman wishes to make a good impression.
- Geographic differences exist in appropriate business dress. Attire is more casual in Florida and California than in New York. In fact, more conservative attire is expected on the East Coast than on the West Coast.

Chapter 6

CULTURAL ATTITUDES, BEHAVIORS, AND CUSTOMS

By observing the attitudes and behaviors of people of a culture, it is possible to gain insight into their values and thus lay the foundation for building effective global business relationships. An understanding of cultural attitudes toward the family, religion, education, and work can be instrumental in fostering intercultural relationships. In addition, attitudes toward equality, status, and social class, as well as cultural variations in public behavior, will be examined to gain a better understanding of other cultures so that cultural interactions will be mutually rewarding.

ATTITUDES TOWARD THE FAMILY

The meaning and importance of the family depends on an individual's own experience as well as on cultural influences. In many countries, people gain a sense of security from their strong family ties. In fact, in most countries of Latin America, North Africa, the Middle East, and Asia, the family unit is so strong that it is viewed as more important than work. This concept is foreign to people of the United States, Canada, and northern Europe, who keep business and family matters separate and, when forced to make a choice between the two, consider work more important than the family.[1]

When an Indonesian visited the United States, he commented on the
differences between the two countries in the importance placed on
the family. He observed that while people of the United States are
hospitable to complete strangers, they do not take care of members
of their own family.[2]

Because the United States is an individualistic culture, people do not feel
committed to staying near their relatives and often move to another part of
the country or the world. They either return to the family for infrequent visits
or sever the family ties permanently. This is not true of people in many countries who maintain family ties throughout their lives. U.S. Americans,
because they value independence and self-reliance, are quite happy moving
from place to place, meeting new people, and facing new career challenges.
Their happiness is not dependent upon staying close to their family.[3]

The word *family* does not have the same meaning in all cultures. In
the United States, family largely refers to the nuclear family. The nuclear
family is defined as including the father, mother, and children. In Mexico,
where even godparents are considered part of the family, their definition of
family would be the extended family, which includes grandparents,
uncles, aunts, and cousins. Likewise, in Arab cultures, a broader definition
of family is used that includes their numerous relatives. Other definitions
of family include a community or an entire culture. In parts of Israel, for
example, members of the community play an active role in raising and
educating children.[4]

Different family systems have evolved to meet the needs of a society. One
system is monogamy—one husband and one wife—which is practiced in
Europe, in parts of Africa and Asia, and in North and South America.
Serial monogamy—multiple monogamous marriages—is practiced in the
United States; people remarry, often numerous times, after the death of a
spouse or following divorce. Polygyny—one man with several wives—is
practiced by followers of Islam and in certain Middle Eastern countries.
Polyandry—one woman with many husbands—is practiced in a number of
Polynesian nations. A consideration in the concept of family is which parent,
father or mother, is the authority figure. Patriarchal families, in which the
father is in control, are typical in Spanish cultures; also Christians and
followers of Islam are usually patriarchal. The children use the father's name.
Matriarchal, or mother-oriented families, are found in Jewish families and
are based on the Judaic code of inheritance through the mother; however,
the children use the father's name, which is also true in patriarchal families.[5]

Cultural variations also exist in the age at which people typically date
and marry, the number of children, the extent to which women work to

contribute to the household, and living arrangements for the elderly. In the United States, dating begins as early as age 13; the average age for marriage is 27 for men and 25 for women. Although a few years ago, the traditional family was made up of a mother, father, and one or two children, this is changing. Numerous family configurations are now common, including single-parent families and married couples without children. Although some elderly family members live with their children, most prefer to live in their own homes for as long as they can care for themselves; they then move to retirement communities. Although this practice is sometimes seen as uncaring and heartless by people of other cultures, it is actually a reflection of the U.S. value of independence and self-reliance, in which children try to help their aging parents keep their dignity and independence for as long as possible. In Canada as well as in many European countries, dating practices, typical ages for marriage, family size, and treatment of the elderly are similar to U.S. customs. In other countries, however, practices are quite different. In India, for example, dating is not customary; some marriages are still arranged, with the bride and groom's consent. Families tend to be large, with the elderly cared for by their children. Dating is, likewise, rare in Iraq. Arranged marriages are common, with the consent of the bride and groom. Large families are the norm; several generations often live in the same house. The family system in Saudi Arabia is similar in some respects to that of India and Iraq. One difference, though, is that men are allowed under Islamic law to have four wives; however, most Saudi men have only one wife. Although families are considered patriarchal, the woman runs the household. In Asian countries, the family is very important. Most young men are expected to be financially secure before marriage. Families tend to be small; many women now work outside the home. Marriages are monogamous, and the divorce rate is lower than in many countries of North America and Europe. The elderly are treated with great respect and are cared for by their children. In fact, people of many other cultures, including Mexicans, Malaysians, Filipinos, and Native Americans, view the elderly as the most important members of the family who are due great respect.[6]

ATTITUDES TOWARD RELIGION

Religious attitudes become apparent when examining the importance of religion in the daily lives of people in various cultures. In the United States, separation of church and state is a deeply held doctrine. This doctrine states that the government will not officially support any religion and will not interfere with a person's practicing any religion. Although people of other cultures may think that this implies that U.S. Americans are not religious, in reality religion is important to people of the United States. Although the United States has never had an official state religion, Christians are in the majority; however, there are numerous non-Christian groups.

Religious observances do not usually interfere with business. Although many people do not work on such religious holidays as Christmas, those who work in supermarkets or restaurants are often asked to work. Religion is highly personal; even within a family, several denominations may be practiced. For that reason, discussing different religious beliefs at family gatherings is not recommended.[7]

Religion is sometimes a factor when conducting business in other cultures. Although religion has little impact on business in Australia, Europe, and North and South America, it would affect business in countries such as Saudi Arabia, the United Arab Emirates, Iran, and Iraq, where Islam is the official religion. Because Muslims stop work five times each day for prayers, people doing business in Islamic countries should be prepared to allow extra time for this daily ritual. In addition, businesspeople may wish to avoid attempting to conduct business during the month of Ramadan, as Muslims must fast from dawn to sunset. Because of religious influences on all aspects of life in Islamic countries, it is advisable to learn about their religious beliefs before traveling there to conduct business.[8]

A Syrian physician, who was participating in a U.S. work exchange program, noted the differences between religion in his country and in the United States. He pointed out that religion in Middle Eastern countries is part of daily life and that even for people who are not especially religious, Islam is an important part of the culture and has an impact on everyone. He added that Middle Easterners consider religion more than praying, which seemed to be the case with religions in the United States.[9]

In many countries of Asia and the Pacific Rim, religion is a way of life. People in some countries practice Buddhism only; in others, people may observe two or three religions. In China, for example, most people practice a combination of Confucianism, Taoism, and Buddhism, whereas Islam has a strong following in the Philippines, Indonesia, and Malaysia. In some countries, numerous temples and mosques are seen everywhere, but in other countries, such as Japan, people are less likely to express their religious beliefs publicly.[10]

Because religion may be a consideration when dealing with people of different faiths, learning about the customs and beliefs associated with the various religions is advisable.

An older woman had been admitted to the hospital for extreme abdominal pain. Since it was the woman's first time to be hospitalized, the nurse explained procedures, including pressing the call bell for help. When the nurse later came by the patient's room for a routine visit and found her in great pain, she asked why she had not used the bell. The patient said that it was against her religion. Because the hospital had little experience with patients who were Orthodox Jews, the staff did not know of the Sabbath prohibition against turning on or off electrical switches. Thereafter, they asked that a family member remain with a patient during the Orthodox Jewish Sabbath so that someone would be available to go to the nurses' station to request help when needed.[11]

ATTITUDES TOWARD EDUCATION

Attitudes toward education vary from countries that believe that education should be accessible to all; to those that believe that education should be limited to a select few. In the United States, people believe that education should be readily accessible to everyone. The easy access to higher education in the United States was noted by Malaysian students who were unable to enter universities in their own country but who were admitted to U.S. universities. Although the Malaysian students compared the U.S. educational system unfavorably to the British approach used in their own country, they acknowledged the possibility that there may be something right about the U.S. system because "Americans put men on the moon."[12] Although in some countries, the objective seems to be to screen people so that education is available to a select few, in the United States, the objective is to have lenient screening standards, if any, so that those who wish to pursue their educational goals may have an opportunity to do so. The U.S. educational system is designed to accommodate students with a variety of abilities and disabilities, including students for whom English is a second language.

In addition to accessibility to all who wish an education, another goal of the U.S. educational system is a literacy rate of 100 percent of its population. Although the goal has yet to be achieved (the adult literacy rate is 99 percent), the ideal remains. Individual U.S. states require young people to attend school until, in most states, the age of 16 or 17 (18 in the remaining states). The educational system is decentralized; states and local boards of education have control of their own educational systems. Unlike in many countries, there is no national ministry of education in the United States. Although people from other cultures sometimes assume that the U.S. Department of Education controls the schools, it does not.

An additional goal of the U.S. educational system is to educate the whole person so that, in addition to academic achievement, students are well rounded and develop social skills through their interactions with other students both inside and outside the classroom. Students are encouraged to participate in sports and school clubs to help in their social development.[13]

When a Taiwanese father enrolled his four brilliant children aged 6 to 13 in a U.S. community college, the president tried to remove them from the school because they had been home schooled and had never even attended an elementary school. A cultural difference in the educational philosophies of the two cultures soon became apparent. In the United States, the learning of social skills, which is best achieved by interacting with other students in elementary school, is an important part of a person's education. In Asian countries, however, academic achievement, rather than social development, is of primary concern.[14]

Most U.S. students attend tax-supported public elementary and secondary schools, which they attend at no cost. Because of the local control of education, students do not take any national tests, as is the case in England, France, and Japan. Because of state and local differences in public education requirements, variations exist from school to school in the quality of education students receive. Private schools, which are expensive because they receive no tax support, are also available. Parents who choose to send their children to private schools may do so because of smaller class sizes, better discipline, higher academic standards, or the religious instruction available to students in some schools.[15]

Sometimes foreign students have problems adjusting to the U.S. educational system. One adjustment includes their relationships with their professors, specifically, the extent of formality considered appropriate between students and professors and the displays of respect students show their professors. In the United States, less formality exists between teachers and students than is the case in many cultures. This informality may take the form of professors who ask that students call them by their first names, a practice that is common in many U.S. graduate schools. Such a practice is especially awkward for Asian students who have been taught to show proper respect to professors by bowing and calling them by their titles and last names. Although some behaviors of U.S. students may seem disrespectful by standards of some foreign students, a closer look at the student-professor relationship will reveal subtle ways in which students show their respect for their professors, including voice tone and vocabulary during interactions. U.S. professors feel it is natural for students to question what they say; foreign students view challenging a professor as disrespectful. This challenging of the professor, however, does not extend to trying to talk the professor into giving them a higher grade. Students from countries where negotiating for a higher grade is considered acceptable must realize that this practice is not acceptable in the United States. In fact, negotiating to get a higher grade is viewed negatively by professors and should be avoided; however, asking for an explanation of the grading of an assignment is acceptable.

Two other areas involving the professor-student relationship are plagiarism and cheating. Plagiarism, which is representing the work of another person as one's own, results in serious penalties in the United States. These penalties include receiving a failing grade on the assignment, failure in the course, or expulsion from the university. The U.S. belief in individualism extends to respecting the ideas and property of another person; U.S. students know that they must acknowledge the source of the ideas they use. Many foreign students, on the other hand, do not see anything wrong with copying another person's ideas because they do not understand the U.S. concept of ownership of ideas.[16] The U.S. concept of cheating is not shared by people of many other cultures. What would be considered helping each other in some countries would be considered cheating in U.S. schools. To avoid the appearance of cheating, U.S. students will often avoid interacting with foreign students in their classes who often seek them out for help with an assignment. Foreign students need to understand U.S. values of individualism, self-reliance, and competition and to realize that these values extend to their schoolwork.

When students in her class of mainly international students talked to each other and exchanged information during exams, despite her warnings that this was considered cheating in the United States, the teacher tried to appeal to students by putting the situation into a cultural context. After explaining that intolerance of cheating in U.S. schools is associated with U.S. cultural values of competition, rather than cooperation, and individuality, rather than working as a group, the teacher was able to gain understanding and to create a positive learning environment.[17]

Another adjustment students from other cultures will need to make to the U.S. educational system is related to the amount of classroom interaction considered appropriate. In some cultures, there is a lot of interaction between students and teachers, whereas in others, there is very little inter-action. In U.S. classrooms, expressing one's own ideas and participating in discussions of assigned topics is encouraged. Criticizing the teacher in front of other students is considered impolite, however. In Algerian class-rooms, students are quite vocal; they criticize and question what the pro-fessor says. In Vietnamese classrooms, on the other hand, talking is prohibited. Classrooms in China are also quiet, a reflection of their respect for silence, knowledge, truth, and wisdom. Mexican classrooms are con-trolled by the teacher, who is in charge of verbal interaction.[18] U.S. fami-lies in foreign assignments will need to check into American schools in the country in which they will be working by accessing such Web sites as http://www.aassa.com/htm/schools.htm and http://overseasdigest.com/schooljobs2.htm.

In their relationships with U.S. students, foreign students would be wise to respect the values and customs of students in the United States. For example, U.S. students are slow to make friends and will not usually initiate a relationship unless they have traveled abroad. Foreign students should, therefore, proceed cautiously when trying to form friendships with U.S. students. When sharing an apartment or dormitory with a U.S. student, foreign students will need to be aware of certain expec-tations of U.S. students. These expectations include being assertive and direct in saying what they want or in explaining what is upsetting them, respecting the privacy and private property of the roommate, and being considerate by doing one's share of the cleaning and cooking and by pay-ing one's share of the expenses.[19]

WORK ATTITUDES, BEHAVIORS, AND CUSTOMS

Work attitudes, a term that refers to how people of a culture view work, are culturally diverse. Some cultures live to work and others work to live. The United States, because it is a work-oriented culture in which people value and reward hard work, is considered a live-to-work culture. People in the United States who do not work are viewed negatively; they are con-sidered lazy and lacking in self-respect. U.S. parents remind their children from an early age of the importance of hard work with such adages as "If you don't work, you don't eat."

Proverbs that reflect cultural attitudes toward work:

"He who wishes to eat the nut does not mind cracking the shell" (Polish proverb).

"He who is afraid of doing too much always does too little" (German proverb).

"Words do not make flour" (Italian proverb).[20]

When U.S. workers are being considered for raises and promotions, their supervisors often look at the person's willingness to work beyond a typical 40-hour week. After all, top-level executives often work 56 hours a week, so those who aspire to executive levels within a company should be willing to do the same. When people are successful, usually measured by salary and/or job title, the assumption is that their success resulted from working long hours, seven days a week. Senior-level U.S. executives work far more than their counterparts in many countries of Europe. They also take only 14 days of vacation annually, compared to executives in many European countries, where businesses are often closed for a month to permit employees to go on vacation.

In many countries of Europe, attitudes toward work are more relaxed than in the United States. Although people of the United States typically work on weekends and holidays, this is not true of a majority of Europeans. They reserve this time to spend with their families. The French, who have the longest vacations of any country in the world (a minimum of five weeks per year), do not work overtime and enjoy their long holidays. Australians, who work fewer hours than any country in the world, also value their free time and look forward to vacation time. Although U.S. Americans usually receive two- or three-week vacations, vacation time is staggered so that business will not be interrupted by having to close while all employees go on vacation.[21]

The 2007 report by the International Labor Organization revealed the average number of hours worked per person, per week, by people in various cultures. The 10 countries with the largest number of working hours per week in 2007 were Singapore (50.5 hours), China (47.1 hours), India (46.9 hours), South Korea (46.0 hours), Mexico (44.7 hours), Japan (43.5 hours), the United States (42.8 hours), Switzerland (41.2 hours), the Netherlands (38.5 hours), and Germany (37.9 hours).[22]

The times people work, take breaks, and eat lunch vary around the world. Generally in the United States, offices are open from 9:00 a.m. to 5:00 p.m. Employees begin work promptly and always look busy even if their work is caught up. Reading the newspaper or visiting with associates, when not busy, is common in many countries in the world, however.

Knowing what the office hours are can be beneficial for planning your work schedule while in another country. Some examples of office hours follow. Iran's business hours are from 9:30 a.m. to 1:00 p.m. and 2:00 p.m. to 5:00 p.m., Saturday through Wednesday, and there is no work from noon until the next morning during the month of Ramadan (the ninth month of the Islamic lunar calendar). In Brazil and Colombia, business hours are 8:00 a.m. to 6:00 p.m., Monday through Friday, with a noon–to–2:00 p.m. lunch time. Peruvians average a six-day workweek of 48 hours.[23] Because office hours vary around the world, you will want to talk with your associates about the proper times to make appointments.

In the United States, breaks and lunch times tend to be on the frugal side. The lunch period is from 30 minutes to an hour, and break times are usually one 15-minute period in the morning with another 15-minute period in the afternoon. Because "time is money" in the United States, workers are expected to adhere to these times to the point that anyone who clocks in and out of work has to clock in and out at lunch time. It is difficult for U.S. businesspeople to understand the Europeans' one- to one-and-a-half-hour lunch break, 20-minute morning and afternoon breaks, plus a 15-minute cleanup time at the end of the workday. Whereas the United States has an average eight-hour workday, Europe has a seven-hour workday.[24]

Although many nations have almost guaranteed employment by a corporation once you are hired, that is not the practice in the United States. The United States has many laws concerning when and how you can fire someone, but it is not unusual for people who do not perform satisfactorily to be let go from an organization. U.S. people know that retaining their position and getting promotions depend on performing the job satisfactorily and on getting along with other workers. In the United States, no position should be considered permanent, although unions and tenure rules try to make positions permanent. In much of Europe and Japan, workers feel as if they will always have a position with the firm. As many firms around the world are having problems paying pensions and surviving economically, this is beginning to change. Likewise, individuals who would never have considered leaving a corporation are now starting to change jobs. In many European countries, if workers are let go for anything but criminal behavior, they will receive generous severance packages. These benefits could be as much as three months' full salary and benefits while they look for a new job.[25] A U.S. firm that wanted to close a plant in Italy, after an unsuccessful attempt to sell the plant, notified the union about their plans. The union went on strike. In Italy, management cannot shut down a plant that is on strike. The U.S. firm fortunately was able to find a buyer, or this could have been a financial disaster. Even though the firm had an Italian lawyer, they were never informed of this legal difference from the U.S. laws.

Although U.S. workers consider their employer simply a place to earn a paycheck, many Asians are more married to their positions and companies than to their spouses. The company's needs come first; the family's needs come second. This difference in the importance of family and company has caused problems when Japanese companies open plants in the United States or elsewhere that do not have this custom of placing the company first. In Japan, it is expected that lower-ranking personnel will not leave for the day until their boss leaves. To do otherwise is disrespectful. Also, the Japanese believe that workers will stay with them for life. They are initially shocked at U.S. turnover rates and the need to constantly retrain people. The Japanese managers also have to change their interview questions because they are accustomed to asking personal questions that are illegal in the United States.

Although in many offices in the world, people would always treat each other with a degree of formality, this fact is particularly true in Europe. Formality varies considerably in U.S. offices. The location of the company (urban or rural), the size of the company, and the type of work that the company does will determine the formality/informality of the organization. An informal atmosphere in U.S. organizations would include the practice of addressing each other by first names, engaging in more small talk concerning families and extracurricular activities, joking, and wearing more casual attire. Many people in the United States enjoy the more informal type of atmosphere.

Showing or not showing emotions at work is culturally determined. Affective cultures that consider open emotions to be acceptable include Kuwait, Egypt, Spain, and Cuba. Examples of countries that feel that it is necessary to mask their feelings by not showing emotions openly include Ethiopia, Japan, and Poland. The United States is in the middle, with some people showing emotion at work and some not showing emotion at work. Although you cannot generalize about showing or not showing emotions by continent, knowing when and where it is appropriate to show emotion is helpful in building global business relationships.[26]

Saying "please" and "thank you" when requesting or acknowledging assistance is expected in the United States. When someone does not say "please" and "thank you," the other people will feel unappreciated or taken advantage of. Saying "please" and "thank you" is not necessarily automatic for people in other parts of the world, however.

A well-mannered German exchange student was staying in an American home, where her house mother did many kind things for her, including driving her to numerous activities. Although the girl was polite in every other way, she never once said "please" or "thank you" to her house mother. Naturally, the house mother felt that her efforts were unappreciated and that she had been taken advantage of.[27]

Making appointments requires different protocol in different countries. In Egypt, you need a letter of introduction; in parts of Africa, China, Latin America, and Saudi Arabia, you need an intermediary to make the appointments. The proper appointment protocol must be acted upon before you leave your home country.

Because of the U.S. obsession with work, people from other cultures have observed that people from the United States even work at relaxing. When they go on vacation, for example, they will plan where to go and what to do to make sure they keep busy the entire time. They do not allow themselves to do nothing because they tend to be action-oriented. Their leisure activities, such as gardening or washing the car, would be considered manual labor in many countries. Visitors from other countries have even commented that U.S. Americans who participate in sports for recreation seem to make work out of it. They approach sports with such seriousness that fun and spontaneity are often missing.[28]

A South American who moved to the United States observed several joggers passing her house in below-zero weather and exclaimed: "These crazy Americans!" While U.S. people view their daily jogging as relaxing and as contributing to their health and fitness, people of other countries do not share their view of what is considered recreation.[29]

To work in harmony with people of other cultures, it is important to consider how they view work. U.S. Americans clearly live to work. This story about Kemmons Wilson, founder of Holiday Inns, emphasizes the importance of hard work to businesspeople of the United States.

Kemmons Wilson, who never received a high school diploma, was invited to give the commencement address to one of the graduating classes at the school he attended. He began his address with this statement: "I really do not know why I am here. I never got a degree, and I have only worked half days my entire life. My advice to you is to do the same. Work half days every day. It does not matter which half you work—the first 12 hours or the second 12 hours."[30]

WOMEN AND WORK

Culture teaches us how to deal with the opposite gender. In many cultures, women are taught to communicate differently, to use different phrasing, to use different tones, and to relate to their femaleness. As women enter upper-management positions in many countries, the genders have tried to ignore the gender-trait stereotyping culture has taught them. Countries have done so in different ways: the United States by legislating equality, in Japan by emphasizing the distinct strengths and qualities of each gender, in Saudi Arabia where men and women are not allowed to interact in the workplace, and in developing nations where there is a high level of inequality between the genders.[31] The preference for the male heirs is apparent in India, where inheritance is through the males, and in Arab nations, where the desire for males is so strong that on their wedding day, newlyweds are wished many sons.[32]

Although it is not always easy to succeed as a woman in business, sometimes being female forces women to think of better ways to succeed. Many men contribute to the glass ceiling women face because of the need many males have to maintain power. Some of the problems women have are that they negotiate differently from men because most feel uncomfortable with haggling and fear that if they negotiate, they may damage their relationship with the company. Many women in the global environment feel their barriers to corporate success are inside the firm rather than from situations outside the firm. Women are often stereotyped as more "human" and are assigned positions in human resources, communications, public relations, and marketing rather than positions that tend to lead to higher levels of management. In the United States, significant salary differences exist between women and men, with women averaging only 76 percent of what male counterparts earn. In some corporations, women are changing this type of environment by joining in existing events or establishing events that mix the genders rather than segregate them.

Studies have found that women equal men when it comes to wanting to pursue an international assignment. Yet, in one recent study of Canada and the United States, out of 13,338 expatriates, only 3 percent chosen to go abroad were women. Although in parts of Asia, South America, and the Middle East, female managers report being mistaken for a wife or secretary, they report that once the error is clarified, they are respected and treated professionally. Except for Saudi Arabia, the remainder of the Arab Gulf States allow women to work alongside men, and the dress code for women is more relaxed. Women from other countries in the Arab Gulf States actually have an advantage because they are not expected to behave according to the social mores of the culture, and they tend to have good cross-cultural management skills because of their sensitivity, communication skills, and community-building behaviors. Many successful female managers say that women need to have more confidence in themselves, they need to have the attitude that they can survive and overcome difficult situations, they need to feel it is acceptable to do things differently, and they need to have an open approach to management rather than a feminine or masculine approach.[33] The bottom line is that women must be treated as people first. Women are just as successful globally as men when given the opportunity.

ATTITUDES TOWARD EQUALITY, STATUS, AND SOCIAL CLASS

Status and social class, although very important in some cultures, are of little importance to most people of the United States. Equality, though, is very important. U.S. Americans sanction the statement in the Declaration of Independence that "all men are created equal." (That statement is, of course, interpreted to mean that men and women are created equal). Although U.S. Americans may sometimes observe violations of this statement of the equality of all people (such as women who are paid less than men doing similar work), they continue to believe that people have equal value and that no one is inherently superior to others. In spite of the purported belief in the equality of all people, distinctions are made between people based on status and position. For example, differences are acknowledged by seating arrangements and order of speaking. Distinctions are also apparent by touch (higher-status people touch lower-status people first) and by characteristics of vocal interactions (higher-status people speak first and talk longer and louder). Two important concepts are important to the U.S. idea of equality: (1) everyone should have a chance to improve their position in life, and (2) everyone deserves to be treated with respect.[34]

People in many other countries are very conscious of status. People in some countries feel that certain people have higher status and are therefore entitled to more respect than those of lower status. India, for example, has a rigid caste system that is determined at birth. The four main castes are religious people, administrators, skilled craftsmen/farmers, and unskilled laborers; people of each caste have their own rights, duties, and status. A fifth group, which is below the main castes, is called the untouchables; these people perform work considered undesirable by others. Interaction between people of different castes is limited. Though the caste system has been officially outlawed, it continues to be a source of tension in India.[35]

People of the United States consider their country a classless society; they cite as evidence of the absence of classes the fact that the country does not have a system of inherited titles, nor is there a formal class structure as is apparent in such countries as India. U.S. Americans maintain that their country is one large middle class. Class and status distinctions, though subtle, exist, however. U.S. people do acknowledge distinctions within the middle class: upper-middle class, mid-middle class, and lower-middle class. Factors that distinguish between the variations within the middle class are usually money, education, and occupation. Even when money is a distinction, how it is earned is a consideration: whether the money was inherited, was made through hard work and determination, or was gained by illegal means. People of the United States have great respect for self-made people but have no respect for people who acquire money through illegal activities. In addition, style, taste, and *savoir faire* are equally important. For example, a drug dealer who had amassed great wealth would not be considered a member of the upper-middle class because of how the money was acquired and because drug dealers rarely have style, taste, and *savoir faire*. The other factors affecting distinctions within the class, education and occupation, can move a person from the lower-middle class to the upper-middle class. For example, someone from a poor family, by completing graduate degrees, can become a scientist, a medical doctor, or a college professor and thus move up to a higher class. Because class is competitive and may change, people who have risen to the upper-middle class level want to make sure their friends and work associates know of their accomplishments by buying a larger home, more expensive automobiles, and other visible symbols of affluence.[36]

Status is also associated with education in several other cultures. In Mexico and a number of South American countries, a lawyer is addressed as *Licenciado*, a very important title. Italians with college degrees are called *Dottore* (Doctor), as are lawyers and architects. German executives and other professionals proudly include titles before their names, as they often suggest their profession or level of education.

In some countries, age is indicative of seniority and is, therefore, deserving of respect. Asians and Middle Easterners have great respect for age, because it is thought that wisdom comes with age. Although rank is important, age takes precedence over rank. In Japan, it is important to know the rank of the people with whom you will interact because people bow lower when meeting someone of high rank. Status is also a factor in who enters a room or an elevator first; the person of higher rank enters first. Then others follow in rank order, with the person of lowest rank entering last. The Chinese also follow this protocol. A foreign guest would be permitted to enter a room or elevator first as a sign of respect for the visitor.[37]

Recognizing differences in status and social class can be important in intercultural encounters. Failure to show proper respect for age, status, wealth, or social position, when these factors are important to members of the culture, may result in unintentionally offending someone with whom you had hoped to establish a business relationship.

CULTURAL VARIATIONS IN PUBLIC BEHAVIOR

Behavior in public is influenced by culture. Public behavior often reflects the values of people of a culture; for example, younger people in some cultures are expected to give up their seats on public transportation to certain people who are considered deserving of special respect. Although this practice is not common in the United States, in Israel and Nigeria, it is customary for younger people to relinquish their seats to expectant mothers, mothers with small children, and the elderly. In addition, what is considered appropriate nonverbal behavior in various cultures (described in Chapter 4) would affect how people behave in public. For example, the aversion of U.S. Americans to being touched in public is apparent. U.S. people will avoid situations where they will be forced into physical contact with others, such as getting on a crowded elevator or train. When they do inadvertently bump into another person, they will apologize. Public touching of people of China, Hong Kong, and Singapore should be avoided. People of Mexico and Japan, on the other hand, are quite comfortable with crowded situations, including pushing through a crowd where touching strangers is inevitable.[38]

Rules for behavior in public observed by people of the United States include keeping to the right when walking down halls, on sidewalks, or other places where people go in opposite directions. Following this rule enables people of the United States to avoid physical contact and to move through crowded places quickly and in an orderly fashion. People who violate the rule of keeping to the right can expect to be met with stares or verbal reminders by other people. In South Korea, on the other hand, people keep to the left when climbing stairs or walking on the street.

U.S. Americans also feel that people should get in line and wait their turn when at the checkout of a supermarket, at the bank, or at a special events ticket office. No special consideration is given to people who are elderly, handicapped, or wealthy. This failure to give consideration to special groups of people in the United States is consistent with the belief that everyone is equal and that no one, regardless of position or status, deserves to go to the front of the line, while others have been patiently waiting for their turn. On the rare occasion that a person tries to break line, others in line will quickly point out the location of the end of the line. When there is no line and several people are waiting for service, the clerk usually asks who is next; those waiting are expected to give an honest reply. The practice of lining up, or queuing, and waiting your turn is likewise customary in Japan and Sweden, where people queue for public transportation and at the theater. In Israel, Mexico, and South Korea, however, there are no queues for anything. Shoving and pushing to get ahead in line is acceptable behavior.

Two Mexican visitors to the United States, who arrived late at the airport for their returning flight to Mexico City, pushed ahead of others waiting in line at airport security and were quickly reported to security officials. Upon being questioned, they admitted to breaking line because they were afraid they would miss their flight. Airport officials, after explaining that waiting in line was expected of everyone, escorted them to the end of the line to await their turn just as everyone else was doing.

A behavior that has been under increased scrutiny in the past few years is smoking in public places.

A visitor from Germany observed that when she lit a cigarette in public places in the United States, people either gave her a dirty look or asked her to put out the cigarette. She commented that she had never even thought about where she smoked when she was in Germany.[39]

Most U.S. cities and states have passed laws prohibiting smoking in such public places as airports, theaters, grocery stores, universities, restaurants, shopping malls, and public buildings. Many businesses have now established smoke-free environments. This prohibition of smoking in public places has no doubt stemmed from pressure from nonsmokers who, after giving careful consideration to the research on the health hazards of smoking—as well as hazards of inhaling secondhand smoke—have insisted on their right to breathe air that has not been polluted with carcinogens. Some companies have refused to hire people who smoke; it is now legal for U.S. companies to refuse to hire people based solely on the fact that they smoke. When smokers are invited to parties at someone's home, they should ask for permission to smoke; often the host will ask that they smoke outdoors out of consideration to nonsmokers who feel entitled to a smoke-free environment. Visitors to the United States will want to be considerate about smoking around other people lest they give offense. Likewise, people of other cultures have rules concerning proper smoking behavior. In Israel and South Africa, asking permission to smoke is expected. Although women should not smoke on the street, men may smoke anywhere. In South Korea and Saudi Arabia as well, women do not smoke on the street. In addition, during Ramadan it is inappropriate to smoke anywhere in public. In Kenya and Argentina, however, smoking in public places—without asking permission—is common.

Voice volume is another public behavior that should be appropriate to the situation, the occasion, and the culture. At a football game in the

United States, fans are expected to make more noise than the same people would when in a theater. Likewise, those who eat at fast-food restaurants usually make more noise than people dining in an expensive restaurant. In France and New Zealand, it is also important to keep the voice level down in public. As a general rule, U.S. people speak in a louder voice than Germans, but they are not as loud as people of Nigeria or Brazil. Visitors to the United States and U.S. visitors to other countries should avoid calling attention to themselves in a negative way by speaking in a voice louder than people near them.[40]

Other behaviors that are considered offensive in public places in some cultures include using toothpicks, spitting on the street, chewing gum, eating or drinking while walking on the street, and showing affection toward members of the opposite gender. Countries that frown on the public use of toothpicks include Canada, New Zealand, and South Korea. Spitting on the street is unacceptable behavior in England but is acceptable in China. Chewing gum is frowned upon in France, Germany, and New Zealand. Eating or drinking while walking on the street is viewed as inappropriate in France, India, Japan, Mexico, and South Korea. Although public displays of affection for members of the opposite gender are common in the United States, this behavior is offensive in China, Egypt, India, Japan, the Netherlands, and Sweden.

Visitors to other countries should be aware of behavior expected in public places. Showing respect for cultural variations in public behavior is much more likely to result in being welcomed in various countries and in being treated with the respect shown for the country's customs.

Country-Specific Information

Cultural attitudes and behaviors for the countries with which the United States conducts most of its international business follow.[41]

Brazil

- Although Brazilian families are traditionally large, smaller families of one to three children are becoming more common. Brazil is a patriarchal society, but the mother has an influence on decisions affecting the home.
- Classes exist in Brazil; people in the middle and upper classes live apart from those in the working class.
- About 70 percent of Brazilians are Roman Catholic, while 20 percent are Protestant.
- Education is compulsory to age 14. The literacy rate in Brazil is 88 percent for males and 89 percent for females.

- Brazilians are hard working. The maximum work week is 44 hours.
- Yawning or stretching in public is rude.[42]

Canada

- Canadians have small families; about one-third of marriages end in divorce; both parents usually work.
- Canadians of Irish, French, and Scottish descent are typically Roman Catholic; others are Protestant.
- Education is free and compulsory from age 6 or 7 to 14 or 15; they have a 99 percent literacy rate.
- Canadians view themselves as hardworking people; they work an average of 32 hours per week.
- Do not sing "Alouette" to Québécois; they view it as condescending.
- Avoid yawning or scratching in public; also, do not use toothpicks or combs in public.

China

- Bringing honor to the family is important; children must respect and practice traditional family values. Most families have one child.
- Rank is very important to the Chinese; they observe a strict hierarchical system that should be respected.
- Most people observe Buddhism, Taoism, and Confucianism; atheism is encouraged by the Chinese government; public worship is discouraged. The state, not religion, dictates morality.
- Less than 10 percent of the population attends a university; the overall literacy rate is 86 percent.
- The Chinese are hard workers; they work an average of 48 hours per week, compared to 43 in the U.S. and 42 in Japan.
- Spitting on the street is common; smoking is banned on public transportation as well as in stores and theaters.

France

- The extended family is just as important as the nuclear family; the average size of the family is one or two children. Pets are considered part of the family and outnumber children.
- The French consider status and rank very important. Most of the population is middle class; however, distinct social classes exist, and the hostility between the classes persists.
- Almost 90 percent of French people are Roman Catholic.

- Education is very important to the French; they provide free schooling to those between ages 6 and 16. France has a 99 percent literacy rate. France's 60 universities are among the world's best.
- The French work 38 hours per week; however, questions about a person's profession are considered intrusive.
- Chewing gum in public is considered inappropriate.

Germany

- The size of the average German family is one or two children. Germany is a patriarchal society.
- Class status is important to Germans. Although all people have equal rights under the law, in reality inequalities exist.
- About one-half of the population is Roman Catholic and one-half is Protestant.
- Education is important to Germans. School is mandatory for those between the ages of 6 and 15. The literacy rate is 99 percent.
- Germans work 39 hours per week; they typically take a full month of vacation, usually in July or August.
- Do not chew gum while conversing; Germans consider this extremely rude.

Japan

- Japan is a patriarchal society; the mother, however, is responsible for raising the children and running the household. Family is very important in Japan; children are taught to have a sense of obligation and responsibility toward the family. Family size is typically one or two children.
- To the Japanese, age equals rank; people who are older have higher status.
- The Japanese practice a combination of Shinto and Buddhism, such as having a Shinto marriage and a Buddhist funeral.
- Education is free and compulsory for students between the ages of 6 and 15. Japan's adult literacy rate is 99 percent.
- The Japanese work longer hours Monday through Friday than U.S. Americans; however, they rarely work on weekends. The average number of hours worked per week is 42 hours, compared to the 43 hours worked by U.S. people.
- When shopping, it is inappropriate to bargain. Store clerks will present your change on a tray without counting it in front of you.
- Do not eat or drink while walking on the street.

Mexico

- Mexicans place high value on the family; families are large, with four or more children common; the father is the authority figure, but the mother has charge of the household.
- Mexico's upper class is the largest of the Latin American cultures. Many Mexicans are at the opposite end of the class scale, however; they work long hours for low pay. Social status is based on education, wealth, friends, and family name.
- Almost 90 percent of Mexicans are Roman Catholic.
- Although education is purportedly free and compulsory for those aged 6 to 15, some fees are required of students, and school attendance is not enforced. The adult literacy rate is 92 percent.
- Mexicans value hard work; they average 43 hours per week. Their *mañana* attitude has caused people from other countries to question their dedication to work.
- When paying for merchandise in stores, always put the money in the person's hand.
- Avoid eating while walking on the street.

South Korea

- Koreans have a patriarchal society; the father and son are given the greatest respect; family members feel a sense of obligation to each other.
- According to Confucian philosophy, everyone has a rank; knowing the ranking system is important. Status is based on gender, age, family background, wealth, and occupation; interactions are determined by a person's place in a social group.
- Confucianism, which is a philosophy rather than a religion, has a strong impact on every aspect of Korean society. About half of the population is Christian.
- Schooling in South Korea is compulsory for those between the ages of 6 and 12. The adult literacy rate is 98 percent.
- South Koreans work 46 hours per week; July and August are vacation months and are not good times for conducting business.
- Do not use toothpicks in public. When forming a line, remember that age and rank are important.

Taiwan

- The people of Taiwan have strong extended family relationships. Although families have traditionally been large, the number of children is now one or two due to a government program aimed at reducing family size. Children are taught to respect and obey their parents.

- About 93 percent of people of Taiwan practice a combination of Buddhism, Confucianism (a philosophy, not a religion), and Taoism.
- Education is important in Taiwan. Schooling is free and compulsory for students between 9 and 15 years of age. The adult literacy rate is 95 percent, but it is close to 100 percent for young people.
- People of Taiwan appreciate diligence and hard work.
- Loud behavior in public is considered rude.
- Avoid embarrassing anyone in public; causing loss of face can damage a relationship.

United Kingdom (England, Scotland, Wales, and Northern Ireland)

- Families are small—usually two or three children; many women work; the number of single-parent families is increasing.
- England has an upper class, a small group of families with wealth and royal connections; class distinctions are apparent by one's education, accent, clothing, and so forth. Most of the population throughout the UK, however, would be considered middle class.
- Education is valued in the UK; their schools are among the best in the world. For students between 5 and 16, school is free and compulsory. Overall literacy rate is 99 percent.
- People of the UK work 40 hours per week; however, work and one's profession are not topics for public discussion.
- Appropriate behavior in public includes standing during the playing of "God Save the Queen" and avoiding loud behavior. Rank should be respected when entering a room; the person of higher rank should be allowed to enter first.

United States of America

- While the traditional U.S. family consisting of a mother, father, and two or three children still exists, single-parent families are becoming common. In fact, almost a third of families are headed by a single parent. In two-parent households, both parents often work. Members of the extended family (grandparents, aunts, uncles, and cousins) do not typically live with the nuclear family.
- The United States has no official church; however, about 80 percent of the population is Christian. Because the U.S. government provides for the separation of church and state, religion does not have much impact on business.
- Education is free and compulsory for those between the ages of 5 and 16. The literacy rate is 99 percent.

- U.S. citizens are known for their work ethic; they believe that work is respectable and should be rewarded; failure to work is viewed with disdain. While most of those employed work an average of 42.8 hours per week, senior-level executives work 56 hours per week.[43]

- Appropriate public behavior includes respecting queues and keeping to the right when walking on sidewalks or other places where people walk in opposite directions. The practice in some cultures of giving up one's seat to the elderly when using public transportation is uncommon in the United States.

- Public behaviors to avoid include chewing gum, spitting on the street, eating/drinking while walking on the street, and using toothpicks in the presence of others.

Chapter 7

DINING AND TIPPING CUSTOMS

People of all cultures send messages by what they eat and by the way they eat. Breeding, upbringing, and education will be revealed in how people behave while dining. Because many business and social encounters involve dining, it is important to be aware of cultural variations in eating styles and mealtime customs as well as food customs and consumption taboos. In addition, during business entertaining, seating and toasting etiquette must be considered. Because people reveal such qualities as generosity (or stinginess) by their tipping behavior, learning the nuances of tipping, especially restaurant and travel tipping, when a guest in other countries is extremely important.

STYLES OF EATING AND PLACE SETTINGS

People of the United States use what is commonly referred to as the American *zigzag* style of eating. Using this style involves holding the knife in the right hand and the fork in the left with the tines down. After cutting a piece of food, the knife is placed on the upper edge of the plate, the fork is switched to the right hand, and the piece of food is eaten with the fork tines up. This switching back and forth of the fork from the left hand to the right and back again is where the term *zigzag* originated.

The arrangement of the plates, glasses, and eating utensils will vary somewhat with the culture; however, the rule that is followed regardless of the culture is that silverware is arranged so that the utensil to be used first is placed on the outside farthest from the plate. Diners then only have to remember to select utensils from the outside and work their way toward the center. Glasses for water and other beverages are positioned to the upper right of the plate, and the bread plate is placed to the upper left of the dinner plate above the fork(s). Utensils for dessert are placed above the dinner plate: the dessert spoon is positioned with the handle facing right, and the fork is placed below the spoon with the handle facing to the left. Napkins may be placed either on the plate, in the coffee cup or wine glass, or to the left of the plate; they may not be placed beneath the forks. American place settings usually place the smaller salad fork on the outside to the left of the plate; the smaller salad knife, when used, is placed on the outside to the right of the plate because it is customary to eat the salad before the meat in the United States. The largest fork and knife, which are used for the meat course, are closest to the dinner plate.

In European and Latin American countries, as well as in many other parts of the world, the Continental or European style of dining is used. When using this style, the fork remains in the left hand, tines down, during cutting and eating the food. Because people in other countries usually eat the entrée before the salad, the larger fork and knife will be to the outside. Because Europeans usually have more courses than U.S. Americans, they will have additional utensils for the added courses, such as a fish fork and/or knife.

People signal when they have finished eating by the placement of the utensils on the plate. When eating American style, the finished position is the placement of the knife on the outside with the blade toward the center of the plate and the fork with the tines up next to the knife at about the 11 o'clock and 3 o'clock position on the plate. Those using the Continental style will indicate that they are finished by placing the utensils in a similar position except that the fork tines are down. During the meal, you would signal that you have not finished by placing the fork and knife in the center of the plate or with the fork placed across the knife near the top of the plate. The Continental resting position is similar: the knife with blade toward the center of the plate is crossed with the fork in the center of the plate with the fork on top of the knife blade.

In addition to these styles of eating, you may encounter other styles when traveling abroad. In Africa, for example, the style may vary from formal English service in larger cities to a community in which you are expected to use the fingers on your right hand to eat from one serving container.

An American became good friends with an Arab while working together in the same shop. When the American was invited to his Arab friend's home for dinner, he noticed that there were no eating utensils on the table. When the guests starting eating with their fingers, the American asked for a fork or spoon, but his Arab friend said that doing so would be an insult to his father. The American was most uncomfortable eating with his fingers.[1]

Because of cultural differences in styles of eating, including the use of utensils, you will want to research the dining customs of people from other cultures with whom you plan to dine. Had the U.S. American in the preceding anecdote researched dining customs in Middle Eastern countries, he would have discovered that people are expected to eat from a common container using the fingers of their right hand. In addition to Middle Easterners, some Filipinos as well as people from India use their fingers to eat from a common platter; refusing to do so would be an insult. Special nuances of eating with the fingers are also important. For example, people from southern India use their entire hand for scooping food, whereas those in northern India place their fingers in the food only as far as the second joint. An important aspect of the custom of eating with one's hands is that the right hand only is used; the left hand is viewed as unclean.

Other countries where knives, forks, and spoons are not commonly used include China, Japan, Korea, and Vietnam; they usually use chopsticks. Even among cultures in which chopsticks are used, variations exist in the shape and length of the chopstick. For example, Chinese chopsticks tend to be longer than those used by the Japanese; in addition, Chinese chopsticks have squared sides, whereas Japanese ones are pointed at one end. The material used also varies, from the metal ones Koreans use to the ones made of ivory, bamboo, or plastic favored by the Chinese. A point of etiquette to remember when eating with chopsticks is that they should not be placed on the table nor should they stand upright in a bowl of rice; they are placed on a chopstick rest or may be positioned together across the upper portion of the dish. Another important point of etiquette is that chopsticks should not be used to point, just as forks or knives are not used for pointing in countries where utensils are used. In addition to chopsticks, soup spoons will be provided in Korean and Chinese cultures. Knives are rarely part of place settings in Asian countries; this custom is perhaps carried over from earlier times when knives were considered weapons.

MEALTIME CUSTOMS

People of the United States usually eat three meals a day, with breakfast around 7:00 a.m. to 9:00 a.m., lunch from 11:30 a.m. to 1:30 p.m., and dinner around 6:00 p.m. to 8:00 p.m. Breakfast may be cereal and juice or eggs, pancakes, or waffles served with bacon or sausage and toast or muffins. Skipping breakfast is not uncommon for working adults. Lunch is usually something light, such as a sandwich, soup, or salad. The largest meal of the day is dinner, which typically consists of meat and potatoes, rice, or pasta, with vegetables, salad, and dessert. Sunday brunch (which combines breakfast and lunch) is a bit different: It is served between 10:00 a.m. and 2:00 p.m. and includes a variety of foods, including fruits and pastries as well as pancakes or waffles, meats, and egg dishes. Fast foods and takeout meals are popular—these may be consumed at the desk, while driving, or taken home to share with the family. Although coffee is the preferred drink in the United States, it is quite weak compared to the coffee served in other countries. Decaffeinated coffee, which is unavailable in some countries, is popular in the United States. Some people prefer tea, but it is often served iced. In fact, if you order tea in a southern U.S. restaurant, the server will assume you wish it served cold with ice unless you specifically order hot tea. Milk, soft drinks, beer, and wine are other popular beverages. The country really does not have a national dish; some foods, however, seem to be associated with a specific region, such as barbecue in the South.

In Argentina, Brazil, Chile, and most other countries of South America, breakfast is eaten between 7:00 a.m. and 9:00 a.m., lunch is around noon to 3:00 p.m., and dinner between 8:00 p.m. and 10:00 p.m. An afternoon refreshment break around 5:00 p.m. to 6:00 p.m. consisting of coffee or tea and a light snack is common. Lunch is the largest meal of the day and typically lasts two hours. South Americans usually have more courses than is common in the United States. In addition to coffee and tea (often served as *café con leche* and *té con leche*—coffee or tea with milk), various alcoholic beverages are served. *Pisco*, a liquor made from grapes and served as a *pisco* sour or *pisco* and Coke, is popular in such countries as Bolivia, Chile, and Peru. In Mexico, alcoholic drinks, in addition to the popular tequila, include mescal, an after-dinner drink made from the maguey plant. (Incidentally, the worm in the bottle is often eaten by Mexicans.) Food specialties vary somewhat with the country. Beef is popular in Argentina and Uruguay, as are some other foods that are uncommon in many countries: intestines, cow brains, and kidneys. Brazilian food has a lot of flavor; in some areas the food is quite spicy. *Arroz con leche* and *arroz con pollo* (rice with milk and rice with chicken, respectively) are popular dishes in most South American countries.

In European countries, a light breakfast of coffee or tea and some type of bread is eaten between 7:00 a.m. and 8:00 a.m., lunch is around 1:00 p.m., and dinner is about 8:00 p.m. to 9:00 p.m. In some countries of Europe, the main meal of the day is lunch, whereas in others it is dinner.

In the countries in which lunch is a light meal, foods commonly eaten include yogurt, sandwiches, salad, or cheese. Food specialties include *moussaka* in Greece (eggplant, ground lamb, and cheese), *caldo verde* (sometimes called "green soup," which is made of kale and mashed potatoes) in Portugal, and the various fish and seafood dishes (including whale meat) in Norway. Special alcoholic drinks include *ouzo* (an anise-flavored liqueur) and *retsina* (a resin-flavored wine) in Greece; *jenever* (gin flavored with juniper berries) in the Netherlands; *aguardente* (a strong local brandy) in Portugal; *glogg* (a hot, spiced wine with liquor) in Sweden, especially at Christmas; *marjalikööri* and *lakka* (berry liqueurs) in Finland; and *aquavit* (from potatoes) in the Scandinavian countries, especially Denmark. Tapas bars are popular in Spain and Portugal; they feature appetizers of snails, squid, shrimp, and octopus served with such drinks as wine and beer. The smorgasbord (similar to a U.S. all-you-can-eat buffet) is popular in Sweden.

In many Asian countries, breakfast is served around 6:00 a.m. or 7:00 a.m., lunch is at noon to 1:30 p.m., and dinner, the largest meal of the day, may be from 6:00 p.m. to 7:00 p.m. or 7:00 p.m. to 8:00 p.m. Breakfast in China may be 1,000-year-old eggs (duck eggs that have been buried in lime, ashes, and mud for three to four months) or rice dishes; lunch might be stir-fried vegetables and soup; dinner usually has a variety of meat dishes served with vegetables, soup, and boiled rice. Alcoholic beverages in China include *mao tai* (a sorghum-based wine) and *shao xing* (a red wine made of rice and served warm); local beers, such as Beijing and Tsing Tao, are also served warm. The alcoholic beverage for which Japan is well known is *sake*, which is made from rice and served warm. In the Philippines, rice is cooked and served with other foods, such as meat and vegetables. Soft drinks and fruit juices are more popular beverages than tea and coffee. Wine and beer are the primary alcoholic beverages, which are typically consumed by men only. In India, their dinner hour is later than in many Asian countries—8:30 p.m. to 10:00 p.m.—so a snack of tea and biscuits may be served around 4:00 p.m. to 5:00 p.m. Alcohol is prohibited in some parts of India; the typical drinks are tea and strong coffee, depending upon whether you are in the northern or the southern part of India. Food can be quite spicy; thus, *paan* (betel leaves stuffed with several spices) will be served at the meal's conclusion to aid in digestion.

U.S. customs that are not shared by people in many other countries include being direct when asked about their appetite and eating rapidly. Americans will often say "I'm starved" when invited to lunch. Such a statement would be very bad manners in Asia. In Asian countries, people will usually say that they are not hungry regardless of whether they are or not. When dining in Asia, finishing a meal before others at the table have finished implies that you are still hungry. Americans should pace themselves so that they finish at the same time as their Asian counterparts.

TABLE MANNERS

Despite the admonitions of many parents to their children to "clean your plate," the United States is not a country where cleaning your plate is expected. In fact, leaving something is customary; it indicates that you have had enough to eat. You are expected to sample everything that is offered. The napkin is placed in the lap immediately upon being seated and is kept in the lap until everyone is ready to leave the table. Slurping or other noises are considered rude; burping is crass. Cutting only a piece or two of meat at once is customary; only small children have their meat cut up all at once. Pass food to others, in a counterclockwise direction, before helping yourself. Ask for items you cannot reach rather than reaching in front of someone. Smoking at the end of the meal is done only with permission of others at the table. Toothpicks are never used at the table. Some U.S. foods are considered finger foods, including sandwiches and fruit.

In the countries of South America, customs related to cleaning one's plate vary. In Bolivia, Peru, Panama, and Guatemala you are expected to eat everything on your plate; leaving food is considered wasteful. In Costa Rica and Colombia, on the other hand, you are expected to leave food to indicate you have had enough to eat. In most countries of South America, food is eaten with utensils rather than the hands; this includes sandwiches and fruit. You are expected to keep your hands in sight and to sample everything you are offered.

In many European countries, including Denmark, France, Germany, Norway, and the Netherlands, you would clean your plate and sample everything offered. Refusing to try a dish is considered impolite. Fruit is peeled, sliced, and eaten with a knife and fork; sandwiches are also eaten with a knife and fork. In England, you are expected to leave some food on your plate.

In most Asian countries, including Japan and Hong Kong, making noises while eating, such as slurping soup and smacking your lips, are considered appropriate. In fact, they indicate enjoyment of the food. Saudi Arabians, as well as people in the Philippines, belch and make other noises during a meal, which is intended to express appreciation for the food. Such noises would be viewed as uncouth by people of Thailand and China.

A friendship developed between two girls who attended a California high school: One was from Japan and the other was Vietnamese Chinese. The Japanese student invited the friend to her home for a birthday dinner. The Japanese family made loud slurping sounds during the meal and appeared to be displeased when the Vietnamese Chinese friend did not.[2]

FOOD CUSTOMS AND CONSUMPTION TABOOS

People in most cultures consume at least some foods that are viewed with surprise or disapproval by people of other cultures. Knowledge of food customs and consumption taboos is important when conducting business in another country.

Although people in the United States eat corn on the cob, it is considered food for animals only in some countries. Other U.S. foods people in some cultures find unusual include marshmallows, popcorn, and grits. Serving dog meat in the United States would never even be considered, but in Taiwan it is viewed as a very desirable meat that is associated with sexual virility; however, it is no longer legal to eat dog meat in Taiwan. In Hong Kong, sea slugs may be on the menu; in Korea, snake meat; in Saudi Arabia, sheep's eyeballs; and in Norway, reindeer. Eating what you are offered is expected, so becoming familiar with special foods associated with the country is recommended so that you are not caught off guard and make derogatory comments about the food customs.

An American college professor upon her arrival in La Paz, Bolivia, for a two-year assignment at the local university, was invited to dine at a well-known local eatery known for its mixed grill—a variety of meats grilled at the table. After sampling one chewy morsel, she asked what it was. The reply: stuffed cow's teats! The lesson she learned: cut the food into thin slices and pretend it is chicken, swallow quickly, and never ask what it is.

Sometimes the surprise is not so much in the type of food that is served, but in how it is served. Foods that people in some countries expect to be served cooked are served raw—and alive!

A Swiss visitor to Japan described his experience eating raw fish at a lavish Tokyo restaurant. After numerous delicacies had been served, the *pièce de résistance* was presented: "A live fish was brought

flopping and gasping to the table and was delicately sliced by the
maitre d' and served a piece at a time."[3]

Some business encounters may coincide with holiday celebrations in
another country. Knowing the special foods consumed during these holidays and the special significance associated with these foods is important.
In the United States, people often eat certain foods on New Year's Day to
bring good luck, such as black-eyed peas and collard greens.

Most ideas about New Year's foods relate to good luck, fertility, or
fortune. Mexicans eat 12 grapes; Germans eat pork, pickled herring,
red cabbage, and lentils; Greeks bake a large loaf of yeast bread
spiced with cinnamon, nutmeg, and orange peel and hide a silver coin
in the dough—whoever finds the coin will be blessed with wealth.[4]

Care must be taken even within the United States to observe food
customs associated with the numerous cocultures. For example, U.S.
Muslim Americans would not consume pork; those whose native country
is India or Pakistan may be vegetarians; and Orthodox Jews do not eat
pork or shellfish.

DRINKING AND TOASTING CUSTOMS

When conducting business internationally, consuming alcohol is an
expected part of building the relationship in many countries. In some countries, declining a drink may be viewed as impolite and an indication that you
do not want to participate in these important rituals. Those who feel they
must decline should offer an explanation. In China and Japan, for example,
where drinking is part of building a business relationship, declining a drink
for health reasons is acceptable. In Japan, it is acceptable to leave the glass
partially full to signal you do not wish more to drink. Rather than participating in the after-dinner drinking in Japan, declining by pleading exhaustion
from jet lag is acceptable. These drinking sessions are important, however,
as business information is often exchanged at these times.

A businesswoman, who often had lunch with a client who typically
had several drinks and who insisted she match him drink for drink,
found her own way of handling the situation. After ordering one
vodka tonic, she stopped at the bar on the way to the ladies' room,
gave the bartender $10, and requested that additional drinks she
ordered should be tonic water only.[5]

Though not a consideration in Islamic countries, drinking sessions are important in other cultures; in fact, refusing to participate may be viewed with mistrust. In Germany, as in some other European countries, drinking with others is associated with openness. It is important to avoid obvious inebriation in Germany, however. Overindulging is viewed negatively in Indonesia, Mexico, and the Philippines as well. Koreans also feel that drinking is an important part of building a business relationship and that refusing to participate in their drinking and singing sessions is an insult and indicates a desire to keep apart from the group. They may, however, expect you to keep promises made while drinking—unlike the Japanese, who do not hold others accountable for what was said while drinking.[6]

Toasting makes a meal more festive. The guidelines for toasting, as well as the words commonly used when making a toast, vary with the culture. In the United States, a toast may be made by either gender and should last about one minute. The host proposes a toast of welcome at the beginning of the meal and another toast to honor the guest of honor. Typical U.S. toasts include "Cheers," "Bottoms up," and "To your health." The guest of honor then responds by toasting the host. At some events, especially large ones, people usually rise for the toast. When toasting people of other cultures, it is a nice gesture to toast in the person's language, such as saying *Slante* when toasting the Irish and *Prosit* when toasting Germans. You can always toast to a person's health; just say "To your health" when toasting in English. The Spanish word *salud* and the Danish word *skol* mean the same thing and are widely understood welcoming toasts. Toasting errors to be avoided include reading the toast, clinking glasses, and drinking when you are being toasted. In addition, it is important to remember that guests who do not drink alcohol may toast with another beverage they may be drinking (except water) or may use an empty wine glass. Toasting with a glass of water may be viewed as disapproval of the toast.

In addition to toasting at business meals, toasting at special occasions, such as at a wedding or anniversary, is common in many countries. When toasts are given at U.S. weddings, the best man usually gives the first toast, followed by the bride's father, then the groom's father.

When invited to attend a traditional Laotian wedding ceremony in California, Mexican-born Clara refused to participate in a toast to the couple, whose tradition it was to pass around the wine glass from which the bride and groom had sipped expecting all to drink from the same glass. She became nauseous about the idea of sharing a glass with other people. Her refusal to drink from the communal glass, though based on hygiene, was viewed as a sign of rejection of the couple rather than a rejection of the practice. Although unable to understand their language, Clara could tell by the voices of the Laotians in attendance that she had unintentionally offended those present.[7]

BUSINESS ENTERTAINING AND SEATING ETIQUETTE

The decision to entertain a foreign guest in a restaurant or in one's home depends on customs of the country and the length of the relationship. People of the United States often entertain business associates in their homes. People of Australia, New Zealand, and Canada also sometimes entertain in their homes. People of Latin America, Spain, and Portugal, on the other hand, do not customarily entertain at home until a personal relationship has been developed. They do most of their business entertaining in restaurants.

When invited for a meal in someone's home in the United States, you will let the host know whether or not you plan to attend. Turning down an invitation is acceptable; however, saying you will attend and then failing to show up is not acceptable. Offering to bring something is considered polite when invited to someone's home; the host's declining is also customary. It is appropriate to bring a small gift anyway, however, and this could be a bottle of wine or flowers. Several types of entertainment are common in the United States, including cocktail parties, buffet dinners, and cookouts. Especially around the holidays, many Americans will have an open house, usually for a two- or three-hour period during which guests stop by for a short period and help themselves to foods available on a buffet table. Arriving within about 15 minutes of the time indicated on the invitation is expected.

In Australia and New Zealand, similar rules apply for entertaining in one's home. You may be invited to join the family for a meal or invited to a buffet dinner in which you are expected to serve yourself. Although most Europeans prefer to use restaurants for business entertaining, people of England and Denmark often invite business guests to their homes.

Business entertaining in restaurants is common in most European countries, Asia, and Latin America. When being entertained in a restaurant, the person who does the inviting does the paying. In some countries, such as in the countries of Asia, the U.S. dutch treat concept does not exist. In fact, offering to pay your part of the bill would be viewed as a lack of appreciation for the host. In most countries, it is considered impolite to order the most expensive item on the menu when someone else is paying. Because dress customs in restaurants vary from quite formal to more casual, you will want to ask about appropriate attire.

In European countries, most business entertaining is done in restaurants, mainly at lunch or in the evening. Business breakfasts are uncommon in most countries of Europe; one exception is in England, where this U.S. habit has become more acceptable in recent years. Another business entertaining difference between England and the rest of Europe is the increased likelihood of your being invited to someone's home. In all European countries, the host should initiate the business discussion, which is usually toward the conclusion of the meal. Spouses are not usually invited to business dinners except in England. This rule varies somewhat with the country. In Spain, for example, when you extend an invitation to your Spanish colleague and wish to include your spouse, by inviting your colleague to bring his or her spouse, you may feel free to bring your own.

Japanese business entertaining may include visits to karaoke bars, where visitors are expected to sing the lead vocal using lyrics displayed on a TV screen and backed up by taped music. Participating in this activity is an indication of your willingness to embarrass yourself publicly, an important part of building rapport with your Japanese business colleagues. Apparently, this willingness to expose your vulnerable side to others becomes easier when sufficiently inebriated. Karaoke is now popular in other parts of Asia as well as in many other countries. Participating in karaoke is expected, so U.S. businesspeople need to decide how they will handle it.

Business school did not teach Chris Engholm how to sing karaoke. But there he was, on stage in a posh Hong Kong nightclub, his new Chinese associates intently awaiting his performance. He knew his inability to mumble a few bars of "Freebird" could be embarrassing to his hosts and devastating to his new business relationships. Still, he froze: "It was a serious thing," Engholm says. His unnerving karaoke experience led him to develop this rule: "If you can't sing, choose a song that you know or demand someone sing with you."[8]

In some African countries, including Ghana and Kenya, you may be entertained in someone's home or at a restaurant. As a guest in someone's home, you will either be served at a dining table or perhaps at a coffee table in the living room. Guests are given a plate and perhaps eating utensils; however, if no cutlery is provided, guests would eat with the right hand. In Kenya, people in the cities use plates and eating utensils. Because men are usually served the best food, a foreign woman would eat with the men. Hotel restaurants are favored for restaurant entertaining;

these usually offer a variety of foods, including those to which foreign businesspeople are accustomed. European-style restaurants are preferred for business entertaining in Kenya and in Egypt. Part of the business entertaining ritual in Egypt is offering a guest tea or coffee; accepting the drink is expected. When Egyptians visit you, extend them the same courtesy.

An Egyptian doing business in the United States finally asked his host what he had done to offend him. The host replied that there was absolutely nothing wrong. The Egyptian then said, "But I've been here for three hours, and you haven't offered me anything to drink."[9]

In South Africa, your initial entertaining will usually be in a restaurant; later you may be invited to their homes. Business entertaining may also include cocktail parties and sporting events. Although spouses are typically invited to business dinners, they are not invited to business lunches.

In Israel, business entertaining is more commonly done in restaurants at lunch rather than at dinner. In Saudi Arabia, the custom of entertaining at lunch and dinner is a fairly recent one, as business dealings with the West have increased. When inviting a Saudi to a business meal at a restaurant, it is customary to suggest that he invite a friend to accompany him.

Seating customs during mealtimes vary with the country. Meals may be eaten while sitting at a table, which is customary in North and South America and in European countries; on the floor, which is common in Japan and India; or on the grass or ground, which is customary in Tonga and most of Polynesia.

In some of the African countries, such as Ghana and Kenya, guests are considered of high status and will be seated at a table, provided one is available. In Nigerian cities, when being entertained in someone's home, you would be served with everyone seated at a table. In villages, however, you would be seated on a floor mat. Your host may indicate where you are to sit; otherwise, sit anywhere. In South Africa, you will wait until your host indicates where you are to sit; honored guests sit near the host and hostess. In India, there is no seat of honor; however, guests are usually seated first. In typical Egyptian homes, you will be seated on carpets with food served on platters, which are placed on low wooden tables. Because no plates or eating utensils will be provided, guests will eat with the right hand. In Egyptian homes of the upper class, however, guests are often seated at a dining table and will be provided with eating utensils.

In Asian countries, seating etiquette is very important, so guests will wait for the host to indicate where they are to sit. In Japan, South Korea, and Taiwan, the most important guest is given a seat facing the door. The highest-ranking host takes a seat at the center of the table, and the guest with the highest rank is placed to the right of the host. Everyone waits for the person of highest rank to begin eating—this high-ranking person waits until everyone at the table has been served before commencing. In China, waiting for the host to suggest when you are to begin each course is polite; touching your food or beverage before being invited by the host to begin is impolite.

People of Germany and France, who typically entertain in a restaurant, seat people based on their status. In both countries, the most important male guest is seated next to the hostess, and the most important female guest sits next to the host. In England, though, the male guest of honor may be placed at the head of the table. In most countries, the position of honor, which is given to the highest-ranking guest, is to the right of the host. In Sweden, however, the highest-ranking guest, after escorting the hostess to the table, sits on her left. When entertaining in a restaurant, the host generally takes the least desirable seat.

TIPPING

Tipping is now expected in many countries, especially in the United States. People who do not tip sufficiently, or those who do not tip at all, are considered stingy. Knowing and observing tipping customs in other countries, including tipping in restaurants, hotels, and other travel-related situations, can affect your personal and corporate image.

The general rule for tipping in U.S. restaurants varies from the 20 percent expected in fine restaurants to the 15 percent considered acceptable in modest restaurants. Most Americans realize that tips are the primary source of income for many servers and feel obligated to tip unless the service is very poor. Even then, most people just tip a bit less than usual and explain to the manager upon departure the reason for the low tip. Other tips expected in fine restaurants include $10 to the maître d'hôtel if you received a good table, 8 percent to the wine steward ($5 minimum), $2 to $5 to the doorman for calling a taxi, $3 to the valet parker for getting your car, and $1 to $2 for the attendants in the ladies' room and the coat check area.[10]

Tipping in U.S. hotels depends upon whether you are staying in an expensive hotel in a large city or in a less expensive one in a small town. People customarily tipped in hotels include the doorman ($1 for opening your car door in a less expensive hotel, $2 in an expensive one, and $1 to $2 for calling a cab waiting nearby), the bellman ($5 to $20, depending upon the amount of luggage and the type of hotel), room service (10 percent to 20 percent), hotel maid ($1 or $2 per person per day), and the concierge ($10 to $20 when a real effort was made to help you).

Taxicab drivers are usually tipped 15 percent to 20 percent, depending upon whether you were given help with your luggage and upon the length of the ride.[11]

In many European countries, a tip of 10 percent to 15 percent is typically included in the restaurant bill; if not, leave the normal 15–20 percent that you would leave in the United States, however, but it is not expected. Taxis are tipped about 10 percent, more when you have luggage.

The chairman of a U.S. consulting company angered a United Kingdom taxi driver when he rounded the fare to the next pound. To express his displeasure at the small tip, the cab driver threw coins out the window at him.[12]

In Singapore, tipping is not customary. People in that country view a tip as a bribe and feel it inappropriate to be bribed to give good service. A service charge is added to bills in most restaurants and hotels; this amount is shared by all employees. When special services are requested, such as room service, it is proper to tip them the equivalent of $1 to $2. Tips to hotel or restaurant personnel and taxi drivers are not expected in Japan as well. The extra service charge of about 10 to 15 percent included in your restaurant or hotel bill is sufficient. Almost the same rule applies in China, except for those who carry your luggage to your hotel room or to and from a taxi. Tipping in restaurants is not customary; the 15 percent added in some restaurants is sufficient.

Tipping guidelines in the countries of South America are quite similar. In most South American countries, tipping is becoming customary in restaurants. A 10 percent tip is considered appropriate and is sometimes included in the bill. Leaving an extra amount, although not required, is appreciated. Tipping taxi drivers and hotel porters is optional, except when they help you with your luggage. In those cases, the equivalent of $1 is appropriate. In Colombia, taxi drivers usually receive a 10 percent tip, depending on the part of the country. Because of these variations within the country, asking at your hotel about tipping taxi drivers is recommended. In many South American countries, it is wise to ask before getting into the taxi what the fare will be. Another suggestion is to ask at the hotel what the usual fare is to your intended destination. Visitors to large Mexican cities frequented by tourists, such as Puerto Vallarta, Cancun, and Acapulco, should be aware that the 15 percent added to the restaurant bill is actually a tax and that a tip of 15 percent to 20 percent is usually expected. In Portugal, there is no place on the bill to add a tip, and no tip is expected.

A U.S. professor with little travel experience, while attending a conference in Puerto Vallarta, ate at a nice restaurant recommended by the hotel concierge where she was staying. When the bill was presented, she noticed that 15 percent had been added. She assumed that this was a gratuity and left no additional amount. As she was leaving, the server ran after her, pointed to the bill and said, "*La propina!*" The professor tried to explain that the tip was included in the bill, but the server was clearly unhappy at receiving no tip.

Tipping in other parts of the world varies. In India, for example, tipping is a necessity if you want to get things done. Rather than a reward for good service, a tip is more like a bribe to open doors. In Saudi Arabia, tipping is becoming more common. Taxi drivers are usually given 10 percent. Because service charges are added to the bill in restaurants, an additional amount is not expected. Servers are poorly paid, however, and appreciate an extra tip. In Egypt, you will want to carry a lot of tipping money for porters, taxis, tour bus drivers, restaurant servers, hotel maids, and guides at historic sites. In South Africa, 10 percent is the usual tip at restaurants; taxi drivers usually receive a tip of 10 to 15 percent of the fare. People who carry your bags receive $1 for each bag; hotel maids receive $5 per week. In Nigeria, the tipping is similar to Saudi Arabia, except for taxi drivers; the tip is included in the flat rate they charge.

Because of cultural differences in tipping customs, researching the country you plan to visit is recommended. Tipping is one of many customs that can positively or negatively affect the success of your relationship with people of other cultures.

COUNTRY-SPECIFIC INFORMATION

Dining and tipping customs for the countries with which the United States conducts most of its international business follow.

Brazil

- Brazilians use the Continental style of eating.
- Avoid eating with the hands; utensils are used even when eating fruit or sandwiches.
- Both hands should be kept above the table during the meal; however, elbows should not be placed on the table.
- Avoid drinking beverages from a bottle or can; drink from a cup or glass.
- Do not eat while walking on the street.

- Food specialties include *feijoada* (black beans with pork, sausage, beef, and tongue), *moqueca* (seafood stew), and *carurur* (pepper, onion, shrimp, and okra mixture).
- When a toast is offered, raise your glass, say *saude* (health!) or *viva* (hurrah!), and take a sip of wine. The person proposing the toast should not tap the glass with silverware to get people's attention, as this is considered impolite.[13]
- A tip of 10 to 15 percent is added to a restaurant bill when the tip is not included.[14]

Canada

- The Continental style is used by a majority of Canadians; some Canadians use the American style.
- Both hands are kept above the table while eating (compared to the U.S. custom of leaving one hand in the lap during the meal).
- Eating on the streets is unacceptable behavior.
- In addition to three meals a day, Canadians have afternoon tea (especially those of English ancestry) or coffee.
- Canadian toasting customs are similar to U.S. customs; "Cheers" is acceptable. In Quebec, *A votre sante* (to your health) is typically used.
- The noon meal in Quebec may last two hours, a French custom.
- Tipping at restaurants is 10–15 percent and is typically included in the bill.

China

- Chopsticks are used for eating; longer chopsticks are used for serving.
- Sampling all dishes presented is considered good manners; leaving something on the plate to indicate satisfaction with the food is customary.
- Seating etiquette is important; wait for the host to indicate where you are to sit.
- Acceptable noises during the meal are slurping soup and belching to express your enjoyment of the food.
- When tea is served following the presentation of food that necessitates use of the hands, dip your fingers into it; do not drink it.
- When hot towels are presented or when fruit is offered, this is a signal that it is time for guests to leave.

France

- The French use the Continental or European style of eating.
- Numerous courses are served at formal dinners in a restaurant; the evening meal is often eaten late, around 10:00 p.m.

- Placing bread on the table, rather than on a bread plate, is common because bread plates are rarely used.
- Cleaning your plate is expected in France; requesting seconds is a positive sign that you enjoyed the food.
- Wine is commonly served at all meals except for breakfast; with the wine accompanying the first course, the host will say *Salut!*; guests may propose a toast with the other courses.
- Fruit is peeled and eaten with a knife.
- Dogs are commonly seen resting beneath café tables; they are often fed from the table.
- Most restaurants include a 15 percent gratuity on the bill; an additional amount for good service is appreciated but not expected.

Germany

- Germans use the Continental style of eating.
- In Germany, you are expected to clean your plate; thus, taking small portions is advisable.
- Knives are used only for cutting foods too tough to be cut with the edge of the fork.
- Although Germany is well known for its beer, wine is typically served with meals.
- German food is heavy and filling; Germans eat a lot of meat, especially pork, and enjoy numerous varieties of sausage.
- In Germany, the main meal is served at noon; Germans eat lightly in the evening.
- The two toasts common in Germany are *Prosit* (more casual and used among friends) and *Zum Wohl.*
- In most restaurants, a tip of 10–15 percent will be added to the bill; an additional tip is given directly to the server when the service has been good.

Japan

- Chopsticks are used for eating; they are shorter than those used by the Chinese.
- Napkins are not provided; guests will be offered a hot towel for wiping their hands.
- Guests pour drinks for each other; do not refill your own glass.
- Leaving food on your plate is considered rude.
- Food specialties include *sashimi* (slices of raw fish), *sushi* (raw seafood, fish, or vegetables wrapped in seaweed), *tempura* (deep-fried seafood

and vegetables), and *fugu* (blowfish, a delicacy that can be toxic unless prepared by a licensed chef).

- Be prepared to remove your shoes in restaurants, in Japanese homes, or in other places where signs indicate that shoes should be removed.
- The host usually makes a toast at the start of a meal; the word to use when toasting is *Kampai!*
- Tipping in restaurants is not customary; in fact, if a tip is offered, it may be refused.

Mexico

- Mexicans usually use the Continental eating style.
- Eating while walking on the street is inappropriate.
- Mexicans typically eat their largest meal of the day in the afternoon, usually from 2:00 p.m. to 4:00 p.m. When it is a business lunch, the person in the group who is oldest usually pays the bill.
- Both hands are kept above the table while dining.
- Cornmeal or flour tortillas are staples; common foods are tacos, mole, *tortas*, *quesadillas*, *enchiladas*, and *tamales*.
- When proposing a toast in Mexico, the proper term is *Salud!*
- Tipping in Mexican restaurants is usually 15 percent; in some cities frequented by tourists, an additional gratuity is expected, which should be placed in the server's hand.

South Korea

- South Koreans eat with chopsticks (except for eating rice, for which a metal spoon is provided); chopsticks should be placed on a chopstick rest or on the table at the conclusion of the meal; when soup is served, a porcelain spoon is provided.
- South Koreans typically sit on the floor when dining.
- Pouring a drink for the person sitting next to you is polite; they will do the same for you.
- Leave something on your plate to signify that your host provided sufficient food.
- Removing your shoes when dining in a South Korean home is polite.
- Because drinking is important in building relationships, expect to be offered more alcohol than you would be offered in many countries.
- When toasting in South Korea, say *Gun-hei* as you raise your glass with your right hand.
- Tipping beyond the service charge added to the bill in restaurants and hotels is unnecessary; exceptional service may be rewarded with a 10 percent tip.

Taiwan

- Chopsticks are used for eating.
- Because seating in Taiwan is arranged hierarchically, it is a good idea to wait for your host to indicate where you are to sit.
- Taiwanese specialties include turtle, squid, jellyfish, and snake. Sampling all food offered is considered good manners.
- Bringing the rice bowl to the mouth and using your chopsticks to move the rice into your mouth is customary.
- Leaving a little food on your plate shows you have had enough to eat; avoid taking the last item of food from the serving platter, as that would also indicate that you are still hungry.
- Food specialties may include such unusual ingredients as dog or snake; however, these ingredients are not commonly used in restaurants.
- Toasting is an important part of business entertaining; it may be done several times during a meal.
- Tipping, though once unnecessary, is now common; in addition to the 10 percent charge added to the restaurant and hotel bills, additional amounts are appropriate for excellent service.

United Kingdom (England, Scotland, Wales, and Northern Ireland)

- The Continental or European eating style is used.
- Lunch is typically light. The main meal of the day is in the evening; an invitation to tea may be an invitation to the evening meal or to afternoon tea.
- Tea is an important part of dining customs; it will be made of loose tea leaves using a large teapot and served with milk, lemon, or sugar.
- Keeping your hands above the table is polite (but no elbows on the table).
- Leaving food on the plate when you have finished eating is appropriate; it signals that you had enough to eat.
- Toasting is common; however, avoid toasting people who are older or who are in positions above you.
- A 10 percent tip is appropriate in restaurants.

United States of America

- The U.S. style of eating is American zigzag style, in which the knife is held in the right hand and the fork in the left, tines down. After cutting a piece of food, the knife is placed along the upper-right edge of the plate; the fork is then switched to the right hand and, with the fork tines up, the piece of food is placed in the mouth.
- People of the United States usually eat three meals a day; the evening meal is typically the largest meal of the day.

- Refusing food offered is impolite; take at least a small amount of whatever is offered.
- Cleaning your plate is not expected in the United States; leaving a small amount indicates that you have had enough to eat.
- The left hand is kept in the lap when not in use for cutting food; eating is done with the right hand.
- Customary U.S. toasts include "Cheers," "To your health," or "Bottoms up."
- Tipping is expected; in U.S. restaurants, the tip should range from 15 to 20 percent, depending upon the service and the restaurant.

Chapter 8

CONVERSATIONAL CUSTOMS
AND MANNERS

When conversing with persons of other cultures or with persons in U.S. cocultures, it is important to know their customs to assure that the intended meaning is conveyed and to avoid unintentionally offending them. For example, in most cultures it is appropriate to engage in light conversation or chitchat before getting down to business. Ignoring this custom would be viewed as rude and insensitive. When selecting a topic for small talk, it is important to recognize that some topics are taboo in both social and business situations, and that in some cultures the use of humor during conversations is inappropriate. The nonverbal aspects of conversations—eye contact, facial expressions, gestures, space, and touch (many of which were included in Chapter 4)—must also be taken into consideration. In addition, the extent to which people of another culture use informal language, such as slang, should be considered.

IMPORTANCE OF CONVERSATION

Conversation is spoken interaction between people; it involves an exchange of information and thoughts. In some cases, this verbal exchange is substantive, whereas in other cases, it is nonsubstantive. Substantive verbal interaction would include discussions of price and terms during intercultural negotiations. Nonsubstantive conversations would include chitchat at social gatherings and light conversation that occurs during the initial stage of negotiation in many countries.

Because conversations between people who know each other well can sometimes have negative consequences, it is reasonable to assume that conversations between people who do not know each other well and between people of different cultures could also present difficulties. A problem with conversation is that once spoken, the words cannot be taken back. A breach of the rules of conversation etiquette when conducting business with a foreign counterpart might have serious consequences. For example, in a conversation with a Saudi Arabian, expressing disagreement publicly would be very inappropriate and would probably be difficult to rectify.

FORMS OF VERBAL INTERACTION

The forms of verbal interaction are repartee, ritual conversation, verbal dueling or argument, and self-disclosure.

In the United States, the preferred form of interaction is sometimes called repartee, which involves speakers taking turns. One speaker says a sentence or two, then glances away to indicate that the other person may take a turn. U.S. persons become irritated when people take long turns; rather than listening, they will wait for a signal that it is their turn to speak. In addition, speaking for too long a period encourages interrupting, which is considered rude behavior by members of the U.S. macroculture. In contrast, Africans and Middle Easterners tend to speak for extended periods of time.

Another form of U.S. conversation is ritual interaction. This form of conversation is culturally based; it involves standard replies and comments in a given situation. When people in the United States use the standard greeting of "Good morning; how are you?" they are not really interested in the other person's well-being; the same is true of the standard reply, "Fine, thanks; how are you?" These standard questions and replies are expected regardless of how the person is actually feeling. These ritualistic comments may vary with the geographic region. For example, in the southern United States, upon taking their departure from friends or colleagues, southerners will say, "Y'all come to see us." The standard reply will be, "We will; y'all come to see us, too." All parties understand that this is not really an invitation; it is just a friendly way to say goodbye. Ritual conversations in other countries may be quite different. Middle Easterners, for example, during ritual conversations will invoke Allah's goodwill, whereas Latin Americans will discuss health issues for long periods of time.

Argument is another type of verbal interaction. U.S. persons have been taught to avoid an argument because they feel it may have a negative impact on the relationship. Although in some countries arguing would be considered an enjoyable pastime, U.S. persons will avoid arguing by changing the subject or even thinking of a plausible reason to excuse themselves from the situation. When they cannot avoid an argument, they try to speak calmly and use few gestures. A form of argument is verbal dueling; this is actually a friendly debate in which one person tries to gain dominance. These interactions are usually lighthearted and are not to be taken seriously. U.S. men, for example, may engage in verbal dueling when discussing sports. They will argue about which team is better or which team is going to win in an upcoming game. Although politics is not an appropriate topic for verbal dueling in the United States, it is appropriate in England, France, and Germany.

Another form of verbal interaction is self-disclosure. Self-disclosure involves revealing information about yourself to enable others to know you. The amount of information people are willing to reveal varies with the culture. In the United States, people reveal little personal information during small talk. Self-disclosure is related to gender; women are more likely to disclose personal information than are men.

SMALL TALK OR CHITCHAT

Getting to know someone usually involves a certain amount of light conversation or small talk. Appropriate topics for chitchat are often related to the culture. U.S. persons are considered masters of the art of small talk. Almost anything of a nonsubstantive nature, such as the day's news, the weather, and the physical surroundings, would be appropriate. Recent movies or television programs, favorite restaurants, and their jobs are other preferred topics for light conversation.

Sometimes topics for small talk will vary according to gender: U.S. men may prefer to discuss cars or sports, whereas women may prefer to talk about their homes or children. In the United States, where people are uncomfortable with silence, becoming adroit at light conversation to fill voids in conversations is expected.

An example of gender differences, as well as cultural differences, in self-disclosure is the experience of a U.S. college student who commented that her male Korean friend seemed uncomfortable when asked about his dating experiences. She said, "I don't understand why. I always talk about dating with my American friends, both guys and girls!"[1]

People of other cultures who also excel at small talk include Australians, the British, Canadians, the French, and South Americans. In some countries, however, small talk seems to pose problems. People of Finland, Germany, Japan, and Sweden, for example, are not particularly skillful at chitchat and encounter difficulty when attempting to engage in such discourse with persons from other cultures. This can be awkward in social gatherings, such as cocktail parties, where people are expected to engage in light conversation with numerous guests over a period of several hours.

The skill of South Americans in the art of chitchat was observed by author Richard Lewis when he attended a cocktail party attended entirely by Latin Americans in Caracas, Venezuela. He said, "There were 300 people present, very little to eat, nobody stopped talking except to draw breath for six hours flat; I do not remember a single word that was said."[2]

In Latin American countries such as Argentina and Brazil, appropriate topics for conversation include sports, the arts, local sights, and international travels. In Chile, asking questions about recommended tourist sights and discussions of Chilean art, history, and literature are appropriate. Likewise, in Venezuela, good topics of conversation include Venezuelan history, art, sports, and food.

In countries of Asia and the Pacific Rim, variations exist both in the importance of small talk and in the topics considered appropriate for discussion. The Chinese, who consider chitchat important during initial meetings, also talk about the weather and travel experiences. In addition, the Chinese feel it is acceptable to ask personal questions about salary and marital status, which would be viewed as inappropriate by U.S. persons. Likewise, South Koreans ask personal questions related to age, religious beliefs, and salary. New Zealanders and Australians, who will start conver with strangers on the street or in the local pub, also like to discuss sports because they enjoy outdoor activities. Other appropriate topics of conversation with people of both Australia and New Zealand are the weather and international politics. Spirited discussions about politics are common; they respect others' beliefs and opinions. In both countries, people enjoy a friendly debate.

In Europe, people from some countries appreciate social conversations, whereas others do not see the value of chitchat. The French, who appreciate small talk, like to discuss art, music, politics, and sports. Italians also like to engage in light conversation; they typically discuss travel, food, art, and wine. Italians are appreciative when visitors admire the beautiful scenery of their country and are complimentary of the food or local hospitality. Germans, on the other hand, do not like to discuss nonsubstantive topics, so conversations with them would probably be limited to such safe topics as sports, travel experiences, and world politics.

During casual conversation, a businessman from Virginia, who was on his first trip to England, asked a man from Scotland about his wife and children. The U.S. businessman was told it was none of his business. When asked about the weather, however, the man from Scotland talked incessantly.[3]

CONVERSATIONAL TABOOS

Conversational taboos are topics considered inappropriate when conversing with people in one's own culture and with people in another culture. Topics considered inappropriate in the United States include religion and politics because they are considered too controversial, and U.S. Americans prefer to avoid arguments. The exclusion of these controversial topics for small talk by U.S. people has at times led people of other countries to erroneously conclude that people of the United States are not smart enough to discuss complex topics. Terrorism and disasters, such as September 11, 2001, are also inappropriate topics for small talk. Some topics are inappropriate because they are too personal. Questions about personal income, how much a person paid for clothes or personal belongings, why they are still single, or why they have no children are too personal; also, comments on body odor and body weight are too personal. (Unless, of course, the person has lost weight, in which case commenting on a person's svelte appearance would be a welcome compliment.)

A U.S. woman and her husband, a German, returned to his country for a visit. She was shocked when her husband's family and friends made comments about his weight gain since living in the United States. His wife's comment: "If my family said that about me, I would be *very* insulted!"[4]

In Saudi Arabia, avoid asking a man about his wife; also avoid political discussions. In Israel, politics is an inappropriate topic for conversation as well; likewise, do not bring up religion. In Egypt, avoid personal questions until you get to know the person better. In Jordan, it is also inappropriate to ask a man about his wife; in addition, do not make negative remarks about the royal family. In Iraq, do not bring up religion and politics; avoid asking personal questions or making comments on birth control policies.

When you converse with people from Nigeria, avoid such words as *witchcraft*, *jungle*, and *hut*. These words have negative connotations; they imply that Africa is a backward country when, in reality, advancements have been made of which the people are quite proud. In South Africa, avoid asking personal questions, such as a person's marital status; also avoid discussions of ethic differences or politics. In Kenya, it is acceptable to ask about a person's children but not the spouse; do not criticize the government.

In Europe, conversational topics to avoid include their personal lives or such personal questions as age or marital status. You would also avoid bringing up your own personal life. In Spain, avoid questions related to a person's occupation. Unlike in the United States, what one does for a living is considered personal. When conversing with Italians, avoid making comments about the Mafia, Italian politics, taxes, and religion. In England, avoid discussions about religion and politics and do not make comments about Scotland or Northern Ireland. Good advice when conversing with Europeans, as well as people in any country, is to avoid bringing up any topic that may imply criticism of their country.

In Australia and New Zealand, avoid discussions of religion, politics, or racial issues. Also, avoid bringing up treatment of the Aborigines, kangaroo population control, or labor disputes in conversations with Australians. Avoid speaking highly of Australia when in New Zealand and vice versa.

In Latin American countries, topics to avoid include politics and religion. In addition to these topics, avoid asking about salary and other personal matters in Brazil. (Brazilians may, however, ask you personal questions, even your marital status and religion.) Also, avoid initiating conversations that would imply criticism of the country, such as economic problems, social class differences, and the government. In Bolivia and Colombia, do not initiate conversations about drug policies or terrorism. In Chile, avoid discussions of wars and comments about social classes. A good rule to observe is to follow the lead of your Latin American host; do not make any derogatory remarks about any aspect of the country, its government, its people and their customs, or their sports teams.

NONVERBAL ASPECTS OF CONVERSATIONS

Nonverbal aspects of conversations include eye contact, facial expressions, gestures, space, and touch. A more detailed coverage of nonverbal communication is included in Chapter 4.

Eye Contact and Facial Expressions

The eyes are important sources of communication during conversations. People in some cultures favor direct eye contact, whereas those in other cultures are uncomfortable with direct eye contact. Facial expressions while conversing are also important; they can confirm or negate the spoken message.

Eye contact is considered very important by persons in the U.S. macroculture. During conversations, people are expected to give direct eye contact. Eye contact is associated with respect and conveys attentiveness. Failure to give eye contact during conversations is viewed with suspicion and is associated with a lack of attention and respect; it is also associated with a lack of self-confidence. Because the United States is a multicultural society, problems with eye contact between persons of the macroculture and those of various microcultures have occurred. People with Asian, African, Caribbean, and Latin American backgrounds have been taught that avoiding direct eye contact shows respect. This avoidance of eye contact, which is interpreted as disrespect by members of the macroculture, has resulted in confrontations between cultural groups in various parts of the United States.

In other cultures, however, maintaining direct eye contact may be associated with disrespect. The Japanese, for example, would view eye contact as rude and disrespectful. Latin Americans and Africans likewise would associate eye contact with disrespect. Eye contact in some cultures depends on social position and gender. In India, eye contact is associated with social position; persons who are of different social classes do not make eye contact. In Egypt, eye contact is associated with gender; men and women who do not know each other avoid eye contact.

Germans, on the other hand, favor intense eye contact that exceeds the comfort level of U.S. persons, who view prolonged stares as often signifying sexual interest either between people of the same gender or the opposite gender. Likewise, in Middle Eastern countries, eye contact is very direct; they make eye contact for prolonged periods during conversations. In Saudi Arabia, making eye contact while conversing indicates respect and is very important.

Facial expressions often reveal messages not being conveyed through verbal exchanges. The Mexican adage "One's face is the mirror of one's soul" illustrates the importance people place on messages conveyed by facial expressions. Some facial expressions are thought to be universal in meaning: fear, anger, disgust, happiness, sadness, and surprise. Cultural variations exist, however, in when and how, as well as to whom, people display these expressions.

One facial expression commonly associated with happiness in the United States is smiling; frowns signify disapproval or disagreement. Smiling during conversations generally means agreement with what the other person is saying or pleasure at receiving the message. In some countries of Asia and the Pacific Rim, people smile often, whereas others do not. People of Thailand, for example, smile a lot; in fact, the country has been referred to as the Land of Smiles. The Japanese smile may be positive or negative; the Japanese may smile when they are frustrated, angry, sad, or embarrassed; they may also smile to indicate happiness. Thus, trying to interpret their smiles may be difficult.

The person taking photos at the Department of Motor Vehicles was surprised when a Japanese man refused to smile for his photograph when requested. The photographer later learned that to the Japanese, smiling for his photo ID would imply a frivolous attitude toward his driving responsibility.[5]

In European countries, people do not smile as readily as do people from the United States. In Latin American countries, people smile frequently; however, the messages conveyed by a smile may vary from "Thank you," to "Please," or "How may I help you?" depending upon the movement of the forehead and eye expressions.

In addition to cultural differences in smiling, gender differences exist that seem to cut across cultural lines. Women smile more often and are more likely than men to return a person's smile.

Gestures and Posture

Gestures are useful in adding emphasis or clarity to conversations. Gestures related to conversations typically include head and hand movements as well as posture.

People of the United States nod their heads up and down during conversations to indicate agreement and will indicate impatience by glancing frequently at their watches. Winking during a conversation in the United States often means that the person is kidding. Canadians, though not known for extensive gesturing, use many of the gestures used by U.S. persons; however, one difference in Quebec is the thumbs-down gesture, which is offensive. Also, people of Quebec use their hands when talking more than people in other parts of Canada.

In Latin American countries, a certain amount of gesturing during conversations is expected. One gesture that should be avoided, though, is the U.S. "OK" gesture, which has a vulgar connotation. During conversations, Brazilians will use a gesture involving scraping the fingers beneath the chin to indicate that they do not understand what the other person has said or do not know the answer to a question. They may also snap the fingers while speaking to emphasize what was said. In Mexico, avoid standing with hands in your pockets while conversing because this is considered rude.

In European countries, variations exist in the types of gestures used during conversations and their meanings. Italians, for example, use a lot of hand gestures when conversing. Their hands are an important part of their interactions with others. People from Scotland, on the other hand, rarely use gestures and other forms of nonverbal communication during conversations. It is important to keep your hands out of your pockets and to speak in a low voice when interacting with people from Scotland.

In Asian countries, such as Japan, people will nod to indicate they are listening. The head nod does not indicate agreement, as is true in the United States. Pointing with the open hand instead of a single finger is customary in China. In Singapore, it is important to pause briefly after the other person has finished speaking to allow him or her to finish the thought. When listening to someone, pause before responding to convey that you have considered carefully what has been said. In India, a part of southern Asia, people do not use a lot of hand gestures. They will shake their head from side to side to indicate agreement and nod the head up and down to signify disagreement. A unique gesture practiced by people in India is grasping the earlobe; this signifies remorse. Gestures to avoid during conversations with people from India include standing with arms crossed, pointing a finger, or winking at a person, which has a sexual or insulting connotation.

Space and Touch

Respecting a person's need for space is an important aspect of interacting with others. Standing too close to people who need a lot of personal space can be intrusive. They may respond by backing away; the issue may then become conversational distance rather than concentrating on the message. This backing away may be viewed as an insult in cultures in which people prefer to stand close together during conversations.

People of the United States like to stand at least a couple of feet away from a person when conversing. When talking to a stranger, they usually prefer even more space. Canadians, too, prefer to interact from a distance of about two feet. Touching, except between good friends, is uncommon during conversations.

People of Iraq stand close together during conversations and will engage in physical contact. In Saudi Arabia, people also stand close together and touch each other while conversing. Remembering not to back away is important, as this would be insulting.

In Asian countries, people dislike being touched by strangers and prefer to keep a respectful distance when interacting with people in important positions. In India, it is important to respect the other person's personal space; an arm's length away is recommended.

INFORMAL AND ALTERNATIVE LANGUAGES

Informal language in the United States includes slang, jargon, provincialisms, acronyms, and euphemisms. Alternative languages used by U.S. cocultures include argot and cant.

Informal language is often used between people who work together and between family members and friends. Slang is an informal nonstandard vocabulary, which may consist of figures of speech, arbitrarily coined terms, or invented words. It has been referred to as *abused English*. Although slang expressions are often coined by teenagers, the truth is that adults also invent various slang expressions. Computer users, in particular, are known for using such slang expressions as *spike* (to describe a sudden increase in voltage) and *crashed* (to describe a computer that is not functional). A slang expression to describe someone who is inattentive is *asleep at the switch*, and to describe a person who has lost an opportunity is to say the person *missed the boat*. Using such expressions in conversations with people who are unfamiliar with their meanings can cause communication problems.

A U.S. businessman, during a conversation in English with his South African business partner, used a phrase that caused the South African to suddenly go silent. The U.S. businessman had assured the South African that he would be kept in the loop regarding a certain aspect of the business plan. Only when the South African contacted the U.S. colleague two weeks later did the U.S. American learn that the phrase he had used meant, in the South African's dialect, that we would keep him pregnant.[6]

Jargon is the technical terminology used by people in specific professions or occupational groups. Financial groups may use such expressions as *red ink*, meaning financial loss; *bottom line*, meaning the actual price; and *rollover*, for reinvestment. Other examples of jargon include *kick around* (discuss), *ballpoint figure* (estimate), *hardball* (a tough approach), and *on the fence* (someone who is undecided).

Provincialisms are expressions that are used by people in a particular region. Although not considered Standard English, these colloquialisms are familiar to persons within the region. For example, people in the South say *y'all*, meaning "you all," and people in other areas will use the word *pop* for soda. Regional variations in pronunciation are also common. In Boston, for example, the letter *r* is added where it does not belong so the word *idea* is pronounced as if it were spelled *idear*. In parts of North Carolina, the sound of the letter *r* at the end of a word is often dropped, so the word *father* is pronounced as *fatha*, and *chapter* is pronounced as *chapta*.

Acronyms are words formed from the initial letters or groups of letters of words in a phrase that are pronounced as one word. An example of an acronym is VAT (value added tax). Initialisms are abbreviations pronounced letter by letter, such as COD (cash on delivery).

Euphemisms are inoffensive expressions used in place of words with negative connotations. Rather than describing people as old, referring to them as *senior citizens* is viewed in a more positive manner. Places where people are buried are rarely referred to anymore as graveyards or cemeteries; the preferred term is *memorial gardens. Customer Service Department* is now considered more positive than Complaint Department.

Argot and cant are considered alternative languages, which are used by those in a subgroup of a community. Argot is a vocabulary used by non-criminal, nonprofessional groups, such as truck drivers who use *smoky* to refer to the highway patrol. Cant is the vocabulary of undesirable cocultures, such as gang members and people who are in prison. For example, gang members would use the term *homegirl* to describe a girl who hangs around gangs; those who are incarcerated would refer to serving a prison sentence as *doing a stretch*.

CONVERSATIONAL HUMOR

As more and more companies conduct business internationally, and as more people travel to other countries, frequent opportunities exist for people to interact in an attempt to develop a good relationship. Humor is used in some countries to establish a relaxed atmosphere before getting down to business.

Types of humor have been categorized as follows: absurdity (ideas that defy logical thinking), exaggeration (overstating sizes or experiences), human situations (situations in which the speaker or situation appear laughable), playful ridicule (sympathetic teasing), and surprise (related to feelings, events, or facts). Absurdity depends upon the other person's understanding that the statement is untrue. Gross exaggeration seems to be used more by people of the United States than by people of other cultures. Serious-minded Germans, in particular, do not appreciate American humor about Texas, which usually involves a great deal of exaggeration. The story about the Mexican who drove as fast as he could for 24 hours trying to get out of Texas but finding it impossible appeals to Americans but sounds far-fetched to Germans. Not understanding that this was a form of humor using exaggeration, a German would typically reply, "He should have used a German car." Although the joke would not be humorous, the response would be very humorous to Germans and also appreciated by the British.[7] Human situations can be humorous, especially those that emphasize your own shortcomings. Teasing can soften the impact when chiding someone for inappropriate behavior, such as arriving late for a meeting; for example, "We'll have to punish you for this." Surprise or an unexpected response can be effective in diffusing a potentially negative situation. For example, a clown falling down may not elicit a laugh, because clowns are expected to fall; however, a prominent politician who falls off the stage provokes loud laughter. By examining these categories of humor, it becomes apparent that each can be used in a positive or a negative manner.

People of the United States use humor in numerous business and social situations. Humor is viewed as an acceptable way to diffuse tension and to convey messages indirectly.

People of the U.S. relax with friends and talk about their lives or relationships, children, careers, and mortgages and laugh at their own foibles or a friend's blunders. They laugh at other people, not to ridicule or make fun, but to indicate they have been there and can appreciate the humor in their situations. Seeing the humorous side of life's traumas helps people gain perspective and share insights.[8]

Although humor is a universal human characteristic, what is perceived as humorous varies from culture to culture. In the United States, presentations are often started with a cartoon, analogy, or joke related to the topic to be covered. The intention is to establish a relaxed atmosphere before getting down to business. In these situations, however, it is considered in bad taste to use off-color humor, sarcasm, and ethnic, racist, or sexist humor. The type of humor used should build someone up rather than diminish the person. In cultures in which playful ridicule is acceptable, it is important to learn to deal with friendly insults. For example, in the United States, because of taboos associated with showing affection between men, they trade insults to indicate that they like each other.

In addition to the United States, most European countries enjoy humor, including during business meetings. The British intertwine humor in their business discussions; they consider understatements as humorous. French humor tends to be intelligent and often at another person's expense. They would not use humor during meetings, however, because it would be viewed as flippant. The French take business seriously and do not use humor to make a point. Italians enjoy humor; they like irony. In business situations, however, they can adopt a more formal and serious attitude. Italian humor can be self-deprecating (humor directed at one's own mistakes and vulnerabilities). German humor, on the other hand, is never self-deprecating. Admitting personal inadequacies, even in jest, is simply not done. Germans do not mix humor with business; they take business seriously and do not appreciate kidding remarks during business meetings.

When a presentation in Germany was begun with a cartoon deriding European cultural differences, no one laughed. As the week progressed, people started laughing both inside and outside the sessions. Only later did presenters learn that cartoons were not appropriate in a professional setting of strangers. Outside the professional meetings, though, Germans would tell jokes in local bars or restaurants.[9]

The Japanese do not understand American humor; in fact, they take what is said quite literally.

In a meeting with Japanese partners, a U.S. businessperson made the statement that the insertion of a certain clause in the contract would blow the deal out of the water; a Japanese colleague asked, "What water?"[10]

Japanese persons find little merit in jokes about sex, religion, or minorities; however, they will laugh out of politeness when a joke is told. Joking or kidding, which is so prevalent in the United States, would be inappropriate in Japan, where courtesy, saving face, and indirectness are so important. The Japanese do not use self-deprecation.

Some humor is acceptable internationally, such as slapstick, restaurant jokes, and humorous stories about golfers. Even so, people of certain countries have their own nuances to make the jokes or anecdotes amusing to members of their own culture. In the United States, for example, sarcasm and kidding accompany humor, whereas in Australia, humor is barbed and provocative. Stated succinctly, people do not all laugh at the same things.

Humor plays a central role in getting to know people of many cultures; it alleviates stress and can lighten and brighten our lives. Oscar Wilde put the use of humor into its proper perspective: "Life is too important to be taken seriously."[11]

Country-Specific Information

Conversation suggestions for the countries with which the United States conducts a majority of its international business follow.

Brazil

- Brazilians are enthusiastic conversationalists and enjoy fast-paced conversations. To avoid being considered unfriendly, match your Brazilian counterpart's enthusiasm.
- Brazilians stand close when conversing and typically touch each other.
- Interrupting others is common among Brazilians and should not be viewed as rude; they are simply showing enthusiasm for the topic being discussed.
- Appropriate topics of conversation include food, sports (especially *futebol*, Brazil's national obsession), the family, and the beautiful beaches and other favorite sights for tourists.
- Avoid initiating discussions about politics, religion, Argentina (Brazil's archrival), or poverty; do not ask personal questions, such as age, marital status, or salary. Brazilians may, however, ask you personal questions and even ask about your political or religious preferences.
- Maintain steady eye contact during conversations; breaking eye contact is insulting.[12]

Canada

- Maintain eye contact during conversations.
- Avoid touching when conversing; Canadians prefer to keep their distance during conversations.
- Remove your sunglasses or hat during conversations.
- Avoid the thumbs-down gesture, which is viewed as offensive; Canadians are conservative when it comes to gesturing.
- Maintain a reserved, formal demeanor.

China

- Use neutral facial expressions; avoid showing emotion when conversing.
- Be modest about your abilities; boasting is considered rude.
- Speak softly; speaking in a loud voice is rude.
- Avoid expansive gestures.

France

- Choose appropriate topics of conversation: sports, art, music, food, wine, and travel experiences.
- Avoid personal topics.
- Expect the French to engage in lively discussions; they enjoy a debate.
- Maintain eye contact during conversations but avoid a prolonged gaze.
- Avoid smiling when passing someone on the street.

Germany

- Avoid using the hands for emphasis during conversations because it is better to appear calm than to use flamboyant gestures.
- Use smiles with discretion because Germans smile only when conversing with people they know well.
- Select safe topics for conversations: sports, travel, and world politics. Remember that Germans prefer to talk about substantive topics rather than engage in small talk.
- Avoid such topics as personal income, family life, and World War II.
- Keep your distance during conversations.

Japan

- Expect the Japanese to ask personal questions; they view it as a way of showing interest.
- Avoid discussing politics, religion, or how much things cost.
- Choose appropriate topics for small talk: for example, food preferences and other topics related to eating.
- Expect periods of silence during conversations because the Japanese value silence.
- Speak softly and avoid showing emotion when conversing.
- Keep your distance during conversations and avoid touching the Japanese.
- Avoid direct eye contact.

Mexico

- Break eye contact frequently while conversing; constant eye contact is perceived as aggressive.
- Feel free to touch the arm or pat the back of the person with whom you are conversing.
- Stand close while conversing; stepping back is considered rude.
- Avoid placing hands on hips or hands in pockets during conversations.
- Choose these topics for small talk: the weather, places visited in Mexico, travel plans, and soccer. Talking about your family or other personal topics is also appropriate.
- Avoid these topics during conversations: politics, the Mexican-American War, and border violations.

South Korea

- Avoid excessive smiling during conversations because this is associated with shallow persons.

- Avoid touching older persons or those of the opposite gender while conversing.
- Stand close to South Koreans during conversations.
- Avoid continuous eye contact because this suggests aggressiveness.

Taiwan

- Maintain a reserved demeanor and talk softly.
- Choose appropriate conversational topics: the weather, travel experiences, and the family. Be prepared for personal questions.
- Avoid such topics as communism and politics.
- Keep your distance when conversing; avoid touching the other person.
- Use a minimum of eye contact.

United Kingdom (England, Scotland, Wales, and Northern Ireland)

- Avoid speaking in superlatives.
- Humor is common in conversations, especially humor that is self-deprecating and sarcastic.
- Be less direct during conversations.
- Avoid touching, and keep your distance while conversing.
- Avoid discussions of politics and religion.

United States of America

- Small talk or chitchat is an important U.S. conversational custom, both in business and social environments.
- Since U.S. persons are uncomfortable with silence, they will initiate small talk.
- Appropriate topics for small talk include sports, travel experiences, the weather, and current events. Avoid controversial subjects, such as religion and politics, or depressing topics, such as world hunger and terrorism. Also avoid asking personal questions, such as a person's age or weight, or questions about money, including a person's salary.
- Humor is often used in both social and business situations. Using humor to begin business presentations is common; the purpose is to create a relaxed atmosphere. U.S. humor may be self-deprecating. Humor laced with racial or sexual undertones is not appreciated.

- During conversations, it is important to stand about an arm's length apart and to avoid touching. U.S. persons are uncomfortable when someone stands too close or touches them.
- People are expected to maintain eye contact during conversations and to take turns speaking. After saying a sentence or two, the person speaking glances away to signal that the other person may speak.
- People of the United States try to avoid arguing and will change the subject or excuse themselves if speakers become argumentative.

Chapter 9

ORAL AND WRITTEN COMMUNICATION CUSTOMS AND ETIQUETTE

Oral and written communication varies around the globe because it is a part of culture. Most of the communication customs and etiquette have developed over time to fit the culture in which they are used. With 97 percent of outgoing international correspondence being sent in English (and 1 percent each in Spanish, French, and German), English is the language of international business. Similar percentages exist for incoming international messages. Because most international people are willing to speak English, their second language, people who speak English as a first language must take the extra step to understand the other culture's written communication customs and etiquette.

LANGUAGE KNOWLEDGE

Although you may not speak the other people's language, if they are speaking and writing to you in English, it may not be as easy for them to express themselves as you think it is. Although much of the Americas, Africa, and Europe write horizontally from left to right (the Russian Federation and Greece use different alphabets but still write horizontally from left to right), the Middle East, Israel, Japan, and China write differently. Both Arabic and Hebrew are written horizontally from right to left. Both Japanese and Chinese are written vertically from right to left. Computers have changed the written text to horizontal lines for Japanese and Chinese. In addition, people who read right-to-left languages read a book or newspaper from what Westerners would consider back to front rather than front to back.

According to one study, language differences were perceived by Chinese, Japanese, North American, and European business executives to be the highest difficulty, followed by the concept of time and punctuality for North American, European, and Japanese executives; the fourth area of difficulty was telephone etiquette by North American, European, and Japanese executives. Language differences, concept of time and punctuality, and telephone etiquette, however, were not perceived as difficulties by the Chinese.[1]

Language can be both unifying and divisive. A common native language ties people together, yet the presence of many different native languages in a small geographic area can cause problems. Both culture and language affect each other. We have the chicken-and-egg dilemma—which came first, the language or the culture? The use of language and culture in creating political, social, economic, and education processes is a consequence of favoring certain ideals over others. Understanding the culture without understanding the language is difficult.

Colonialism caused many areas of the world to lose or replace their native languages with the colonial language. Because people in the colonies spoke the colonizers' language, the colonizers treated them from an ethnocentric viewpoint. Many areas of the world that once were colonized are now trying to regain their native language in an effort to regain their ethnic identity.[2]

Because most U.S. Americans are immigrants and have learned English, their native languages are no longer spoken in the United States. Although many U.S. citizens may not speak the languages of their ancestors, many of the thought patterns have been passed from generation to generation, such as how one greets male and female friends, male and female family members, one's spouse and children, or an acquaintance. When people continue to speak their native language, it is because expressing their thoughts is easier in their native language. Because language determines your cognition and perception, if you are removed from your linguistic environment, you no longer have the conceptual framework to explain ideas and opinions easily.[3]

Language functions as a way of shaping a person's experience and not just as a device for reporting that experience. People adhere to the connections of their language to communicate effectively. Both structural and semantic aspects of a language are involved with culture. The structural aspect includes phonetics and syntax. The syntactic aspect of language is influenced by and influences perception and categorization, and the semantic aspect of language deals with meaning.

The idea that language controls our views and thoughts is what linguistic determinism studies. Languages that are similar still represent different social realities of life. So, the more languages are different, the more difficult it becomes to understand another culture's thought patterns and ways of viewing the world. Although language equivalencies often exist between languages, it is difficult for one person to understand another's language reality or for that person to explain his/her reality to someone from a different culture.

Many times it is an absence of an exact translation, such as the English word for snow, that causes communication difficulties. Although the Norwegians have 16 words for snow, they call snow many different words, depending on the type of snow that has fallen. Because the Norwegians live in a snow-covered area of the world, the exact description of snow is very important to them; however, for most English-speaking people, the type of snow does not matter. Consequently, in English we have only one word for the concept of snow.[4]

Social structure also affects language. Culture, subculture, social context, and social system are part of social structure. Language and speech are either restricted or elaborated. The restricted code includes the oral, nonverbal, and paralinguistic communication channels. Because we use restricted codes with people whom we know very well, the people receiving the message have a good understanding of what we are saying because these codes share common interests or experiences. With the shared experience, it becomes unnecessary to elaborate; and the messages tend to be shorter when we are communicating with someone who understands what we are saying. Best friends or people who have worked together for a period of time are good examples of people who anticipate what one another are going to say because of their shared experiences. Elaborated codes are used when we are not sure the other person will understand us. When we are working with people from other cultures, there is a high probability that we will have to use more elaborated coding if we are going to be successful in getting our message across. Although the verbal channel is used in elaborated codes, we have to be sure that the nonverbal and paralinguistic channels do not convolute the message.[5] In countries where you have many nationalities, it becomes important to use elaborated codes to be sure you are understood.

ORGANIZATION OF MESSAGES

If you are going to use English with nonnative speakers of English, it is important to understand the words people will probably learn first. You must remember that your vocabulary, complete with slang, would be very difficult for a new speaker of English to follow because most people with English as a second language have a limited vocabulary of between 3,000 and 4,000 words. An excellent reference for becoming acquainted with this limitation is P. H. Collin, M. Lowi, and C. Weiland's *Beginner's Dictionary of American English Usage* (Lincolnwood, IL: NTC Publishing Group, 2002). Understanding the business communication of the new culture, a small knowledge of how their language is structured, and how people properly respond to each other socially in business situations will help you get your message across in a new culture.

Two common errors that occur in business between native and nonnative speakers of the language being spoken are lexical errors and syntactic errors. Lexical errors are content errors in meaning, such as using a word that is close in pronunciation or spelling. Syntactic errors include the order in which the words appear in the sentence. Syntactic errors are easier for the native speaker of a language to discover, because they are obvious. For example, "The polyfoam breaks easily during shipping" might appear as "Polyfoam for package is easily to break out when shipped." Lexical errors include items that are close in sound or spelling, such as using "expect" when "accept" is correct for an invitation.

Guidelines that have been developed to decrease misunderstanding between people not speaking a language on the same level follow.

- Use common meanings of words that have multiple meanings or choose words with only one meaning. Avoid uncommon words.
- Use action verbs.
- Avoid making verbs out of nouns.
- Be aware of words within the same language that change meanings between cultures.
- Be aware of different spellings for the same word.
- Avoid slang and sports terms.
- Use single-word verbs rather than two-word verbs.
- Use the formal tone and correct punctuation.
- Use the other country's salutation and closing; avoid using first names in salutations.
- Conform to rules of grammar.
- Use short, simple sentences; avoid compound and compound-complex sentences.
- Clarify the meaning of words that have more than one meaning.
- Adapt the tone of the letter to the reader and try to capture the flavor of the language.

- Avoid acronyms, emoticons, and abbreviations in writing letters, faxes, or e-mail messages.
- If photocopies are appropriate, ask for a list of people who should receive them.[6]

Many organizations have internal magazine publications for employees. Items must be considered when writing such publications to make them global in scope. When a person from one culture writes about a culture with which they are not familiar, people from the culture who read the article often feel like an animal in the zoo. It may be well to have a person at each location submit articles to prevent them from seeming exotic and having cultural stereotypes rather than the cultural diversity of the location. If the president is writing a message to all employees, he or she would do well to remember the different religions of employees around the world as well as the different seasons around the world. If an executive wants to wish employees a seasonal greeting, the executive should direct it to those where it is currently that season rather than to all employees around the globe; the same is true of religious holidays. It is also important to consider the placement of the stories because languages are written in different directions on paper. Countries that write left to right consider the top left corner the most noticeable and important place in the paper; countries that write right to left consider the top right corner the most visible and important. Photographs can be a problem culturally. If you are sending publications containing photographs to countries where women are expected to be completely covered, you would not want to include photographs of scantily clad women. Photographs in which everyone is smiling are seen as very typically U.S. by many European and Asian countries. Hierarchical cultures regard photos of employees in casual clothing as disrespectful. Colors of the publication, in general, should be subdued and professional.[7]

WRITING TONE AND STYLE

Because there are numerous stories of U.S. businesspeople, as well as people from other countries, being insensitive to people of cultures different from their own, it is especially important to learn the verbal and nonverbal communication styles so these styles will not be misread and blunders made. The largest blunder is often that these misreadings are made without the person's awareness that they are even making an error. Blunders such as keying in all capital letters or all lowercase letters that are very difficult to read in your own language, let alone a second language, are examples of being insensitive to another culture. If it is a culture that is collectivistic, then being very direct would be seen as very impolite by the collectivistic culture. Other examples are not being aware of the way numbers and dates are written in other cultures and not using honorific titles in salutations. Awareness by expatriates of the impact of verbal and nonverbal style differences in intercultural business communications is dependent on their success.[8]

Most countries have a more formal, traditional tone and writing style than is typical in the United States. Directness is not valued in most cultures the way it is in the United States, and this direct style may make a positive message be received negatively.

The direct approach is used for beginning good news, direct requests and inquiries, and neutral messages; the indirect approach is used for bad news and persuasive messages in the United States. When using the direct approach, the most important or positive news is given first, then the reasons, alternatives, and the goodwill close. The indirect approach, however, when used for negative messages, begins with a buffer to soften the bad news in the message. The buffer sets the tone of the letter without saying anything unpleasant. In persuasive messages, too, the indirect approach is used; the message starts with a statement that gets the reader's attention. Although U.S. and Korean business letters use direct and indirect request strategies, Japan and Taiwan will tend to use a buffer with both. The structure used for direct requests in the United States and Korea is *please* plus the imperative ("Please get back to me by Wednesday"). Indirect requests are written differently in the United States and Korea. Korean letters prefer requests ("We trust you will replace the container"). U.S. letters avoid "wishful" requests; they call for a specific action ("Your replacing the container is appreciated"). In individualistic countries, such as the United States, the "you" approach is used; however, in a collectivistic country, they use an inclusive approach, such as "we" or "our." By using the inclusive approach, no one person is singled out or caused to lose face. Collectivistic cultures also believe that because the work is the result of the whole team, the whole team, not one individual, is responsible for the results.[9]

Women are not considered to be serious businesspeople in many parts of the world and are not expected to be as direct as many U.S. women are. Because businesswomen are not the norm in many parts of the world, businesswomen must be cautious of their tone and word choice to be taken seriously. In order to avoid having comments taken as flirtatious by men, statements must be worded carefully. By giving compliments indirectly, from the company rather than from the woman herself, the comments will not be misconstrued. It also helps to soften very direct words, such as "would appreciate" rather than "must" or "expect."[10]

Germans occasionally use buffers; however, they are more direct with negative news than many other cultures. Latin Americans, in general, do not use buffers; however, they also will not give negative news because they feel it is discourteous to do so.[11] When two different cultures are doing business together, they must be able to read between the lines. In order to read between the lines, you need knowledge of what proper business communication is in the other culture. Differences, such as the way the Japanese always begin a message with a seasonal greeting, although not an appropriate way to begin a U.S. letter, might be a nice gesture for a U.S. person when writing to a Japanese businessperson. By using phrasing common in the other culture, you are showing sensitivity to the writing style of the culture. Likewise, the Japanese present negative news in a positive manner to the point that other cultures have a difficult time realizing that it is negative. Comments that are present in Japanese letters that are generally missing from U.S. letters include seasonal and weather-related comments, congratulations to the recipient, and apologetic comments.[12]

The Japanese will begin all letters (good and bad news) with a statement about the season: "Rice paddy fields are ready to be planted."

French letter endings are formal.[13] An awareness of the differences between the format, tone, and style of written communication can help to develop a global business relationship. When you receive a letter that is addressed to "Dear Professor Roberta H. Krapels," you will know that part of the culture of the person writing the letter is to show great respect for titles and positions. These style and tone differences between cultures should be ignored, however, and attention paid to the meaning of the letter. Although the use of politeness is very common for many cultures, do not let it distract you. It is important as a writer or reader to keep these cultural differences in mind as you read and write correspondence.

People of other cultures tend to write longer letters than do people of the United States. As a sign of relationship building, U.S. businesspeople need to delete parochialism and ethnocentrism from their writing. Having knowledge of the other culture will help to temper U.S. businesspeople's writing tones.

Although it is not necessary to write to people of other cultures as they may write to you, your writing must be clear. Humor in intercultural writing does not come across, and do not be oversensitive to salutations, such as "Dear Boy" from a Filipino who is really saying you are one with their family, or the Middle Eastern dramatic and emotional letter writing styles.[14]

LETTER FORMATS

Letter format styles are different across countries. Some countries, such as France, still use the indented letter style with closed punctuation, such as France. Latin American countries prefer the modified block format, which features the date and closing lines beginning at the center and paragraphs beginning at the left margin.[15] In the United States, the preferred format is the block format (all lines beginning at the left margin) or the modified blocked (date and closing beginning at the center and paragraphs blocked). Either standard punctuation (colon after the salutation and comma after the closing) or open punctuation (no punctuation after either the salutation or the closing) is used in U.S. letters. Many countries use the U.S. format for their letters, particularly when communicating with people of the United States. Use the overstrike function, symbol function, or multinational insert function of your word processing software to add special accent marks, or diacritics, used in other languages (e.g., *mañana*, *crudités*, and *crêpe suzette*).

The inside address varies from country to country. In the United States, the title and full name are placed on the first line, street number and street name on the second line, and city, state, and ZIP code on the last line. In Germany, the title (*Herr, Frau,* or *Fräulein*) goes on the first line with the full name, then the street name followed by the street number on the second line, and ZIP code, city, and state on the last line. The recipient's title (*señor, señora, señorita*) goes on the line above the person's name in Spanish-language cultures.[16] The street name is followed by the street number in Mexico and South America. Observe the styles used in letters that are sent to you to see the different formats that are used around the world.

The date is also placed differently in letters around the world. U.S. letters place the date before the inside address, whereas the French place the date after the inside address. In French letters, the inside address is typed on the right side, with the ZIP code preceding the name of the city (84040 MARSEILLES); however, in U.S. letters, the inside address is on the left. In French letters, the salutation is followed by a comma rather than a colon or no punctuation, which is used in the United States. A formal complimentary close is used in French business letters, with the writer's title preceding the writer's name. Use your incoming correspondence as a format for your return mail.

Follow U.S. guidelines for addressing the envelope if you do not know the correct form.

Mr./Mrs./Ms./or appropriate title plus first then last name
Street number followed by street name

City, state, and ZIP code

The country name is typed in full capital letters

Note the country and city are sometimes at the beginning and sometimes at the end of the address in the following examples.

Herr Dieter Neidlinger	JAPAN, Tokyo	Mr. George St. Clair
BASH Gmbh	Hachioji-shi	5230 Kirkside Cove
500 Hiller Due	47–25 Nanyodai	Memphis, TN 38117
GERMANY	Nakamura Yoko	USA

Although we single-space business letters in the United States, other countries may use single or double spacing in their letters. The company name in the complimentary close of U.S. letters, if used, is typed a double space below the complimentary close, then the name of the writer is typed four lines below the company name with the title typed below the writer's name. In German letters, the company name is also placed below the complimentary close, but the writer's name and position are not typed in the signature block. Surnames will precede the given name in the signature block in Japan and China. Many Far Eastern businesspeople are familiar with the U.S. way of writing names, and you need to be sure they have not already written their name as first name and last name in deference to the U.S. culture rather than surname and given name, which is normal in their culture.

The formality of salutations and complimentary closings varies from country to country. The English equivalent of the German letter salutation would be "Very Honored Mrs. McKee," and in Latin American countries, "My Esteemed Dr. Frink." The English equivalent of other countries' complimentary closing is "Very respectfully yours."[17] Diplomatic titles are very important to the holders of these titles and should be addressed as shown in the following table.

Diplomatic Titles[18]

Written Forms of Address and Salutations

Title and Address Form	*Salutation*
Ambassador	
His/Her Excellency (name)	Excellency: (or)
The Ambassador of (country)	Dear Mr./Madame Ambassador:

Chargé d'Affaires

The Honorable (name)	Dear Sir/Madame:
Chargé d'Affaires of (country)	Minister:
The Honorable (name)	Dear Sir/Madame:
The Minister of (country)	Dear Mr./Madame Minister:

Consul General

The Honorable (name)	Dear Mr./Ms. (name):
Consul General of (country)	

Consul

The Honorable (name)	Dear Mr./Ms. (name):
Consul of (country)	

CALENDARS

Although many people who have been economically involved with the United States may use our Western Gregorian calendar, many of the countries that businesspeople are involved with may not use it. Other calendars include the Arabic, Hebrew, and Chinese calendars. It is best to use both calendars' dates on all memos and correspondence in order to avoid any confusion.[19] By using both calendars, it will also help ensure that you remember holidays and religious festivals in the other country. *The World Almanac* is a good source of information on the different types of calendars.

Even when countries are using the Western calendar, they may write the date differently. For example, the date 5/10/20—, means May 10, 20—, in the United States and October 5, 20—, in Turkey. Some countries use commas to write the date, such as 5,10,20—; some use periods, such as 5.10.20—; and some use slashes 5/10/20—. Some countries write the date 10 May 20— or 20— May 10. Knowing which format the countries you do business with use is very important. The best rule is to always key the month as a word rather than a number because that clarifies the situation no matter in what order the day, month, and year are written.

NUMBERS

Decimal points are not the same the world over. Whereas in the United States people would write 68.5, in Europe it would be written 68,5. The period is also used for separating thousands in Europe: 7.652 is equal to 7,652 in the United States. In some countries, the decimal may be located halfway up the line such as 68·5. Another area of confusion is what is a billion and what is a trillion. In the United States, Russia, France, Italy,

Turkey, Brazil, and Greece, a billion has nine zeros (1,000,000,000) but is called a milliard in Russia, Italy, and Turkey; in Germany, Austria, the Netherlands, Hungary, Sweden, Denmark, Norway, Finland, Spain, Portugal, Serbia, Croatia, and some South American countries, what they call a billion has 12 zeros (1,000,000,000,000), which is equal to the U.S. trillion. Some other interesting differences you may see is a one (1) written so that it looks like a V, sevens written with a slash across the middle that can be mistaken for a Y or a 4, eights that start at the bottom loop rather than the top loop, and zeros that may be crossed.[20] Although the British government announced in 1974 that all government reports and statistics would use the United States system for billion, you would want to check twice when doing business in Britain.[21]

A misplaced comma cost Lockheed $70 million, according to James A. "Micky" Blackwell, president of Lockheed's aeronautics division. However, Lockheed would not name the company that held them to the misplaced comma price.[22]

ELECTRONIC MESSAGES

Thomas L. Friedman has dubbed the new electronic means of communicating as the "Steroid Flatteners." The prevalence of digital, mobile, personal, and virtual wireless connectivity means everyone can run their office from wherever they are as long as the technology is available. A surprising fact is that China is more wired than the United States.[23] Electronic messages are sent via the telephone, facsimile, and electronic mail (e-mail). Such factors as speed and reliability of transmission, as well as cost and convenience, must be taken into consideration when selecting which type of electronic message is most appropriate.

Telephone

Aspects of protocol related to successful intercultural communication include telephone manners and cyberspace etiquette, sometimes referred to as netiquette (network etiquette). Many intercultural encounters are via the telephone. When talking on the telephone, the initial impression is formed mainly by vocal quality (70 percent) rather than on the words spoken (30 percent). Thus, opinions are formed more on how something is said and the voice tone rather than on what the person actually says.[24]

Good telephone manners include answering the phone promptly (first or second ring), identifying yourself properly by giving your department and your name, and being courteous at all times, including the frequent use of "please" and "thank you." Successful telephone communication involves recognizing and avoiding behaviors that typically irritate others. Being put on hold has been identified as the single most irritating behavior. When the telephone call is to another country, being put on hold can go beyond irritation. Other negative behaviors that should be avoided include mouth noises, not paying attention, and having a negative or rude attitude. A positive behavior appreciated by callers is "the voice with a smile." Callers also appreciate a cheerful attitude.

When voice mail is used, be brief but complete when leaving a message. Include your name, company, the date, and the time of the message. Give your phone number slowly and include a brief summary of what the call concerns. Leaving a voice mail may be seen as rude in many countries rather than efficient. You also must realize that sometimes connections are poor and the receiver may not be able to understand who you are or what you are saying.[25]

Facsimile (Fax)

The use of fax messages is increasing as a quick method of communication between countries. Points of etiquette regarding fax transmission follow.

- Calling ahead to confirm the fax number and allowing the person to switch the line to the fax machine in case the fax shares a telephone are very helpful. This will also alert the person that you are sending a message. You should send the message immediately because you are disabling their ability to receive telephone calls.

- Sending documents that are longer than 10 to 15 pages, personal or confidential information, and negative news should not be done using a facsimile.

- Using the fax when impressions are important should be avoided. Printed documents that have been faxed are not always as crisp and clean looking as the original document, nor can you control the paper quality.[26]

In many countries, global businesses have found the facsimile (fax) machine to be more dependable than the mail service. If the telephone system is of poor quality, however, then the fax machine may not be any better than the mail. Countries that have very stormy seasons generally will have poor mail and phone service during those time periods. Another problem is the regularity of maintenance and delivery service in remote areas. Telecommunication satellites, cell towers, and cell phone service are becoming more dependable in many locations around the globe.

Faxes require the same good writing skills that letters or e-mails require. When sending production schedules, budgets, or other types of written information, use a cover letter or transmittal sheet so that the receiver knows to whom the fax is directed, from whom the material originates, and how many total pages are included.

Electronic Mail (E-Mail)

The Internet and e-mail are connected to major cities around the world. Because e-mail sends documents in their original format as attachments, it has become a very convenient way to send documents. Normally, e-mail printouts are clearer than those from a fax machine. Again, the quality of the infrastructure in the country is important to the quality and dependability of e-mail, faxes, and telephone service, and the cost for these services may be much higher than the cost to which you are accustomed.

E-mail as a communication medium has not been totally adopted by non-Western countries, and one reason given for this is different communication preferences.[27] Culturally based resistance is common if proper managerial intervention does not take place so culture has an important role in technology adoption.[28] It has been found that people with high-powered distance values perceive e-mail as not fulfilling their desired goal of social interaction with individuals.[29]

For your international e-mail, use the same good writing skills you would use for a letter. The format is a memorandum form with the TO, FROM, DATE, and SUBJECT already stated. Because of this automatic formatting, you would not use an inside address in the body of the e-mail. Rather than using a proper salutation as you would in writing a letter, address the receiver by name in the first sentence (e.g., "Mr. Chou, your kindness is greatly appreciated"). Avoid first names unless the person has given you permission to use the first name. Your electronic mailbox should be checked at least once a day, but two or three times is probably a better idea. Responses should be made within 24 hours. Messages should be concise and brief; no more than two screens should be used. An electronic "signature" is necessary because, unlike a letter, it is not on company letterhead.[30] When composing an e-mail message, you must consider your receiver's e-mail habits and resources. If English is the receiver's second language, be sure to use words that you are sure will be understood and state points clearly. Use normal grammar and paragraphing and use politeness markers such as "please" or "this might work," because nonverbal cues are absent. Do not use jokes or informal idioms, and edit carefully.[31]

Rules of e-mail etiquette should be observed. The following are examples of improper netiquette: If you type in all caps, it is the same as shouting. You should not speak ill of someone; doing so is called dissing. Sending vicious or insulting messages is called flaming and should not be done. Sending mass messages is called spamming and is wasteful of the receiver's time.[32] Avoid the use of humor and sarcasm globally because it is probably going to be misinterpreted. Cultural variations exist in what is perceived as humorous. Also, maintain a positive tone rather than even a slightly critical one.[33]

A company is responsible for information leaked into cyberspace; employees should be very careful about the messages they send. A good rule to follow: If you would not want your message posted on the company bulletin board, do not send it via e-mail. Hitting the delete key does not necessarily remove the message or a trail from your computer.[34]

Choosing a channel by which to send a message is something that needs to be thought about. The advantage of e-mail is its low preparation and fast delivery time as well as being personal and convenient for the receiver. The disadvantages of e-mail include the lack of confidentiality and the lack of nonverbal interaction.[35] Also, not all countries use e-mail as frequently as do people in the United States. Internet access is available to 68.8 percent of the people in the United States (third highest of the top 20 countries); almost 75 percent of the residents in Sweden; 72.5 percent of the people in Hong Kong; 66 percent of the residents of the Netherlands, Australia, and Canada; 58.5 percent of the residents of the United Kingdom; and 52.2 percent of Japanese residents.[36] Some other suggestions to avoid misunderstanding include spelling out the name of the month, including country codes in telephone numbers, and indicating whose time zone you are referring to when you wish to make contact at a specific time of day.

COUNTRY-SPECIFIC INFORMATION

Oral and written communication customs and etiquette for the countries with which the United States conducts a majority of its international trade follow.

Brazil

- Speak Portuguese or English. Portuguese is the national language of Brazil; speaking Spanish is offensive.
- When greeting someone say *Oi* (Hi) or *Como vai* (How are you?); parting expressions are *Tcháu* (Goodbye) or *Ciao* (Bye).[37]
- Spell and pronounce names of your Brazilian colleagues correctly; mispronouncing or misspelling someone's name is an insult.
- Forms of address to use in written correspondence include *Doutor* (doctor), *Professor/Professora* (professor), *Padre* (priest), *Senhor* (Mr.),

Menina (Miss), and *Senhora* (Mrs.). Titles are used with given names for doctor, professor, and priest; titles are used with family names for Mr., Miss, and Mrs.[38]

- The style of written communication includes comma splices and run-on sentences, which are incorrect in English. The indirect style of digression used by Brazilians makes understanding the train of thought of the writer difficult.[39]

Canada

- Canadians are polite listeners and writers.
- Canadians are more formal than people in the United States.
- Canadians tend to be in the middle of the scale between direct and indirect writing style.

China

- People of China make more syntactic errors when changing from Chinese to English.
- Chinese tend to understate or convey meanings indirectly.
- Chinese use vague terms and double negatives; but they use indirect criticism.
- Chinese are concerned with maintaining harmony.
- Chinese restate positions in a repetitious fashion.
- Chinese discuss changes before changing a position as a group.
- Chinese speak humbly and negatively of their supposedly meager skills and those of their subordinates and their family.
- Chinese write names with the family name first followed by the given name.

France

- French tend to use the indented style for business letters. The French place the name of the originating city before the date (Norvège, le 15 décembre 20—).
- French use the "we" attitude and the indirect apology.
- French type the surname in all capital letters.
- French consider titles important; formality is also important.

Germany

- Due to structural differences in languages, the verb often comes at the end of the sentence in German; in oral communication, Germans may not immediately understand what you are saying.

- In Germany be honest and direct; stick to the facts. Germans are low-context people; everything is spelled out.
- Use first names only when you are told it is correct to do so.
- Germans send lengthy, detailed communications to employees.

Japan

- Add "-san" to another person's name but never to your own. Always refer to yourself by your last name and the name of your organization.
- Begin your letters with a salutation followed by a comment about the season or weather.
- Do not use the word "no"; they may not understand what you mean if you use it.
- Begin all messages with a buffer, a kind remark about a gift, kindness, or patronage. Then include the main message and close with best wishes for the receiver's health or prosperity.[40] Japanese people who do business internationally are adjusting and changing the way they write. They are using a shorter seasonal greeting and are writing the business message sooner. Studies show that Japanese businesspeople are using both deductive and inductive writing patterns.[41]
- They have many different meanings for the word "yes."
- Prefer faxes, letters, and telephone conversations to e-mails.[42]

Mexico

- Mexicans seem overly dramatic and emotional to U.S. persons. They rise above and embellish facts; eloquence is admired.
- Mexicans like to use diminutives, making the world smaller and more intimate. They add suffixes to words to minimize importance.
- In Mexico, rationale involves two types of reality: objective and interpersonal. Mexicans want to keep people happy for the moment. When asked directions, if they do not know the answer, they will create directions to appear to be helpful.
- Mexicans show respect by using titles. Titles are used alone or with the family name. Officials are addressed by their position, such as Señor Presidente.

South Korea

- Use the following greeting when writing to the South Koreans "To my respected (title, family name, first name) . . ."[43]
- Be sure not to use triangle shapes in presentations, as they have a negative connotation. South Korea is a culture of symbolism.[44]
- Do not write a person's name in red ink, as this means the person is deceased. Use colors of ink other than red.[45]

Taiwan

- Use an expert Taiwanese translator because Chinese characters are not the same in Taiwan and China.
- Use their title and family name when addressing or writing to a Taiwanese.[46]

United Kingdom (England, Scotland, Wales, and Northern Ireland)

- People of the UK do not use a period after Mr, Mrs, Ms, or Dr; people of the UK are very conscious of forms of titles and addresses and expect others to use them appropriately.[47]
- People of the UK do not use middle initials when writing their names.[48]
- Today, addressing someone in the UK is less formal than it was a few years ago. The class system is becoming less rigid. If you do not know someone well, however, you need to use his or her title and surname. When writing about someone in a letter, you would include after the name the abbreviations for military and civil orders and decorations, highest degree or diploma, professional memberships, and professions. In the typed signature line, include in parentheses the title you prefer to use, such as Ms.[49]

United States of America

- The direct approach is used for U.S. letters that start with good news, with direct requests and inquiries, and with neutral messages; the indirect approach is used for bad news and persuasive messages.
- A buffer is used to begin negative messages to soften the bad news. The buffer tells what the letter is about but does not suggest a positive or negative response.
- The "you" approach is the preferred writing style rather than the "we" style used in collectivistic countries.
- U.S. letters avoid "wishful" requests; instead, they request action.
- The preferred letter styles are block, with all lines starting at the left margin, and modified block, with the date and closing lines beginning at the center and the paragraphs blocked.
- The letter format commonly used in the United States features the date before the inside address, which is followed by the salutation. Letters are single-spaced.

Chapter 10

ETIQUETTE FOR INTERNATIONAL BUSINESSWOMEN

Women are increasingly being afforded opportunities in the international business arena. These opportunities often take the form of representing U.S. companies during interactions with foreign-owned corporations in the United States, traveling to other countries to negotiate business contracts, or serving in overseas assignments.

To enhance their chances for competing successfully in the world of global business, women should upgrade their business etiquette skills. As Leonard points out, "Etiquette alone will not enable you to reach your targeted goal. It will give you the extra edge that will make the difference between you and the competition."[1] She further emphasizes the importance of etiquette to business success: "Like it or not, management equates good manners with competence in business and poor manners with incompetence."[2]

Women interested in assignments involving international business interactions must acknowledge that women are not regarded the same in all cultures, a fact that has been well documented. Prejudices continue to exist regarding the competency of women in the global workplace. However, many women who have worked internationally have reported favorable experiences and, in fact, have stated that being a woman has worked to their advantage. These international businesswomen have remarked that resistant attitudes they have observed are directed more toward local businesswomen rather than toward foreign women.[3]

Several years ago, one U.S. firm experimented with the use of female sales executives to make cold calls on Dutch businesses. The company found that these saleswomen were able to gain access to Dutch executives more often than salesmen. "Whether because of surprise, politeness, curiosity, or even chivalry, being a woman served as a distinct advantage."[4]

Companies have discovered that women have unique characteristics that make them successful in intercultural encounters. Women, according to research, are viewed as being superior to men in interpersonal skills; they are more patient and willing to spend the necessary time to build rapport with their international colleagues. Women are often more accustomed than men to realizing the importance of social amenities, such as writing thank you notes and giving gifts, which are considered an important part of conducting business in some cultures. In addition, women are perceived to be better listeners, more willing to accept the values of other people, more sympathetic, and more understanding than men. In addition, women are typically less competitive than men; this characteristic is viewed as an advantage in problem-solving situations.[5]

An international female consultant stated: "I've found that international experience, decision-making authority, and sound judgment are valued everywhere—and far outweigh any consideration of gender when it comes to getting the deal done."[6]

GUIDELINES FOR WOMEN IN INTERNATIONAL BUSINESS

To be successful in international business, women will want to become knowledgeable about the behavior expected of them in various cultures of the world. Guidelines for women who work in international business include the following:

- Conduct research on countries with which you expect to conduct business to determine attitudes toward women and the extent to which they are respected in the business world; vow to respect cultural differences and to avoid being judgmental.
- Be prepared to make adjustments in your attitudes, attire, and behaviors to accommodate expectations of the foreign country.
- Avoid aggressive behavior, a stereotype of U.S. women. This behavior is viewed negatively in most countries. Remain calm; avoid emotional outbursts.
- Expand your knowledge of foreign languages; concentrate on the ones you are most likely to need in your international encounters. Language training

will enhance your credibility and will ensure that you are not at the mercy of translators who may not always convey your intended message.

- Establish your credibility at the outset; make sure your educational background, position, and professional expertise are known to your foreign counterparts. Asking someone who is mutually respected to introduce you is recommended.

A businesswoman from Chicago explains her experience with credibility in foreign countries: "When I conduct business in most countries, I am consciously aware that my male colleagues have more credibility than I do, just because of gender differences. In most countries women are not expected to have significant positions of authority, so I am frequently viewed in the same way. I feel I have to work doubly hard to establish my credibility before I can effectively conduct business."[7]

Another businesswoman who has worked overseas made this additional observation: "I lose points when I walk through the door without laying the groundwork. Businessmen tend to assume that I don't have the necessary background information, and they try to backtrack and explain the basics if I don't establish first that I have a thorough understanding of the subject matter."[8]

- Be on time for business meetings and appointments. Being "fashionably late," a practice some U.S. women view as acceptable for social events, is not appropriate for business commitments. Even in countries with lax attitudes toward punctuality, U.S. persons are often expected to be on time.
- Behave professionally at all times—professional attitude, professional attire, and professional demeanor.
- Project self-confidence through erect posture; a strong (not loud), unemotional voice; and a positive visual image through attire that is elegant yet conservative.[9]
- Be flexible when it comes to expectations from men in the host culture. Permit them to treat you as a woman first; e.g., allow them to open doors for you without comment. Ignore behavior you consider inappropriate, such as kissing your hand or addressing you in an informal manner.[10]

RECOMMENDATIONS FOR WOMEN TRAVELERS

Women who work internationally will probably travel as part of their jobs. By following a few guidelines, especially those related to safety and health, women can make their travel experiences favorable ones.

Safety must be a top priority for women travelers. In addition to taking certain safety precautions before leaving, women should practice rules of safety during travel—whether by airplane or by automobile. Further, safety guidelines during hotel stays as well as while walking on streets should be followed.

One international businesswoman offers this advice on safety for women travelers:

Do not schedule your arrival into a country during the middle of the night. Never cut corners when it comes to safety: Take a taxi rather than the subway and use valet parking. Choose a nice hotel and eat there. Be personable but private; if you converse with a man at a bar, do not leave with him to go anywhere.[11]

Safety precautions women should take prior to departure include making copies of such travel documents as driver's license, passport, plane tickets, and credit cards that can be left with a friend who may be contacted in case these documents are stolen or lost. In addition, before making final travel plans, check online sources to determine whether the countries on your itinerary are involved in civil unrest or are under threat of terrorist attack. Online travel advisories should also be checked for severe weather problems or for such disasters as floods or earthquakes. Another suggestion is to look at catalogs that feature products such as leather pouches that can be worn next to the body to conceal money or other items of value. Luggage stores or travel shops also offer personal safety devices, such as alarms, that women may wish to purchase to provide a sense of security.[12]

Women who travel by air should follow all safety rules, including keeping their seat belts buckled during the flight and following all instructions given by flight attendants. Whenever possible, selecting a seat near an emergency exit is recommended. When planning to travel by automobile, women should determine in advance if an International Driver's License is required and whether their U.S. automobile insurance policy provides coverage in foreign countries. Some businesswomen who travel overseas simply prefer to avoid driving in foreign countries because of the added stress associated with differences in rules of the road abroad; they take taxis or hire local drivers for special side trips, such as sightseeing.[13]

Hotel safety is of utmost importance for women, especially those traveling alone. When checking in, women should request a hotel room on a floor between the second and seventh floors to make walking to the ground level possible in case of an emergency. When registering, women need to make sure that others do not know their room number. Upon reaching their room, women should also check for escape routes in case of fire. Additional hotel safety guidelines for women include putting jewelry, money, and other valuables in the safe-deposit box provided in the room or at the front desk; checking to see that doors to connecting rooms, to balconies, or to the outside are locked; keeping a "Do Not Disturb" sign on the outside door when inside the room; and refusing to open the door when someone knocks. The concierge can provide suggestions for safe restaurants and information about parts of the city that are unsafe for women.[14]

Street safety requires constant vigilance. Women travelers often do not feel safe walking alone on the streets, especially in countries that are known to have problems with pickpockets. In some countries, children have become quite skilled at distracting foreign visitors with sales of souvenirs or other wares while their "partners in crime" are stealing jewelry, money, or other valuables. Women who decide to walk on the streets should take special precautions, including wearing a handbag with a strap that is placed around the neck; the bag is held close to the body. Wearing the handbag underneath a long jacket or topcoat is also a good idea. Women may wish to take along an alarm in case they feel threatened. Flirtatious comments from local men are not unusual in some countries; when complimented, simply say "Thank you" and continue walking.[15] In the event that you decide to take a taxi back to your hotel, keep matches from the hotel with you (which typically contain the name, address, and phone number of the hotel) to show cab drivers who do not speak your language your intended destination. Women who usually take an early morning jog may decide to forego this practice while in another country unless the concierge indicates the location of safe places to jog.[16]

Health precautions to take to avoid or minimize illnesses prior to departure include determining if vaccinations are recommended for your destination country, checking to see that your health insurance covers travel overseas, and making sure you have extra prescription medications, feminine hygiene products, and other items that may not be readily available at your destination, such as medication for pain, sleep, diarrhea, headache, and motion sickness. Suggestions for staying healthy during your trip include drinking plenty of water (bottled), limiting intake of alcohol to avoid dehydration, washing hands often, getting ample sleep, and avoiding uncooked foods such as fruits (unless they are peeled) and salads. Exercise can be beneficial in maintaining good health; packing a jump rope can be an excellent way to get some exercise in your room.[17]

APPEARANCE

Dressing appropriately for international business encounters is especially important for women because of cultural variations that exist in what is considered acceptable attire. Unlike men, women must be concerned not only with style, but with color and coverage as well. In some countries, for example, pantsuits and short skirts are inappropriate for business; in others, only muted colors are acceptable for business attire. Further, in some countries, women are expected to wear clothing that provides good coverage; higher necklines and longer skirts are expected. Because of cultural variations in dress, international businesswomen sometimes make mistakes in selecting what to wear. When this happens, taking quick action is recommended.

When the former director of a large medical association entered a Cairo hotel conference room wearing a long-sleeved business suit with a skirt covering the knees, she immediately realized that she had more skin showing than the other women. She hurried back to her room and changed into a pantsuit.[18]

Although international businesswomen are expected to dress conservatively, they should retain their femininity. Dressing in a feminine style does not, however, mean dressing provocatively. Attire can be feminine without calling attention to one's sexuality.

An American diplomat was overheard one night making this statement about a French businesswoman: "She looked terrific, she smelled so good, and she was in a plain black cover-up dress. All you saw was her face: mysterious, chic, sexy. Everyone in the room wanted to talk to her."[19]

Making a positive initial impression by dressing appropriately enhances a woman's credibility and her chances for successful dealings with people from other countries. U.S. women who plan to conduct business internationally should always be mindful that dress is more formal and conservative in most other countries. In addition, quality—in dress, accessories, and jewelry—is very important in many countries. In addition, U.S. businesswomen should be aware that the casual attire that is acceptable in some U.S. firms is not appropriate for business abroad. In fact, the very casual attire (shorts, halter tops, and short skirts) U.S. women often wear when sightseeing and engaging in other nonbusiness activities is inappropriate in many countries.[20] The importance of dress and appearance for both international businesswomen and businessmen was emphasized earlier in Chapter 5.

SOCIAL GRACES

Knowledge of social skills can make the difference between losing a potential client and closing a deal. Lack of social skills can result in unintentionally offending prospective international businesspeople. Social graces can enable women to present themselves with authority and confidence. The most important social skills when interacting with people of other cultures involve greetings, introductions, business cards, dining, tipping, and gift giving.

Polite greeting etiquette for women in the United States has changed somewhat over the years, especially when it comes to handshakes. At one time, U.S. women could choose to shake hands in both business and social settings. The current rule of U.S. etiquette is that women are expected to shake hands in business situations but may choose not to shake hands on purely social occasions. The nature of the handshake for U.S. women at one time depended upon the geographic area of the country. Southern women were more likely to give a soft handshake than northern women. Now, all U.S. businesswomen are expected to give a firm handshake and direct eye contact when greeting others.

U.S. women will need to prepare themselves for cultural variations in greetings and will want to modify their behavior to show proper respect. For example, the Japanese usually bow when greeting others, a behavior perceived as subservient by some U.S. Americans. The direct eye contact expected during greetings by U.S. persons is viewed as disrespectful by many Asians and some Latin Americans. In India, the *namaste* (called the *wai* in Southeast Asia) is the appropriate greeting. This greeting involves putting the palms of the hands together at the chest as if praying and bending the head slightly forward. While U.S. businesswomen would not be expected to use these greetings on the initial visit, they should probably be prepared to use them on subsequent visits.

Even in countries where people typically shake hands, U.S. women should be prepared for more than the one or two pumps common in the United States. In addition, when visiting countries where women are not usually included in business dealings, local businessmen may be unsure of the proper greeting procedure. Women should always offer their hands first but should not take offense if the foreign host does not reciprocate.[21]

It is not customary to shake hands with businesswomen who are Orthodox Jews. Indications that the businesswoman is an Orthodox Jew are when she is wearing any type of head covering or a knee-length skirt with opaque tights worn beneath it so that no skin shows.[22]

People who make introductions should remember to mention the name of the person of higher rank first; they should give the person's name, title, and company (in that order) when introducing an international visitor to the company's executive. During introductions, women should be sure to give their credentials but should not dwell on their education, accomplishments, or expertise. Having a colleague emphasize a woman's achievements is a more subtle way to convey her credentials.[23]

Exchanging business cards is an important part of encounters with businesspersons in other countries. Since the business card plays such an essential role in relationship building, it would be wise to have cards for every country on your itinerary printed in the local language on the back of your cards. Because of the negative associations with certain colors in many countries, use white paper with black ink for business cards. When designing their business cards, U.S. businesswomen should be sure to include all their credentials, such as a title that is easy to translate into another language. Titles such as Specialist or Consultant are too vague; titles such as Director or Vice President for Sales are more easily compared to titles in other countries. Also include all telephone numbers (with international codes) and your e-mail address. Learning proper procedures for exchanging business cards is likewise important. For example, when presenting your card in Japan or South Korea, use both hands and position the card so that the recipient can read it. In the Middle East, Southeast Asia, and African cultures (except Israel), use only your right hand to present and accept business cards as the left hand is reserved for taking care of bodily functions.[24] More specific guidelines for greetings, introductions, and business card exchange are included in Chapter 2.

Since many business and social encounters involve dining, it is important to be aware of cultural variations in eating styles and dining customs. For example, in many cultures, the European style of eating is used rather than the American zigzag style. In addition, in some countries, cleaning one's plate is customary; but in other countries, leaving food on the plate to signify that you have had enough to eat is expected.[25] It is also important to learn the nuances of tipping, especially restaurant and travel tipping, when visiting another country. Dining and tipping customs were explained in more detail in Chapter 7.

Gift giving is an integral part of building global relationships. Women seem to be adept at understanding the subtleties of gift giving but may be unaware that some gifts considered appropriate in the United States would be inappropriate in other cultures. Flowers, for example, are appropriate gifts in most cultures. However, the type of flower, number, and color are important considerations when selecting flowers to avoid inadvertently sending a negative message. For example, carnations are funereal in France and Germany, four is a negative number in China, and red, yellow, or white have special significance to Mexicans and are inappropriate flower choices.[26] More detailed information on gift giving was covered in Chapter 3.

DINING ALONE

Dining alone can be a problem for businesswomen who travel; many say that they are uncomfortable eating alone and simply order room service to avoid it. Here are some suggestions for solo dining for women travelers:

- Choose restaurants in U.S. business hotel chains, such as Marriott and Hyatt, where it is common to see other businesswomen dining alone.
- Look for upscale department stores, such as Harrods in London, that have restaurants with solo seating to accommodate shoppers. Shopping malls also have eating areas where women are frequently seen eating alone.
- Ask your hotel concierge about restaurants where it is common for women to dine alone; also ask about local dinner theaters where you can watch a show while eating.
- Look for restaurants that have a dining/lounge area where diners can sit alone and perhaps enjoy piano music while having a light meal.
- Ask to be seated in a private area or where you can look out a window.
- Bring along a book to read; women should be aware, however, that this behavior is considered rude in many nice restaurants.

Some international businesswomen have suggested dining at off hours—either early or late—when there are usually few diners. Others have booked city tours that include stopping to dine at a restaurant featuring local cuisine; this can be a good opportunity to enjoy the company of other travelers.[27]

One businesswoman uses business trips to lose a few pounds. She dines with clients in the evenings, but when she does not have business commitments, she visits the local grocery and buys fruit and vegetables to take back to her room.[28]

SEXUAL HARASSMENT, GENDER DISCRIMINATION, AND DATING

Sexual harassment has been defined as "unwelcome behavior of a sexual nature that makes someone feel uncomfortable or unwelcome in the workplace by focusing attention on her (or less commonly, his) gender."[29] Sexual harassment in the U.S. workplace may result in disciplinary action, including lawsuits.

A U.S. worker was disciplined for sexual harassment when he placed on his desk a photo of his girlfriend clad in a bikini. The picture was visible to other workers; some were women.[30]

Examples of sexual harassment in the United States, in addition to the preceding example, include asking for sexual favors in return for some special treatment such as a salary increase or promotion, telling jokes that have sexual content, and unwelcome touching.

In other countries of the world, however, sexual harassment is not clearly defined. What is perceived as sexual harassment in the United States may be viewed as acceptable behavior in other parts of the world. When faced with perceived sexual harassment in other countries, women should consult trusted colleagues in the host country to determine if the behavior is considered harassment in their country and to ask for suggestions on how to respond. In some countries, women will probably be advised to ignore the behavior. Simply asking the person to stop the harassment is certainly appropriate. If this is ineffective, it may be wise to start recording offensive incidents including the date and description of the behavior in case it becomes necessary to report the conduct to a supervisor, a local attorney, or your firm's U.S. attorney.[31]

Gender discrimination in the workplace occurs in most countries. Women receive lower salaries and fewer promotions than men worldwide. They are often treated as subservient to men and are sometimes subjected to sexually explicit comments and derogatory remarks. In Asian companies, for example, female workers are typically asked to serve tea; in addition, Asian businesswomen are asked questions about marital status, children, and age—questions that would not be asked of men. While this treatment of women was once considered acceptable in many U.S. firms, it is no longer tolerated by U.S. businesswomen. Research shows that Asian women continue to feel inferior to men; the stereotype that women are the less capable and weaker gender continues. In Japan and Korea, it is considered proper etiquette for men to enter rooms and elevators ahead of women. The opposite is true in the United States: men permit women to precede them. In many European countries, comments of a sexual, flirtatious nature and off-color jokes are quite common. In Italy and France, men often comment on women's physiques and touch women inappropriately. The excessive flattery by Latin American males is not appreciated by U.S. women; such behavior is not tolerated in U.S. offices.[32]

One U.S. businesswoman said that both European businessmen and businesswomen were more flirtatious than she was comfortable with. Although she said she tried to "roll with the punches" and avoid getting angry, she found it stressful sometimes to determine which behaviors were viewed as normal for Europeans and which ones were considered inappropriate.[33]

The best advice on dating for women on international assignments is: Do not do it. Dating international colleagues is simply inappropriate. Even flirting with overseas associates is not smart. Spending time in the hotel bar is not a good idea, as it may suggest to men that you are seeking company. (Besides, drinking too much is not the way to make a good impression when conducting business abroad.) Activities that would suggest a romantic relationship, such as going to a disco with a male colleague, should likewise be avoided. Remember that mixing business and pleasure will complicate the business relationship and may jeopardize your career.

"Although there are no 'nevers' in real life, consider the risk before you act. Ask yourself: 'Is there a chance my behavior could be misunderstood?' If the answer is yes, then don't say it, don't do it, don't wear it, don't go."[34]

In conclusion, women are increasingly visible in the world of international business because they are well suited for global interactions. One U.S. female international executive stressed the advantages women enjoy when working globally. She said: "Women are naturally more caring, nurturing, and better listeners. They like to help and to respond to people's needs. This is consistent with most business cultures around the world because everything is based on relationships. This works in favor of women."[35]

The first step toward successful international encounters for women is learning the proper etiquette in other countries and, of course, learning about the culture before departure. Women interested in working in the world of international business would benefit from the advice of one U.S. international businesswoman: "My basic strategy for doing business consists of being polite, competent, and in unfailing good humor. Develop the knack of treating every person as if he or she is the most important person you are meeting that day. People invariably react positively when you treat them in a positive manner. That has worked well for me in the United States and in every country I have visited on business."[36]

COUNTRY-SPECIFIC INFORMATION

Country-specific information on etiquette for international business-women for the United States and for the countries with which the United States conducts most of its international business is provided in the following sections:

Brazil

- Women in Brazil are increasingly achieving positions in upper management as well as directorships; however, women are rarely in positions as presidents of large domestic or international firms. Women also hold political positions, including serving as members of the Supreme Court, as state governors, and as city mayors.[37]

- Since Brazilian women are considered the most liberated of those in the Latin American countries, professional women from other countries will be able to deal with Brazilian male colleagues without incident.[38]

- Women are expected to dress fashionably, even when shopping, and in a feminine manner. Pantsuits, skirted suits, and dresses are typical attire; elegant dresses are the norm when invited out for an evening of entertainment. Women should also pay attention to grooming, as Brazilians notice such details as manicured nails and carefully applied makeup.[39]

- Shaking hands with everyone upon arrival and departure is expected; handshakes are often lengthy and accompanied by touching on the shoulder, kissing, or hugging. Women usually kiss each other on both cheeks during greetings; married women receive two kisses (one on each cheek), and single women receive a third kiss (alternating left, right, left cheek).

- Brazilians have two surnames, with the mother's surname preceding the father's surname. After marriage, the woman takes her husband's surname. Brazilian businesswomen typically use their father's surname. Using a person's first name is usually inappropriate (until invited to do so); however, addressing older women or women of high rank with *Doña* plus their first name is appropriate.[40]

Canada

- Women are not only accepted but also well represented in business and government in Canada.

- Canadian women expect men to rise when they enter a room.

- The handshake is customary when meeting someone; in addition, kissing on the cheeks is a common greeting in Quebec.

- Titles with last names are used until invited to use first names; Ms., Miss, and Mrs. are female titles used, except in Quebec where *Madame* (Mrs.) and *Mademoiselle* (Miss) are used.[41]

China

- Economic and social inequality for Chinese women continues. Chinese women hold few managerial positions in business. However, life is improving for women; their literacy rates have increased in recent years, and more women are now enrolled in higher education. They hold about one-third of official jobs and one-fifth of parliamentary deputy positions.[42]

- U.S. businesswomen traveling to China will receive no special consideration because of their gender.

- Although the Chinese usually bow when greeting each other, U.S. persons are usually greeted with a handshake.[43]

- During greetings, the most senior person is acknowledged first. Formality is important. When a title is used, it precedes the person's given name; otherwise, use the person's family name followed by the first name.[44]

France

- French women hold few top positions in business except in the fields of art, advertising, fashion, and cosmetics. While French men do not generally accept the women of France in business, they usually accept women from other countries, especially from Canada and the United States.[45]

- Equal rights for women is a belief held by many French people, but equality is not a reality.

- When addressing people they do not know well, the French are quite formal and do not even use last names; they simply address people as *Monsieur* (Mr.), *Madame* (Mrs.), or *Mademoiselle* (Miss). As is true in many countries, using someone's first name is unacceptable until invited to do so.[46]

- French men are flirtatious and often comment on a woman's appearance, behavior viewed as acceptable in France.

- Foreign businesswomen are advised to forgo their usual assertive business manner and to behave in a low-key manner when conducting business in France.[47]

Germany

- German women are not treated as equal to men in status or salary despite the fact that gender equality is guaranteed by German law. While German women have not been perceived as having the ability to supervise males in the workplace, this attitude appears to be changing, as evidenced by the 2005 election of Angela Merkel, Germany's first woman chancellor.[48]

- Foreign businesswomen will be shown respect by German men provided, of course, they behave professionally, dress conservatively, and exhibit business knowledge.

- Women initiate the handshake in Germany; a firm handshake is expected.
- When addressing someone, use the person's business or courtesy title and last name until invited to use the first name.[49]

Japan

- Many Japanese women now hold high-ranking positions; however, despite the fact that women comprise half of the Japanese workforce, the majority hold lower-level staff positions.
- Women from other countries may not receive the respect in Japan that is given them in Europe and in many other countries. For example, they may not be served first and may not be given the seat of honor.
- When greeting the Japanese, use a handshake with a light grip and quick release.
- Use a person's title and last name when being introduced; high-ranking persons are addressed by title instead of last name. The Japanese follow the last name with *san*, which represents Mr., Mrs., and Miss.[50]

Mexico

- Mexico has traditionally been a male-dominated culture; however, Mexican women are now holding more important positions in business and politics; they are becoming visible in such professions as the law, medicine, and teaching.
- Foreign businesswomen may encounter some problems doing business in Mexico, especially if the Mexican businessmen they are working with are unaccustomed to dealing with women holding positions of authority.
- International businesswomen should avoid being aggressive; however, they should be very professional and should convey their skill and competence to gain the respect of Mexican men.
- Businesswomen from other countries may not appreciate the flirting and complimenting that is characteristic of Mexican men. This behavior is simply part of the culture; no disrespect is intended.[51]
- Handshakes are the usual form of greeting, but wait for Mexican women to initiate the handshake. Mexican women may kiss each other on the cheek when greeting.
- Use titles (*Señor*, *Señora*, and *Señorita*) with the last name. To show respect for older Mexicans, use the titles *Don* or *Doña* followed by the first name. Avoid calling people by their first name until asked to do so.[52]

South Korea

- In South Korea, women are not viewed as equal to men.
- Most South Korean women who work are employed as teachers, secretaries, or assembly workers.

- International businesswomen may encounter some difficulties conducting business in South Korea since men typically hold decision-making positions.
- When greeting South Koreans, bend the upper body slightly while shaking hands.
- Western women may offer their hand first when greeting a South Korean man. However, men should wait for a South Korean woman to initiate a handshake; she may choose to nod when greeting someone rather than to extend her hand.[53]

Taiwan

- Taiwanese women are now starting to hold positions of responsibility.
- Alert prospective Taiwanese business associates to the presence of a Western woman on your U.S. team, since the Taiwanese are accustomed to working with men.
- A handshake is the common form of greeting; the senior person is greeted first.
- Business cards are exchanged during the greeting; it is customary to present the card with both hands with the card facing the recipient. Business card information should be translated into Mandarin on the back of your regular business card.
- Address people of Taiwan with their title and last name until you are invited to use their first name.[54]

United Kingdom (England, Scotland, Wales, and Northern Ireland)

- Women of the U.K. have made progress in politics and in the business world; they enjoy equality and power. However, people in the United Kingdom expect men to show women respect, such as rising when women enter a room and holding doors open for them.
- Although handshakes are the usual form of greeting in the United Kingdom, women do not usually shake hands during greetings and introductions, so it is a good idea to permit women to initiate the handshake. The handshake is brief and not as firm as the U.S. handshake.
- When greeting and conversing with others, use last names until you are invited to use their first name.[55]

United States of America

- U.S. women hold positions of prestige and leadership in government, business, and education. They are independent and are able to accomplish as much as men using their own style. However, U.S. women do not receive the same salary as their male counterparts. In fact, women managers earn 81 cents to a man's dollar, according to a 2010 report.[56]

- While U.S. women do not expect special treatment in the workplace, the majority appreciate polite behavior from men, such as rising when women enter and leave a room and opening doors for women and allowing them to enter first.[57]

- U.S. businesswomen expect to be treated with respect; they do not appreciate terms of endearment, such as "honey" and "sweetie," in the work environment. Demeaning terms, such as "broad" and "dame," are likewise offensive.

- Touching of U.S. businesswomen should be limited to the handshake; affectionate hugs or kisses are not appreciated.

- Use the title Ms. and last name when addressing a U.S. businesswoman until she indicates how she wishes to be addressed. Since the United States is a country where first names are used rather quickly after meeting someone, some women will prefer to be called by their first name.

- U.S. women shake hands during greetings and introductions in business situations. In social situations, however, they may choose not to shake hands.[58]

Chapter 11

INTERNATIONAL NEGOTIATION ETIQUETTE

International negotiation involves "discussions of common and conflicting interests between persons of different cultural backgrounds who work to reach an agreement of mutual benefit."[1] The etiquette of international negotiation involves knowledge and use of proper procedures and behaviors to assure that an agreement is reached amicably—an agreement that emphasizes what the two parties have in common and deemphasizes possible conflict.[2]

Guidelines for proper negotiation etiquette depend somewhat on whether the culture is high context or low context. In high-context cultures, the nonverbal aspects of communication are important; communication is indirect; and silence is used to communicate. In low-context countries, the message is explicitly stated; messages are direct; and nonverbal aspects are unimportant. The following recommendations for intercultural negotiators are directed toward low-context negotiators (such as those from the United States, Germany, and Switzerland) who are negotiating with high-context adversaries (such as the Japanese, Chinese, Latin Americans, and Arabs):[3]

- Study your opponents' culture and history to be prepared for the negotiation; learn the language.
- Work on establishing a personal relationship with members of the opposing team.
- Acknowledge that members of the opposing team may not understand your message and that what you say will be interpreted according to the other culture's background.

- Be aware of nonverbal messages you may be sending through your body language; try to read between the lines; what your opponents are not saying may be as important as what they are saying.
- Since status and face are important in some cultures, establish yourself and your adversaries as equals; avoid anything that would lead to loss of face, such as public criticism, losing your temper, or unpleasant surprises.
- During negotiations, leave room to bargain. Start high and save a trump card for the final round.
- Be patient; allow your opponents sufficient time for making decisions.
- Remember that face-conscious negotiators must feel that they are leaving with a favorable outcome.[4]

NEGOTIATION PREPARATION

Successful international negotiation etiquette requires attention to negotiation preparation, including selection of the site, team members, and interpreters.

Negotiation preparation begins before departure. Although the meeting site is not very important to U.S. negotiators, it may be important in other countries. In some countries, such as Asia and Latin America, you are expected to go to their country, especially for a first meeting, as they are more comfortable in their own country.[5] Problems associated with negotiating on the other company's turf include having to deal with jet lag and cultural shock, in addition to contending with another language and business practices that are unfamiliar. If the negotiations take place at your company, you have the home field advantage. You are not tired from travel, you have access to your office staff, and your foreign colleagues will speak your language and will need to adjust to your way of conducting business. However, you are responsible for all the social amenities associated with your foreign colleagues' visit, including transportation, meals, and entertainment. More specifically, meet their flight, take them to their hotel, and send a car to take them to and from the meeting; feed them; and make sure that evening entertainment is provided so that they do not sit alone in their hotel rooms at night.[6] This would be a good time to remember the Platinum Rule: Do unto others as they would have done unto them. In other words, attempt to accommodate the customs, preferences, and needs of your international guests insofar as possible. Needless to say, this means doing some research to determine cultural differences in dining and entertaining.[7]

The selection of team members should be done with care. Important considerations include gender and age as well as the rank, expertise, and personalities of potential team members. Including someone on the team who is from the culture you wish to do business with or who has at least spent some time there is recommended. Selecting someone with expertise in the host-culture language is often a good idea. When you plan to include a woman on your team, it may be wise to alert the other culture so that they can become accustomed to the idea. This would be especially important when negotiating with countries that do not typically include women on their teams. (Etiquette for women negotiators is covered in a later section of this chapter.) The number of team members should also be considered. On U.S. and Mexican teams, the number is usually two to three, while it may be four to seven on Japanese teams. When in doubt, ask about the number of team members the opposing team has so that each side will be equally represented. Keep the same team members during negotiations.[8]

TRANSLATION AND INTERPRETATION ISSUES

Unless one of the team members is fluent in the host-culture language, it may be necessary to secure the services of an interpreter. Select the interpreter carefully as this person can determine the success or failure of the negotiation. A missed negative, for example, can prove disastrous. If you hire a professional interpreter in the host culture, try to find one who is bicultural. This person can alert you to local customs that may have an impact on your presentation and may provide useful suggestions on cultural differences in nonverbal behaviors that may affect the effectiveness of your presentation. Allow sufficient time to meet with the interpreter to provide written materials that would be helpful in understanding your business proposal and to explain any technical terms. Even when using an interpreter, it is a good idea to give your closing comments in the language of the host country.[9] However, make sure your use of the language is accurate to avoid possible embarrassment.

President John F. Kennedy, in an effort to show his solidarity with West Berlin citizens just after the Berlin Wall had been built, said: "*Ich bin ein Berliner.*" The translation of that phrase is, "I am a jelly-filled doughnut," a popular pastry in Berlin.[10]

When conversing in English with people in a country whose primary language is other than English, you will increase the chances of being understood correctly if you use short sentences and words; avoid humor; avoid jargon, slang, and idioms; and provide examples whenever possible. In situations in which people do not have a common language, the services of an interpreter may be needed.

When using a translator, it is important to realize that the translation may not be the meaning intended. In his book *Blunders in International Business*,[11] Ricks points out numerous errors in translations that have proved embarrassing, to say the least, and in some cases have had a negative impact on sales.

- The message "Buy American Made," which was to be placed on T-shirts trying to convince consumers to buy U.S.-made cars, rather than Japanese-made automobiles, was translated into Japanese as "Buy an American Maid."[12]
- A U.S. manufacturer advertised its car battery as "highly rated"; after translation, the battery, when introduced in Venezuela, was described as "highly overrated."[13]

Interpreters selected to help people who do not share a common language should be both bilingual and bicultural to assure that the intended messages are conveyed. Suggestions for using interpreters in business situations include the following:

- Become acquainted with the interpreter prior to your interaction with the intended business associate; find out about cultural differences in nonverbal behaviors, such as eye contact and gestures, as well as local customs regarding small talk.
- Ask the interpreter to apologize for your lack of ability to speak the other person's language.
- Speak slowly and avoid words with multiple meanings; for example, use the word *expensive*, which has only one meaning, rather than the word *high*, which has more than 30 meanings. When you must use technical terms, review them with the interpreter in advance.
- Suggest that the interpreter translate in phrases or short sentences, rather than waiting until the end of a long sentence.
- During the conversation, speak to your colleague rather than to the interpreter.
- Learn a few words and phrases in the other person's language so that your parting comments will be in your colleague's language.

A final thought when using interpreters is to avoid sarcasm or innuendos, because they are difficult to translate. Try to state concepts in more than one way to be sure the point you are making is understood. Also, remember that the word you have used may not have an exact duplicate in the other language. Not all languages have the same verb tenses; many verbs have multiple meanings. In the English language, for example, the verb *get* can mean to buy, borrow, steal, rent, or retrieve. When interpreters are bicultural and have ethnic compatibility with persons for whom they will be translating, the chances of a successful translation increase.

RELATIONSHIP BUILDING

Building a relationship, which is not very important in the United States, is important in a number of countries, including those of Latin America. To start building a relationship, it is important to have an introduction. A professional reference by someone who is highly regarded in the host culture is helpful; a personal introduction is of value in opening doors. People wishing to conduct business with governmental employees in Latin America will need to use an intermediary to get an appointment. The time spent in relationship building is well worth the effort. A good place to start is meeting with your international colleagues for lunch or dinner. Just keep in mind that table manners count and that business is not to be discussed during these times when the two teams are getting to know each other.[14]

An international consultant emphasizes the importance of table manners when dining in other countries, especially in France. "The French get quite disturbed watching an American switch the fork and knife back and forth between hands. Although it is the norm in America, only peasants and vagrants in France eat this way. So it can be embarrassing for a Frenchman to be seen in an exclusive restaurant, even with a prominent American business executive, if that executive appears unsophisticated."[15]

Gift giving is also important to building a relationship in many countries. Asians will usually initiate the gift giving; U.S. negotiators should not attempt to "outdo" a gift from Chinese or Japanese negotiators. As Lewis points out, "It is a game you are not going to win anyway."[16] Remember not to open gifts in the presence of Asians and Arabs because of the possibility that someone will lose face. Additional tips for international gift giving are included in Chapter 3.

OPENING TALKS

Opening talks begin promptly in most cultures and include a short time for small talk, especially in the United States and Australia. The Swedes also value promptness and typically engage in small talk. People of Finland, on the other hand, do not engage in small talk; they get right down to business. The length of small talk varies; in Spain and Italy, small talk may last for 10–30 minutes while waiting for everyone to arrive. In Germany, however, small talk is very brief; after formal introductions, everyone gets down to business.[17]

Opening the presentation with a joke, which is a common practice in the United States and most European countries, would not be considered appropriate in some countries. Germans, for example, take business seriously and do not feel that jokes are appropriate during negotiations. Because of the risk of telling a joke that no one understands or that may be offensive to some people in attendance, it is better to avoid humor when conducting business internationally. Although Asians will laugh at jokes to be polite, they do not appreciate jokes about religion, sex, or minorities and usually do not understand U.S. humor.[18]

Agendas are common in such countries as the United States and Sweden; an agenda is an indicator of a well-planned meeting. Agendas are not considered in a positive manner, however, in such countries as the Middle East and Latin America. In fact, they are considered a hindrance to successful negotiations. The Japanese also do not typically use agendas, perhaps because of the tendency of Japanese negotiators to discuss a number of topics simultaneously.[19]

DISCUSSIONS AND AGREEMENT

During the discussion phase of negotiations, a variety of nonverbal behaviors may be displayed; these behaviors will have different meanings, depending upon the culture. The French enjoy debating, so a lively discussion can be expected from them. Negotiators from Argentina sometimes become emotional. Spanish negotiators may argue with each other to the extent that Asians may conclude that they are fighting. Smiling may signify happiness with the progress of the negotiations by Germans, Britons, and Scandinavians. However, among Asians, the smile often indicates a lack of understanding. In addition, Asians may say "Yes," which does not typically signify agreement. "Yes" may actually mean, "Yes, I understand."[20]

At the close of negotiations, delays are common in some countries, so it is wise to allow extra time for the completion of the deal. Delays are common in India as well as in Asian and Latin American countries.[21] While the final step is usually the signing of the contract, the nature of the contract may be different from contracts to which U.S. negotiators are accustomed. The contract is viewed as binding in the United States; however, in Asian countries, it is a guide for future negotiations. As a result, negotiations may continue for some time after both parties have signed the agreement.[22]

TYPICAL NEGOTIATION MISTAKES

Mistakes that are sometimes made during negotiations may negatively affect the outcome. Talking too much and failing to listen are two of these mistakes. People from other countries have pointed out that U.S. Americans are guilty of these mistakes. One New Zealander expressed his frustration with this alleged characteristic of people from the United States. He said, "If you Americans can't learn to shut up and listen more often, could you at least lower your volume?"[23] Showing discomfort with silence is another mistake that is commonly made. Remaining silent after you have asked for your international colleague's business will result in a more positive outcome than continuing to talk; a period of silence will give the other side an opportunity to consider your request. U.S. negotiators, who are uncomfortable with silence, should consider the following well-known quotations on the importance of silence.

"It is better to remain silent and be thought a fool than to speak out and remove all doubt."

—Abraham Lincoln

"Never miss a good chance to shut up."

—Will Rogers

Other mistakes made by negotiators include making a negative initial impression, failing to ask important questions, assuming understanding by representatives of the other culture, using unfamiliar and slang words, interrupting the speaker, failing to read nonverbal cues, failing to note key points, and making statements that are irritating or contradictory.[24]

ETIQUETTE FOR WOMEN NEGOTIATORS

Women who are members of international negotiation teams should be aware of how they are perceived in the world of global business.

"Women have a tremendous advantage over men in international negotiating. They very often are adept at reading nonverbal cues sent out during a negotiation. Studies show that men primarily pick up general ideas and conclusions from a conversation, while women often get more information from body language, intonation, voice pitch, and eye movements."[25]

In addition to getting a feel for how they are viewed in various cultures, businesswomen should polish their social skills to avoid unintentionally offending people with whom they wish to conduct business. The consequences of failing to observe rules of appropriate social behavior can be serious as emphasized by Rossman: "A businesswoman who unknowingly breaks a social taboo may find other doors in the same locale permanently closed. On the other hand, businesswomen who take the time to become attuned to cultural considerations can negotiate contracts, make deals, and more important, open entire markets for their companies."[26]

The following 10 guidelines for women planning to negotiate internationally are offered by Axtell:

- Be aware of cultural variations in behavior to better understand actions of international counterparts.
- Do not expect to be treated equally; acknowledge that even in the United States, women and men are not treated equally.
- Show respect for the norms of the host culture and try to work within the norms of their system.
- In advance of your encounter with members of the host culture, study their history, food, languages, literature, and other specifics of the culture. Recognize, however, that despite studying a culture prior to visiting it, embarrassing errors can still be made.

An experienced international businesswoman asked her Australian male host to join her for lunch. She wondered why her colleague was rather cool toward her during the meal. What the businesswoman later learned was that by singling him out in front of his "mates," she had unknowingly caused him much embarrassment.[27]

- Find a mentor who has experience in international business who may be able to open doors for you; expand your network of international contacts.
- Act with diplomacy, tact, self-confidence, and self-control; behave in a professional manner at all times.
- Because of the importance of building personal relationships, be patient, flexible, and compassionate.
- Maintain a good sense of humor; acknowledge that you will make mistakes; learn to see the humor in the situation.
- Recognize the importance of humility, a key to success in many international encounters.
- Differentiate between gender differences and cultural differences; when difficulties arise, women sometimes assume that gender differences are at the root of the problem when, in fact, the difficulty may be cultural differences.[28]

Additional suggestions for women who wish to be successful international negotiators include becoming knowledgeable about the negotiation topics and associated issues, preparing a plan for the negotiation including goals and alternatives, and demonstrating a cooperative attitude conducive to discussing and resolving conflict.[29]

COUNTRY-SPECIFIC INFORMATION

Country-specific information on international negotiation etiquette for the United States and for the countries with which the United States conducts most of its international business is provided in the following sections:

Brazil

- Portuguese is the primary language; have handout materials in Portuguese. Although English is spoken, it is a good idea to have at least one member of your negotiating team who speaks Portuguese. Do not speak Spanish.
- Keep the same team members throughout the negotiation.
- Consult a Brazilian accountant or lawyer for issues related to the agreement; bringing your own legal counsel may be resented.
- Upon meeting members of the Brazilian negotiating team, shake hands with everyone. Use titles with the last name; however, sometimes Brazilians introduce themselves using their titles and first names. It is not necessary to bring a gift at the initial meeting.
- During the relationship-building stage, remember that soccer is a good topic of conversation; avoid discussions of politics and Argentina, Brazil's traditional rival.
- U.S. persons should not refer to themselves as Americans since Brazilians view themselves as Americans also.
- When making agreements, remember that Brazilians use periods for punctuating thousands; for example, 3,340 would be punctuated 3.340.
- Present a gift during a social event after the formal negotiations are concluded.[30]

Canada

- Canada is a bilingual country; English is the primary language in all provinces except for Quebec, where French is the primary language. English Canadians are low-context communicators, while French Canadians are high-context communicators. Written materials should be prepared in French and English in Quebec.

- Canadians are conservative, reserved, and very formal; however, they appear to be open and friendly. They observe strict rules of etiquette. French Canadians in particular are very protocol-conscious.
- Negotiation team members are selected for their expertise, knowledge, and prior negotiation experience.
- Time is important to both English and French Canadians. Negotiations are expected to begin and end promptly.[31]
- When meeting Canadian businesspeople, give a firm handshake and eye contact. Use titles and last names until Canadians suggest using their first names.
- Business gifts are appropriate after the contract is signed; gifts are opened in front of the giver. A gift from your country is a good choice; however, a gift may be a meal or another type of entertainment.[32]

China

- Patience is necessary when negotiating with the Chinese; developing a relationship before conducting business is important, so plan to make numerous trips before finalizing an agreement.
- Business cards should be printed in gold ink in Mandarin Chinese on one side and in black ink on white paper in English on the other.
- Address most people using their professional title (Doctor, President) or "Mr." "Mrs.," or "Miss" and their last name. Remember that in China, the surname comes first; the given name is last.
- Rank is important; address the highest-ranking person first.
- Use black and white for business materials; colors have special significance in China, so it is best to avoid the use of color in presentations and handout materials.
- Bringing your own interpreter to meetings is recommended.
- When preparing contracts, remember that the Chinese write the date with the year first followed by the month and then the day.
- Exchanging gifts is customary, but only after all negotiations are concluded. The Chinese will decline a gift three times before eventually accepting it. Gifts will not be opened in the presence of the giver. Gifts to avoid include white flowers, clocks, and handkerchiefs (which are associated with death) as well as knives and other cutlery (which signal a desire to sever the relationship).[33]

France

- The French take pride in their language; they will expect you to speak French or to apologize for not speaking their language. It is highly advisable to have at least some members of your negotiating team who speak French.

- Building long-term business relationships is important to the French.[34]
- When conducting business with the French, manners, status, education, family, and individual accomplishments are keys to success.[35]
- During introductions, use titles with last names; when speaking French, use the *vous* form until given permission to use *tú*.
- Have business cards printed in French on one side (include your academic credentials) and in English on the reverse side. Treat business cards given by the French with respect.
- Be aware of the importance of hierarchies. Learn who the higher-ranking persons are and cultivate their friendship.
- Business gifts are not appropriate at the first meeting. Gifts at later meetings should be tasteful and may include books or music; avoid gifts containing your company logo or a bottle of wine since fine wines are French specialties.[36]

Germany

- Third-party introductions are necessary; appropriate references include lawyers and bankers.
- Punctuality is especially important to Germans; arriving even five minutes late for an appointment or a meeting is an insult.
- Allow sufficient time for negotiations, as Germans feel it takes time to do a good job.
- Although meetings may be conducted in English, translate all promotional materials into German. Make sure your proposal is precise and detailed and that your presentation is well organized and professional. Using an interpreter is recommended.[37]
- Status is important. People of higher status enter a room first.
- Take an ample supply of business cards. One side of the business card should be printed in German, the other side in English. Education is respected, so include advanced degrees on the card. In addition, include the date your company was founded if it has been in business for a long time.
- Conversations with Germans when getting acquainted should not include personal questions or political questions that may prove embarrassing. Sports of all types, especially soccer, are recommended topics of conversation.
- During business discussions, do not make attempts at humor; Germans take business seriously and do not smile in business situations. Maintain poise and self-control. Be direct, but be honest as Germans dislike exaggeration.
- Business gifts that are small, inexpensive, and of good quality are preferred. Imported liquor or wine, electronics, or gifts from your country

are appreciated. Beer is not a wise choice; any foreign beer you choose could probably not compete with German beer.[38]

Japan

- The traditional greeting in Japan includes a bow; when dealing with people from other cultures, a handshake is often included with the bow.

- Exchanging business cards is important; have cards printed in English on one side with the Japanese translation on the reverse side. The business card should be presented with the Japanese side facing the recipient; cards are also received with both hands. Business cards are treated with respect and should not be placed in one's pocket. They are examined carefully before placing them in a briefcase or business card holder.

- Be punctual; being late for meetings and appointments is rude.

- Intermediaries who are not associated with either company and who are of the same rank as the Japanese negotiators are recommended, especially in conveying bad news. Use a Japanese lawyer, not one from a U.S. firm.

- Remember that throughout the negotiations, "yes" or "we will consider it" may actually mean "no."[39]

- After the contract is signed, it is permissible to continue to negotiate, as contracts are not viewed as final agreements.

- Gift giving is important to the Japanese. Gifts are often given at initial business meetings. Since wrapping is important, having gifts wrapped after arriving in Japan is recommended. Appropriate gifts include electronic gadgets or imported cognac or Scotch; avoid giving four of anything.

- Follow these additional guidelines during negotiations: Be polite, be indirect, and use "I'm sorry" when appropriate. Avoid humor; avoid hard-sell, high-pressure techniques; and do not compliment individuals as Japan is a group-oriented culture.[40]

Mexico

- Building a long-term relationship is important in Mexico; maintaining contact with Mexican colleagues between visits is recommended.

- Include an upper-level manager on your negotiating team, as status is important in Mexico. Mexican negotiators are typically selected based on education, family connections, and influence; they are usually male and occupy high-level positions.[41]

- Because Mexicans are concerned with status, staying at a prestigious hotel and dining at fine restaurants are recommended.

- Since Mexicans avoid saying "no," written agreements are essential to make sure that the oral "yes" does in fact signify agreement.[42]

- During negotiations, an emotional approach is more effective than a logical one. In other words, emphasis should be on trust, pride, and personal benefits rather than on the details of the contract.

- When negotiating with Mexicans, anticipate their need to finance purchases; expect to work out financing issues.[43]

- Time is more relaxed in Mexico. People are considered more important than tasks. Being on time for meetings is important; however, be prepared to wait.

- Here are some final reminders when negotiating with Mexicans: They place great importance on diplomacy, courtesy, tact, respect, and good manners. Also remember that Mexicans, unlike U.S. persons, are not risk takers and have a pessimistic attitude in situations involving risk.[44]

South Korea

- Building a relationship is important before conducting business in South Korea; allow time to get to know your South Korean counterparts, which may necessitate making several trips before a contract is signed.

- Business cards are important and are given out often; have the cards printed in Korean on one side and in English on the reverse side. Use your right hand when offering your card. Avoid writing on a business card or treating it with disrespect.

- When selecting negotiation team members, remember to include older, senior executives from your company, as age and status are important to South Koreans. Women are not usually included on negotiating teams, so tell your South Korean counterparts in advance if a woman will be on your team to give them time to adjust to the idea.

- While concern for promptness was not important in the past, South Koreans now consider time in much the same way as do U.S. businesspersons. Thus, being on time for meetings and appointments, as well as for social engagements, is important.

- Written materials may be in English; presentations may also be in English. However, having a translator available is recommended to make sure your proposal is clear.

- During the initial stage of negotiations, begin with a bid that will permit compromise. South Koreans, while starting with an extreme position, expect to compromise to achieve a "win-win" outcome.

- During meetings, remember that South Koreans tend to give a response that is pleasing to the other side and may be uncomfortable saying "no." Rather, South Koreans may use nonverbal signals, such as tipping back the head, squinting, or sucking air through the teeth, to convey a negative response.

- A written contract is important.

- Final suggestions when negotiating with the South Koreans include showing respect for the elderly, complimenting others, and being modest about your accomplishments. Do not criticize anyone publicly; this includes criticism of the competition.[45]

Taiwan

- Arrange for a personal introduction if possible.

- Business cards are important; have the cards printed in Mandarin Chinese (using gold ink) on one side and in English on the reverse side. Treat business cards with respect.

- The negotiating team should include older, senior-level executives as Taiwanese respect age and seniority. Since women are not usually included on negotiating teams, advise your Taiwanese counterparts if you plan to include a woman on your team to give them time to become accustomed to the idea.

- Allow ample time to build a relationship with the Taiwanese; patience is required, especially when dealing with delays. Several trips to Taiwan may be necessary before a contract is signed.

- During negotiations, keep in mind that the Taiwanese consider saying "no" to be rude, so when they say "maybe," it usually means "no."

- Avoid embarrassing another person; face-saving is important in this culture. Also avoid criticizing competitors.

- Bargaining is common during negotiations; expect to make concessions.

- Final suggestions for negotiating with the Taiwanese include being honest, sincere, modest, and respectful—especially to the elderly and to high-ranking Taiwanese team members; refrain from emotional displays, speaking loudly, or using excessive hand gestures during conversations or when making presentations.[46]

United Kingdom (England, Scotland, Wales, and Northern Ireland)

- Although there are slight behavioral differences in people from the four major regions, punctuality is expected throughout the United Kingdom.

- Introductions are often made by third parties; these third parties have no additional duties. Be prepared with business cards during introductions.

- Sending your senior executives to negotiate with your UK counterparts is recommended because they are usually treated with greater respect.

- Observing rules of etiquette is important on both business and social occasions in the United Kingdom; these rules include appropriate attire, proper table manners, and a calm, composed demeanor. Emotional outbursts are inappropriate.

- UK negotiators can be ruthless and tough, yet they are tolerant and willing to compromise; avoid hard-sell techniques; UK negotiators are direct and are typically interested in short-term results; their skill in negotiation should not be underestimated.
- Remember that the British are rather formal and value their privacy. Thus, asking personal questions and controversial topics should be avoided. They are often critical of themselves and use self-effacing humor; however, it is unwise to participate. Simply listen and remain silent.[47]

United States of America

- U.S. negotiations take place at a more rapid pace than in many other cultures. Bringing a final contract and having it signed at a first meeting is not uncommon. Statements such as "Let's get to the point" indicate a desire to speed up the negotiation process and reach a decision.
- Building a relationship with prospective clients is unnecessary. After a brief period of chitchat or small talk, getting right down to business is the norm.
- During small talk, U.S. persons may ask about a person's profession or job; this is not considered intrusive. Other conversation topics may include travel, music, books, and sports; however, controversial topics, such as religion, politics, and money, are inappropriate.
- Exchanging business cards is not as important as it is in many cultures. Usually, business cards are exchanged only if there is a reason to get in touch with the person later. The U.S. practice of writing on business cards and putting them in a wallet or back pocket is not viewed as disrespectful.
- Punctuality is extremely important. Being on time for business appointments and meetings is expected; however, arriving a few minutes late for social engagements is acceptable.
- Business meetings may take place at breakfast or lunch; the host invites and pays.
- U.S. space requirements should be considered during negotiations. Standing too close (up to 18 inches) can cause discomfort for U.S. persons.
- Using cell phones and other electronic devices during meetings, though quite rude, is common. The practice is understandably irritating to people from other cultures.
- Remember that U.S. negotiators are uncomfortable with silence, tend to be informal, value honesty, and expect an agreement to be honored. They are not concerned with saving face and are quick to offer constructive criticism, which may cause discomfort or embarrassment for negotiators from other cultures.[48]

NOTES

PREFACE AND ACKNOWLEDGMENTS

1. Gregory Rodriguez, "Americans Fret over Another Deficit—Our Lack of Manners," *The Commercial Appeal*, April 17, 2011, V2.

INTRODUCTION

1. Joe Burris, "Overseas, We're Seen as Ugly Americans," *The Commercial Appeal*, October 22, 2006, M3, M4.

2. Emily Ross, "It Pays to Be Well Mannered," *BRW*, August 26–September 1, 2004, 64.

3. Gary Stoller, "Doing Business Abroad? Simple Faux Pas Can Sink You," *USA Today*, August 24, 2007, B1.

4. Ibid.

5. Michael Powell, *Behave Yourself! The Essential Guide to International Etiquette* (Guilford, CT: Globe Pequot Press, 2005), 5.

6. Nan Leaptrott, *Rules of the Game: Global Business Protocol* (Cincinnati, OH: Thomson Executive Press, 1996), 35.

7. Lillian H. Chaney and Jeanette S. Martin, *The Essential Guide to Business Etiquette* (Westport, CT: Praeger, 2007), 155.

CHAPTER 1: TRAVEL CUSTOMS AND TIPS

1. P. Christopher Earley and Elaine Mosakowski, "Cultural Intelligence," *Harvard Business Review* 82, no. 10 (2004): 139.

2. P. Christopher Earley and Randall S. Peterson, "The Elusive Cultural Chameleon: Cultural Intelligence as a New Approach to Intercultural Training for the Global Manager," *Academy of Management Learning and Education* 3 (2004): 110.

3. James Gray Jr., *The Winning Image* (New York: AMACOM, 1993), 68–71.

4. Sally Walker Davies, "Incessant Chatter Tops Travel Gripes," *The Commercial Appeal*, April 1, 2007, M3.

5. Roger E. Axtell and John P. Healy, *Do's and Taboos of Preparing for Your Trip Abroad* (New York: Wiley, 1994), 66.

6. Ibid., 70.

7. Ibid., 71–72.

8. Ibid., 73–74.

9. Ibid., 42–44.

10. Ibid., 49.

11. Susan Bixler, *The New Professional Image*, 2nd ed. (Avon, MA: Adams Media, 2005), 235.

12. Marshall Missner, *Ethics of the Business System* (Sherman Oaks, CA: Alfred, 1980), 5–6.

13. Roy J. Lewicki, David M. Saunders, and John W. Minton, *Essentials of Negotiation*, 3rd ed. (Homewood, IL: Irwin/McGraw-Hill Higher Education, 2003), 487.

14. Thomas Donaldson and Thomas W. Dunfee, "When Ethics Travel: The Promise and Peril of Global Business Ethics," *California Management Review* 41 (1999): 49, 52, 55–57.

15. Ibid., 49–50.

16. Missner, *Ethics of the Business System*, 5–6.

17. Lewicki, Saunders, and Minton, *Essentials of Negotiation*, 544–46.

18. Christopher Engholm and Diana Rowland, *International Excellence* (New York: Kodansha International, 1996), 130.

19. Thomas L. Friedman, *The World Is Flat* (New York: Farrar, Straus and Giroux, 2005), 110.

20. Christopher Engholm, *When Business East Meets Business West* (New York: Wiley, 1991), 238.

21. Engholm and Rowland, *International Excellence*, 133.

22. Engholm, *When Business East Meets Business West*, 239.

23. Roger E. Axtell, *The Do's and Taboos of International Trade* (New York: Wiley, 1994), 62.

24. Robert T. Moran, Philip R. Harris, and Sarah V. Moran, *Managing Cultural Differences*, 8th ed. (Burlington, MA: Elsevier Butterworth-Heinemann, 2011), 199.

25. Norine Dresser, *Multicultural Manners*, 2nd ed. (New York: Wiley, 2005), 95.

26. Roger E. Axtell, *The Do's and Taboos of Hosting International Visitors* (New York: Wiley, 1990), 152–53.

27. Larry A. Samovar and Richard E. Porter, *Communication between Cultures*, 5th ed. (Belmont, CA: Wadsworth/Thomson Learning, 2004), 295.

28. Lillian H. Chaney and Jeanette S. Martin, *Intercultural Business Communication*, 5th ed. (Upper Saddle River, NJ: Pearson/Prentice Hall, 2011), 74.

29. Barbara Davis and Roberta H. Krapels, "Culture Shock and Reverse Culture Shock: Developing Coping Skills," in *2005 National Business Education Association Yearbook*, ed. James C. Scott (Reston, VA: NBEA, 2005), 117.

30. Chaney and Martin, *Intercultural Business Communication*, 75.

31. Ibid., 76.

32. Ibid.

33. Ibid.

34. Ibid.

35. Lillian H. Chaney and Jeanette S. Martin, "Cultural Shock: An Intercultural Communication Problem" (paper presented at the annual convention of the Association for Business Communication, Montreal, Quebec, October 1993).

36. Chaney and Martin, *Intercultural Business Communication*, 76.

37. Gary Fontaine, "Skills for Successful International Assignments to, from and within Asia and the Pacific: Implications for Preparation, Support, and Training," *Management Decision* 35 (1997): 632.

38. Ibid.

39. Richard W. Brislin, *Cross-Cultural Encounters: Face-to-Face Interaction* (New York: Pergamon, 1981), 277–78.

40. Dresser, *Multicultural Manners*, 134–35.

41. Mary Murray Bosrock, *Put Your Best Foot Forward: Asia* (St. Paul, MN: International Education Systems, 1997), 136.

42. Richard D. Lewis, *When Cultures Collide: Leading across Cultures* (Boston: Nicholas Brealey, 2006), 96–97.

43. *CultureGrams, Brazil* (Ann Arbor, MI: ProQuest CSA, 2010), 100.

44. *CultureGrams, Canada* (Ann Arbor, MI: ProQuest CSA, 2010), 127.

45. *CultureGrams, China* (Ann Arbor, MI: ProQuest CSA, 2010), 148.

46. *CultureGrams, France* (Ann Arbor, MI: Proquest CSA, 2010), 248.

47. *CultureGrams, Germany* (Ann Arbor, MI: Proquest CSA, 2010), 267–68.

48. *CultureGrams, Japan* (Ann Arbor, MI: ProQuest CSA, 2010), 360.

49. *CultureGrams, Mexico* (Ann Arbor, MI: Proquest CSA, 2010), 467–68.

50. *CultureGrams, South Korea* (Ann Arbor, MI: ProQuest CSA, 2010), 684.

51. *CultureGrams, Taiwan* (Ann Arbor, MI: ProQuest CSA, 2010), 720.

52. *CultureGrams, United Kingdom* (Ann Arbor, MI: ProQuest CSA, 2010), 775–76.

53. Jeanette S. Martin and Lillian H. Chaney, *Passport to Success: The Essential Guide to Business Culture and Customs in America's Largest Trading Partners* (Westport, CT: Praeger, 2009), 54.

54. World Intellectual Property Organization, "WIPO-Administered Treaties," http://www.wipo.int/treaties/index.html.

CHAPTER 2: LANGUAGE, GREETINGS, INTRODUCTIONS, AND BUSINESS CARDS

1. Mary Kay Metcalf, "Etiquette Tips for Today's Global Economy: What to Know before You Go," *Direct Marketing* 61 (1999): 22.

2. Helen Spencer-Oatey, "Rapport Management: A Framework for Analysis," in *Culturally Speaking: Managing Rapport through Talk across Cultures*, ed. H. Spencer-Oatey (London: Continuum, 2000), 20.

3. Mary Murray Bosrock, *Put Your Best Foot Forward: USA* (St. Paul, MN: International Education Systems, 1999), 122.

4. Roger E. Axtell, *Do's and Taboos around the World* (White Plains, NY: Benjamin, 1993), 30–32.

5. Bosrock, *Put Your Best Foot Forward: USA*, 92.

6. Norine Dresser, *Multicultural Manners*, 2nd ed. (New York: Wiley, 2005), 189.

7. Elizabeth Devine and Nancy L. Braganti, *The Traveler's Guide to Latin American Customs and Manners* (New York: St. Martin's Griffin, 2000), 1; Elizabeth Devine and Nancy L. Braganti, *The Traveler's Guide to Asian Customs and Manners* (New York: St. Martin's Griffin, 1998), 14; Elizabeth Devine and Nancy L. Braganti, *The Traveler's Guide to African Customs and Manners* (New York: St. Martin's Griffin, 1995), 82, 131; Axtell, *Do's and Taboos around the World*, 7.

8. Dresser, *Multicultural Manners*, 189.

9. Larry A. Samovar and Richard E. Porter, *Communication between Cultures*, 5th ed. (Belmont, CA: Wadsworth/Thomson Learning, 2004), 216.

10. Ibid.

11. Utroska, "Management in Europe," 24.

12. Axtell, *Do's and Taboos around the World*, 8.

13. Carol Turkington, *The Complete Idiot's Guide to Cultural Etiquette* (Indianapolis, IN: Alpha Books, 1999), 181.

14. Robert T. Moran, Philip R. Harris, and Sarah V. Moran, *Managing Cultural Differences*, 8th ed. (Burlington, MA: Elsevier Butterworth-Heinemann, 2011), 305.

15. Michael Powell, *Behave Yourself! The Essential Guide to International Etiquette* (Guilford, CT: The Globe Pequot Press, 2005), 16.

16. Jeanette S. Martin and Lillian H. Chaney, *Passport to Success: The Essential Guide to Business Culture and Customs in America's Largest Trading Partners* (Westport, CT: Praeger, 2009), 54.

17. Roger E. Axtell, *Gestures* (New York: Wiley, 1998), 226–27.

18. Jan Yager, *Business Protocol: How to Survive and Succeed in Business*, 2nd ed. (Stamford, CT: Hanacroix Creek, 2001), 112.

19. Ann Marie Sabath, *International Business Etiquette: Asia and the Pacific Rim* (New York; ASJA Press, 2002), 34.

20. Samovar and Porter, *Communication between Cultures*, 215.

21. Yager, *Business Protocol*, 116.

22. Sabath, *International Business Etiquette: Asia and the Pacific Rim*, 89.

23. Nan Leaptrott, *Rules of the Game: Global Business Protocol* (Cincinnati, OH: Thomson Executive Press, 1996), 166.

24. Sabath, *International Business Etiquette: Asia and the Pacific Rim*, 156–57.

25. Christopher Engholm, *When Business East Meets Business West* (New York: Wiley, 1991), 94.

26. Leaptrott, *Rules of the Game*, 169.

27. Axtell, *Gestures*, 136.

CHAPTER 3: SOCIALIZING

1. Dennis A. Pitta, Hung-Gay Fung, and Steven Isberg, "Ethical Issues across Cultures: Managing the Differing Perspectives of China and the USA," *Journal of Consumer Marketing* 16 (1999): 248.

2. Erin C. Johnson, Amy L. Kristof-Brown, Annelies E. M. Van Vianen, Irene DePater, and Megan M. Rigsby, "Expatriate Social Ties: The Impact of Relationships with Comparable Others and Host Country Nationals," *Academy of Management Proceedings* (2002), H4.

3. Gary Fontaine, "Skills for Successful International Assignments to, from and within Asia and the Pacific: Implications for Preparation, Support, and Training," *Management Decision* 35 (1997): 640–41.

4. Roger E. Axtell, *Do's and Taboos of Hosting International Visitors* (New York: Wiley, 1990), 92.

5. Richard W. Brislin and Eugene S. Kim, "Cultural Diversity in People's Understanding and Uses of Time," *Applied Psychology: An International Review* 52 (2003): 365.

6. John Boslough, "The Enigma of Time," *National Geographic*, March 1990, 109.

7. Lawrence H. Wortzel, *Global Strategies Management* (New York: Wiley, 1985), 496.

8. Nadeem M. Firoz and Taghi Ramin, "Understanding Cultural Variables Is Critical to Success in International Business," *International Journal of Management* 21 (2004): 309.

9. Donald A. Ball and Wendell H. McCulloch Jr., *International Business: The Challenge of Global Completion* (Boston: Irwin, 2001), 276.

10. Brislin and Kim, "Cultural Diversity in People's Understanding and Uses of Time," 367–68.

11. Ibid., 368–71.

12. Ibid., 371–72.

13. Carol Ezzell, "Clocking Cultures," *Scientific American* 287, no. 3 (September 2002): 74–75.

14. John S. Mbiti, *African Religions and Philosophy* (New York: Praeger, 1969), 17.

15. Axtell, *Do's and Taboos of Hosting International Visitors*, 93.

16. Yuji Tsunda, *Language Inequality and Distortion* (Philadelphia: John Benjamin, 1986), 116.

17. June Cotte and S. Ratneshwar, "Timestyle and Leisure Decisions," *Journal of Leisure Research* 33 (2001): 396–409.

18. Brislin and Kim, "Cultural Diversity in People's Understanding and Uses of Time," 378–79.

19. David Victor, *International Business Communication* (New York: HarperCollins, 1992), 233.

20. Edward T. Hall, *The Silent Language* (Garden City, NY: Doubleday, 1959), 24.

21. Marjabelle Young Stewart, *The New Etiquette* (New York: St. Martin's, 1997), 246–47.

22. Christopher Engholm, *When Business East Meets Business West* (New York: Wiley, 1991), 228.

23. Mary Murray Bosrock, *Put Your Best Foot Forward: Europe* (St. Paul, MN: International Education Systems, 1995), 153; Mary Murray Bosrock, *Put Your Best Foot Forward: South America* (St. Paul, MN: International Education Systems, 1997), 213–14; Mary Murray Bosrock, *Put Your Best Foot Forward: Asia* (St. Paul, Minn.: International Education Systems, 1997), 136.

24. Cynthia Barnum and Natasha Wolniansky, "Glitches in Global Gift Giving," *Management Review* 78, no. 4 (April 1989): 61–63.

25. Bosrock, *Put Your Best Foot Forward: Asia*, 233–34.

26. Engholm, *When Business East Meets Business West*, 227.

27. Roger E. Axtell, *Do's and Taboos around the World* (New York: Wiley, 1993), 115–45; Stewart, *The New Etiquette*, 246–49.

28. Robert T. Moran, Philip R. Harris, and Sarah V. Moran, *Managing Cultural Differences*, 8th ed. (Burlington, MA: Elsevier Butterworth-Heinemann, 2011), 12–13.

29. Paula Caligiuri and Rosalie Tung, "Comparing the Success of Male and Female Expatriates from a US-based Multinational Company," *International Journal of Human Resource Management* 10 (1999): 778.

30. Paula Caligiuri and Mila Lazarova, "A Model for the Influence of Social Interaction and Social Support on Female Expatriates' Cross-Cultural Adjustment," *The International Journal of Human Resource Management* 13 (2002): 764.

31. Ibid.

32. Ibid., 765.

33. Ibid.

34. Ibid., 766.

35. Rosalie L. Tung, "American Expatriates Abroad: From Neophytes to Cosmopolitans," *Journal of World Business* 33 (1998): 136.

36. Nancy K. Napier and Sully Taylor, "Experiences of Women Professionals Abroad: Comparisons across Japan, China, and Turkey," *The International Journal of Human Resource Management* 13 (2002): 843.

37. Tung, "American Expatriates Abroad," 130.

38. Camille P. Schuster and Michael J. Copeland, "Executive Insights: Global Business Exchanges—Similarities and Differences around the World," *Journal of International Marketing* 7 (1999): 67–68.

39. Jeanette S. Martin and Lillian H. Chaney, *Passport to Success: The Essential Guide to Business Culture and Customs in America's Largest Trading Partners* (Westport, CT: Praeger, 2009), 48–49.

40. Michael Powell, *Behave Yourself! The Essential Guide to International Etiquette* (Guilford, CT: Globe Pequot Press, 2005), 18.

41. Martin and Chaney, *Passport to Success*, 49.

42. Ibid., 53.

43. Ann Marie Sabath, *International Business Etiquette: Latin America* (Franklin Lakes, NJ: Career Press, 2000), 60.

44. Pitta, Fung, and Isberg, "Ethical Issues across Cultures," 16.

45. Bosrock, *Put Your Best Foot Forward: South America*, 141, 206.

46. Elizabeth Devine and Nancy L. Braganti, *The Traveler's Guide to Asian Customs and Manners* (New York: St. Martin's Griffin, 1998), 14.

47. John Mole, *Mind Your Manners* (Sonoma, CA: Nicholas Brealey, 1995), 4.

48. Peggy Kenna and Sondra Lacy, *Business Japan: A Practical Guide to Understanding Japanese Business Culture* (Chicago: Passport Books, 1994), 28.

49. Samovar and Porter, *Communication between Cultures*, 217.

50. Letitia Baldrige, *Letitia Baldrige's New Complete Guide to Executive Manners* (New York: Rawson Associates, 1993), 265–66.

51. Nan Leaptrot, *Rules of the Game: Global Business Protocol* (Cincinnati, OH: Thomson Executive, 1996),167.

52. Ibid.

53. Bosrock, *Put Your Best Foot Forward: Asia*, 444–50.

54. Ibid., 481–87.

55. Leaptrott, *Rules of the Game*, 327.

CHAPTER 4: GESTURES AND OTHER NONVERBAL COMMUNICATORS

1. Edward T. Hall and Mildred R. Hall, *Understanding Cultural Differences* (Yarmouth, ME: Intercultural Press, 1990), xx.

2. Roger E. Axtell, *Gestures: The Do's and Taboos of Body Language around the World* (New York: Wiley, 1998), 17.

3. Ibid.

4. Gordon R. Wainwright, *Body Language* (Lincolnwood, IL: NTC/ Contemporary Publishing, 1999), 51–52.

5. David A. Victor, *International Business Communication* (New York: HarperCollins, 1992), 218.

6. James C. Scott, "The Colorful World of International Business," *Business Education Forum* 57 (October 2002): 40.

7. Thomas J. Madden, Kelly Hewett, and Martin S. Roth, "Managing Images in Different Cultures: A Cross-National Study of Color Meanings and Preferences," *Journal of International Marketing* 8 (2000): 90–107.

8. Norine Dresser, *Multicultural Manners* (New York: Wiley, 2005), 68–69.

9. Ibid.

10. Marc Gobé, *Emotional Branding: The New Paradigm for Connecting Brands to People* (New York: Allworth Press, 2001), 79.

11. Dresser, *Multicultural Manners*, 63.

12. David A. Ricks, *Blunders in International Business*, 4th ed. (Malden, MA: Blackwell, 2006), 32–33.

13. Scott, "The Colorful World of International Business," 42.

14. Ricks, *Blunders in International Business*, 32–33.

15. Wainwright, *Body Language*, 134.

16. Lillian H. Chaney and Jeanette S. Martin, *Intercultural Business Communication*, 5th ed. (Upper Saddle River, NJ: Prentice Hall, 2011), 121.

17. Ibid., 120.

18. Chuck Shepherd, "News of the Weird," *The Times*, January 17, 2007, 28.

19. Larry A. Samovar and Richard E. Porter, *Communication between Cultures*, 5th ed. (Belmont, CA: Wadsworth/Thomson Learning, 2004), 187–88.

20. Ibid.

21. Fred E. Jandt, *An Introduction to Intercultural Communication*, 4th ed. (Thousand Oaks, CA: Sage, 2004), 136.

22. Axtell, *Gestures*, 6.

23. Everett M. Rogers and Thomas M. Steinfatt, *Intercultural Communication*, (Long Grove, IL: Waveland Press, Inc., 1999), 84–85.

24. Joe Burris, "Overseas, We're Seen as Ugly Americans," *The Commercial Appeal*, October 22, 2006, M4.

25. John T. Molloy, *New Women's Dress for Success* (New York: Warner Books, Inc., 1996), 135.

26. Dresser, *Multicultural Manners*, 62.

27. Donald W. Klopf and James C. McCroskey, *Intercultural Communication Encounters* (Boston: Pearson Education, 2007), 228.

28. Dresser, *Multicultural Manners*, 193.

29. Lillian H. Chaney, "Curb Appeal," *OfficePro* 66, no. 6 (August–September 2004): 28–29; Lillian H. Chaney and Julie A. Lyden, "Impression Management: The Office Environment," *Supervision*, April 1996, 5.

30. Victor, *International Business Communication*, 222–24.

31. Ricks, *Blunders in International Business*, 30.

32. Victor, *International Business Communication*, 222–24.

33. Dresser, *Multicultural Manners*, 52.

34. Wainwright, *Body Language*, 157–58.

35. James Poon Teng Fatt, "Nonverbal Communication and Business Success," *Management Research News* 21 (1998): 4–5.

36. Ibid., 4.

37. Wainwright, *Body Language*, 157–58.

38. Jeanette S. Martin and Lillian H. Chaney, *Passport to Success: The Essential Guide to Business Culture and Customs in America's Largest Trading Partners* (Westport, CT: Praeger, 2009), 53.

39. Terri Morrison and Wayne Conaway, *Kiss, Bow, or Shake Hands: Latin America* (Avon, MA: Adams Media, 2007), 49.

40. Martin and Chaney, *Passport to Success*, 53.

41. Ibid.

CHAPTER 5: DRESS AND APPEARANCE

1. Mary Mitchell, *The First Five Minutes: How to Make a Great First Impression in Any Business Situation* (New York: Wiley, 1998), xiii.

2. Victoria Seitz, *Your Executive Image* (Holbrook, MA: Adams Media, 2000), 36.

3. Cash (1985) and Harris et al. (1982) as cited in Richard J. Ilkka, "Applicant Appearance and Selection Decision Making: Revitalizing Employment Interview Education," *Business Communication Quarterly* 58 (September 1995): 16.

4. Michael Korda, *Power: How to Get It, How to Use It* (New York: Random House, 1975), 56.

5. Patricia A. Thompson and Brian H. Kleiner, "How to Read Nonverbal Communication," *The Bulletin*, September 1992, 82.

6. Sherry Maysonave, *Casual Power: How to Power Up Your Nonverbal Communication and Dress Down for Success* (Austin, TX: Bright Books, 1999), 3.

7. Karyn Repinski, *The Complete Idiot's Guide to Successful Dressing* (New York: Alpha Books, 1999), 7.

8. Mitchell, *The First Five Minutes*, 58–59.

9. John T. Molloy, *New Women's Dress for Success* (New York: Warner, 1996), 61–62; Seitz, *Your Executive Image*, 55; Susan Bixler, *The New Professional Image*, 2nd ed. (Avon, MA: Adams Media, 2005), 46, 58.

10. Susan Morem, *How to Gain the Professional Edge* (New York: Facts on File, 2005), 61–64.

11. Bixler, *The New Professional Image*, 55.

12. Fred E. Jandt, *An Introduction to Intercultural Communication*, 4th ed. (Thousand Oaks, CA: Sage, 2004), 140.

13. Molloy, *New Women's Dress for Success*, 61–62; Seitz, *Your Executive Image*, 55; Bixler, *The New Professional Image*, 58.

14. Repinski, *The Complete Idiot's Guide to Successful Dressing*, 28–29.

15. Mitchell, *The First Five Minutes*, 35.

16. Nancy Tuckerman and Nancy Dunnan, *The Amy Vanderbilt Complete Book of Etiquette* (New York: Doubleday, 1995), 492.

210 NOTES

17. Barbara Pachter and Marjorie Brody, *Complete Business Etiquette Handbook* (Paramus, NJ: Prentice Hall, 1995), 316.

18. Repinski, *The Complete Idiot's Guide to Successful Dressing*, 196–99.

19. Stephanie Armour, "Companies Rethink Casual Clothes," *USA Today*, June 27, 2000, 2A.

20. John T. Molloy, *New Women's Dress for Success* (New York: Warner, 1996), 213.

21. Graham Button and Joshua Levine, "No Bathrobes, Please," *Forbes*, November 6, 1995, 130.

22. Richard B. Elsberry, "Clothes Call," *Office Systems* 14 (September 1997): 25, 60.

23. Pachter and Brody, *Complete Business Etiquette Handbook*, 317.

24. Bixler, *The New Professional Image*, 234.

25. Repinski, *The Complete Idiot's Guide to Successful Dressing*, 194–96.

26. Bixler, *The New Professional Image*, 234.

27. Sue Fox, *Etiquette for Dummies* (Foster City, CA: IDG Books Worldwide, 1999), 294.

28. Letitia Baldrige, *Letitia Baldrige's New Manners for New Times* (New York: Scribner, 2003), 164–72.

29. Mary Murray Bosrock, *Put Your Best Foot Forward: South America* (St. Paul, MN: International Education Systems, 1997), 105–7.

30. Tuckerman and Dunnan, *The Amy Vanderbilt Complete Book of Etiquette*, 78–79.

31. Jan Yager, *Business Protocol*, 2nd ed. (Stamford, CT: Hannacroix Creek Books, 2001), 111.

32. Mary Murray Bosrock, *Put Your Best Foot Forward: Asia* (St. Paul, MN: International Education Systems, 1997), 126.

33. Mary Murray Bosrock, *Put Your Best Foot Forward: Europe* (St. Paul, MN: International Education Systems, 1995), 84–85.

34. Norine Dresser, *Multicultural Manners* (New York: Wiley, 1996), 54–55.

35. Carol Turkington, *The Complete Idiot's Guide to Cultural Etiquette* (Indianapolis, IN: Alpha Books, 1999), 309–10.

36. Elizabeth Devine and Nancy L. Braganti, *The Travelers' Guide to Middle Eastern and North African Customs and Manners* (New York: St. Martin's Press, 1991), 194.

37. Terri Morrison and Wayne A. Conaway, *Kiss, Bow, or Shake Hands*, 2nd ed. (Avon, MA: Adams Media, 2006), 158.

38. Norine Dresser, *Multicultural Manners*, 2nd ed. (New York: Wiley, 2005), 56.

39. Jeanette S. Martin and Lillian H. Chaney, *Passport to Success: The Essential Guide to Business Culture and Customs in America's Largest Trading Partners* (Westport, CT: Praeger, 2009), 50; Terri Morrison and Wayne A. Conaway, *Kiss, Bow, or Shake Hands: Latin America* (Avon, MA: Adams Media, 2007), 50.

CHAPTER 6: CULTURAL ATTITUDES AND BEHAVIORS

1. David A. Victor, *International Business Communication* (New York: HarperCollins, 1992), 78–79.

2. Ibid., 79.

3. Alison R. Lanier, *Living in the U.S.A.*, 5th ed. (Yarmouth, ME: Intercultural Press, 1996), 26.

4. Larry A. Samovar and Richard E. Porter, *Intercultural Communication: A Reader*, 10th ed. (Belmont, CA: Wadsworth/Thomson Learning, 2003), 119.

5. Lillian H. Chaney and Jeanette S. Martin, *Intercultural Business Communication*, 5th ed. (Upper Saddle River, NJ: Pearson Prentice Hall, 2011), 38.

6. Ibid., 42.

7. Mary Murray Bosrock, *Put Your Best Foot Forward: U.S.A.* (St. Paul, MN: International Education Systems, 1999), 57–59.

8. Fred E. Jandt, *An Introduction to Intercultural Communication*, 4th ed. (Thousand Oaks, CA: Sage, 2004), 237.

9. Gary Althen, *American Ways: A Guide for Foreigners in the United States*, 2nd ed. (Yarmouth, ME: Intercultural Press, 2003), 119.

10. Ann Marie Sabath, *International Business Etiquette: Asia and the Pacific Rim* (New York: ASJA Press, 2002), 10.

11. Norine Dresser, *Multicultural Manners* (New York: Wiley, 1996), 133–34.

12. Althen, *American Ways*, 101–2.

13. Ibid., 102–9.

14. Dresser, *Multicultural Manners*, 48–49.

15. Lanier, *Living in the U.S.A.*, 163–65.

16. Althen, *American Ways*, 244.

17. Dresser, *Multicultural Manners*, 40–41.

18. Donald W. Klopf, *Intercultural Encounters*, 2nd ed. (Englewood, CO: Morton, 1991), 121–22.

19. Althen, *American Ways*, 242–43.

20. Donald R. Utroska, "Management in Europe: More than Just Etiquette," *Management Review* 81 (November 1992): 24.

21. Fons Trompenaars and C. Hampden-Turner, *Riding the Waves of Culture*, 2nd ed. (New York: McGraw-Hill, 1998), 70–71.

22. Bosrock, *Put Your Best Foot Forward: USA*, 115–16.

23. Joe Griffith, *Speaker's Library of Business Stories, Anecdotes, and Humor* (Englewood Cliffs, NJ: Prentice Hall, 1990), 376.

24. Lennie Copeland and Lewis Griggs, *Going International: How to Make Friends and Deal Effectively in the Global Marketplace* (New York: Penguin Books, 1985), 128.

25. International Labor Organization, *Yearbook of Labour Statistics 2003*, 62nd ed. (Geneva, Switzerland: ILO Publications, 2003).

26. Mary Murray Bosrock, *Put Your Best Foot Forward: South America* (St. Paul, MN: International Education Systems, 1997), 221.

27. Utroska, *Management Review* 81, 23.

28. Althen, *American Ways*, 191.

29. Ibid.

30. William H. Bonner and Lillian H. Chaney, *Communicating Effectively in an Information Age*, 2nd ed. (Mason, OH: Thomson Learning, 2004), 365.

31. David Victor, *International Business Communication* (New York: HarperCollins, 1992), 96–99.

32. Larry A. Samovar and Richard E. Porter, *Communication between Cultures*, 5th ed. (Belmont, CA: Wadsworth/Thomson Learning, 2004), 117–18.

33. Robert T. Moran, Philip R. Harris, and Sarah V. Moran, *Managing Cultural Differences*, 8th ed. (Burlington, MA: Elsevier Butterworth-Heinemann, 2011), 127–48.

34. Althen, *American Ways*, 14–15.

35. Samovar and Porter, *Intercultural Communication*, 72–73.

36. Lanier, *Living in the U.S.A.*, 24–26.

37. Roger E. Axtell, *Gestures: The Do's and Taboos of Body Language around the World* (New York: Wiley, 1998), 11.

38. Carol Turkington, *The Complete Idiot's Guide to Cultural Etiquette* (India, IN: Alpha Books, 1999), 56, 68, 217, 255, 266, 321, 331.

39. Althen, *American Ways*, 231.

40. Ibid., 232–33.

41. *CultureGrams* (Ann Arbor, MI: ProQuest CSA, 2010): *Brazil*, 97–100; *Canada*, 125–28; *China*, 145–48; *France*, 245–48; *Germany*, 265–68; *Japan*, 357–60; *Mexico*, 465–68; *South Korea*, 681–84; *Taiwan*, 717–20; *United Kingdom*, 773–76.

42. Terri Morrison and Wayne A. Conaway, *Kiss, Bow, or Shake Hands: Latin America* (Avon, MA: Adams Media, 2007), 45.

43. International Labor Organization, *Yearbook of Labour Statistics 2007*, 66th Issue (Geneva Switzerland: ILO Publications, 2007).

CHAPTER 7: DINING AND TIPPING CUSTOMS

1. Norine Dresser, *Multicultural Manners*, 2nd ed. (New York: Wiley, 2005), 79–80.

2. Ibid., 80–81.

3. Roger E. Axtell, *Do's and Taboos around the World* (New York: Wiley, 1993), 10.

4. Ibid., 86.

5. Susan Bixler and Lisa Scherrer Dugan, *Five Steps to Professional Presence* (Avon, MA: Adams Media, 2001), 200.

6. Maurice E. Schweitzer and Jeffrey L. Kerr, "Bargaining under the Influence: The Role of Alcohol in Negotiations," *Academy of Management Executive* 14, no. 2 (2000): 47–57.

7. Norine Dresser, *Multicultural Manners* (New York: Wiley, 1996), 87.

8. Kevin Brass, "Success Starts with Karaoke," *NWA World Traveler*, March 2005, 36.

9. Elizabeth Devine and Nancy L. Braganti, *The Travelers' Guide to Middle Eastern and North African Customs and Manners* (New York: St. Martin's Press, 1991), 44.

10. Letitia Baldrige, *Letitia Baldrige's New Manners for New Times* (New York: Scribner, 2003), 150–51.

11. Ibid., 152–54.

12. Gary Stoller, "Tipping Can Trip Up Any Globe Trotter," *USA Today*, September 11, 2007, 6B.

13. Jeanette S. Martin and Lillian H. Chaney, *Passport to Success: The Essential Guide to Business Culture and Customs in America's Largest Trading Partners* (Westport, CT: Praeger, 2009); Michael Powell, *Behave Yourself! The Essential Guide to International Etiquette* (Guilford, CT: Globe Pequot Press, 2005), 18.

14. Stoller, "Tipping Can Trip Up Any Globe Trotter," 6B.

CHAPTER 8: CONVERSATIONAL CUSTOMS AND MANNERS

1. Gary Althen, *American Ways: A Guide for Foreigners in the United States* (Yarmouth, ME: Intercultural Press, 2003), 40.

2. Richard D. Lewis, *When Cultures Collide: Leading across Cultures*, 3rd ed. (Boston: Nicholas Brealey, 2006), 89.

3. Gary Stoller, "Doing Business Abroad? Simple Faux Pas Can Sink You," *USA Today*, August 24, 2007, B1.

4. Althen, *American Ways*, 36.

5. Norine Dresser, *Multicultural Manners*, 2nd ed. (New York: Wiley, 2005), 20–21.

6. Ivan Misner, "Networking Etiquette Around the World: How Not to Embarrass Yourself When Networking in Another Country," *Business Credit* 108, no. 8 (2006): 42.

7. Lewis, *When Cultures Collide*, 13.

8. George Barbour, "Want to Be a Successful Manager? Now That's a Laughing Matter!" *Public Management* 80 (July 1998): 6.

9. Lewis, *When Cultures Collide*, 14–15.

10. Ibid., 15.

11. Linda Farrell, "You've Got to Be Kidding: Humor as a Fundamental Management Tool," *Records Management Quarterly* 32 (1998): 6.

12. Mary Murray Bosrock, *Put Your Best Foot Forward: South America* (St. Paul, MN: International Education Systems, 1997), 207–8; Ann Marie Sabath, *International Business Etiquette: Latin America* (Franklin Lakes, NJ: Career Press, 2000), 55.

CHAPTER 9: ORAL AND WRITTEN COMMUNICATION CUSTOMS AND ETIQUETTE

1. Wei-lin Dou and George William Clark Jr., "Appreciating the Diversity in Multicultural Communication Styles," *Business Forum* 24 (1999): 58.

2. Gary P. Ferraro, *The Cultural Dimension of International Business*, 4th ed. (Upper Saddle River, NJ: Prentice Hall, 2001), 20.

3. Larry A. Samovar and Richard E. Porter, *Intercultural Communication: A Reader*, 10th ed. (Belmont, CA: Wadsworth, 2002), 153; Gary R. Weaver, "American Identity Movements: Cross Cultural Confrontations," in *Culture, Communications, and Conflict*, ed. G. R. Weaver (Needham Heights, MA: Simon & Schuster, 1998), 72–77.

4. Carley H. Dodd, *Dynamics of Intercultural Communication*, 5th ed. (Boston: McGraw Hill, 1998), 121.

5. Samovar and Porter, *Intercultural Communication*, 153.

6. Dorothy I. Riddle and Z. D. Lanham, "Internationalizing Written Business English: 20 Propositions for Native English Speakers," *Journal of Language for International Business* 1 (Winter 1984–1985): 1–11.

7. Angela Sinickas, "Avoiding Global Misunderstandings," *SCM* 8 (2004): 2–3.

8. Dou and Clark, "Appreciating the Diversity in Multicultural Communication Styles," 54–55.

9. Mi Young Park, W. Tracy Dillon, and Kenneth L. Mitchell, "Korean Business Letters: Strategies for Effective Complaints in Cross-Cultural Communication," *Journal of Business Communication* 35 (1998): 340.

10. Mary A. DeVries, *Internationally Yours* (Boston: Houghton Mifflin, 1994), 3.

11. Roger N. Conaway and W. J. Wardrope, "Communication in Latin America," *Business Communication Quarterly* 67 (2004): 472.

12. Shoji Azuma, "How Do Japanese Say 'No' in the Written Mode?" *Academy of Managerial Communications Journal* 2 (1998): 27.

13. Iris I. Varner, "A Comparison of American and French Business Correspondence," *Journal of Business Communication* 25 (1988): 59.

14. Roger E. Axtell, *Do's and Don'ts of Hosting International Visitors* (New York: Wiley, 1990), 93.

15. Conaway and Wardrope, "Communication in Latin America," 471.

16. Ibid.

17. Varner, "A Comparison of American and French Business Correspondence," 59.

18. Mary Murray Bosrock, *Put Your Best Foot Forward: Europe* (St. Paul, MN: International Education Systems, 1995): 54.

19. Nadeem M. Firoz and Taghi Ramin, "Understanding Cultural Variables Is Critical to Success in International Business," *International Journal of Management* 21 (2004): 309.

20. John Bermont, *How to Europe: The Complete Travelers Handbook* (Midland, MI: Murphy & Broad, 2004), 416.

21. *Names of Big Numbers*, http://www.unc.edu/~rowlett/units/large.html

22. Alexander Nicoll, "Misplaced Comma Costs Lockheed $70m," *Financial Times*, June 18, 1999, 1.

23. Thomas L. Friedman, *The World Is Flat* (New York: Farrar, Straus and Giroux, 2005), 160–61.

24. Mary Mitchell, *The Complete Idiot's Guide to Etiquette* (New York: Alpha Books, 2000), 164.

25. Angela Sinickas, "Avoiding Global Misunderstandings," *SCM* 8 (2004): 2.

26. Charlotte Ford, *21st-Century Etiquette* (Guilford, CT: Penguin Putnam, 2003), 22–23; Audrey Glassman, *Can I FAX a Thank-You Note?* (New York: Berkley, 1998), 71–72.

27. Charles Ess, *Culture, Technology, Communication: Towards an Intercultural Global Village* (New York: State University of New York Press, 2001), 17.

28. Richard T. Watson, Teck Hua Ho, and K. S. Raman, "Culture: A Fourth Dimension of Group Support Systems," *Communications of the ACM* 37 (1994): 45–55.

29. Linjun Huang, Ming-Te Lu, and Bo K. Wong, "The Impact of Power Distance on Email Acceptance: Evidence from the PRC," *Journal of Computer Information Systems* 44 (2003): 98.

30. Ann Marie Sabath, *Business Etiquette: 101 Ways to Conduct Business with Charm and Savvy* (Franklin Lakes, NJ: Career Press, 1998), 57.

31. Mary Munter, Priscilla S. Rogers, and Jone Rymer, "Business E-Mail: Guidelines for Users," *Business Communication Quarterly* 66 (2003): 27, 28, 33.

32. Nat Segaloff, *The Everything Etiquette Book* (Holbrook, MA: Adams Media, 1998), 169.

33. Samantha Miller, *E-Mail Etiquette* (New York: Warner Books, 2001), 112.

34. Ibid., 96.

35. Sharon B. Kenton and Deborah Valentine, *Crosstalk: Communicating in a Multicultural Workplace* (Upper Saddle River, NJ: Prentice Hall, 1997), 9.

36. Internet Penetration Statistics, Internet Penetration Rate—Top 20 Countries, http://internet.worldstats.com.

37. Michael Powell, *Behave Yourself! The Essential Guide to International Etiquette* (Guilford, CT: Globe Pequot Press, 2005), 16.

38. Mary A. DeVries, *Internationally Yours: Writing and Communicating Successfully in Today's Global Marketplace* (Boston: Houghton Mifflin Company, 1994), 23.

39. Robert T. Moran, Philip R. Harris, and Sarah V. Moran, *Managing Cultural Differences*, 7th ed. (Burlington, MA: Elsevier Butterworth-Heinemann, 2007), 381.

40. Suburo Haneda and Hirosuke Shima, "Japanese Communication Behavior as Reflected in Letter Writing," *Journal of Business Communication* 19 (1982): 19–21.

41. Ryuko Kubota, "A Reevaluation of the Uniqueness of Japanese Written Discourse," *Written Communication* 14 (1997): 472.

42. Detmar Straub, "The Effect of Culture on IT Diffusion: E-Mail and FAX in Japan and the U.S." *Information Systems Research* 5 (1994): 23–47.

43. Nan Leaptrott, *Rules of the Game: Global Business Protocol* (Cincinnati, OH: Thomson Executive Press, 1996), 166.

44. Ibid.

45. Ibid., 167.

46. Ibid., 169

47. James C. Scott, "Dear ???: Understanding British Forms of Address," *Business Communication Quarterly* 61 (1998): 53.

48. Angela Sinickas, "Avoiding Global Misunderstandings," *SCM* 8 (2004): 2.

49. Scott, "Dear ???," 52–54.

CHAPTER 10: ETIQUETTE FOR INTERNATIONAL BUSINESSWOMEN

1. Melissa Leonard, "Avoid the 'Fatal' Faux Pas," *ABA Banking Journal* 96, no. 5 (2004): 10.

2. Ibid., 14.

3. Mary Murray Bosrock, *Put Your Best Foot Forward: Mexico/Canada* (St. Paul, MN: International Education Systems, 1995), 71.

4. Roger E. Axtell, Tami Briggs, Margaret Corcoran, and Mary Beth Lamb, *Do's and Taboos around the World for Women in Business* (New York: John Wiley & Sons, 1997), 28.

5. Tracey Wilen, *International Business: A Basic Guide for Women* (n.p.: Xlibris Corporation, 2000), 176.

6. Anne Fisher, "Overseas, U.S. Businesswomen May Have the Edge," *Fortune*, September 28, 1998, 304.

7. Wilen, *International Business: A Basic Guide for Women*, 31–32.

8. Sheida Hodge, *Global Smarts: The Art of Communicating and Deal Making Anywhere in the World* (New York: John Wiley & Sons, 2000), 182.

9. Nan Leaptrott, *Rules of the Game: Global Business Protocol* (Cincinnati, OH: Thomson Executive Press, 1996), 218.

10. Bosrock, *Put Your Best Foot Forward: Mexico/Canada*, 72; Wilen, *International Business: A Basic Guide for Women*, 31–32.

11. Axtell, Briggs, Corcoran, and Lamb, *Do's and Taboos around the World for Women in Business*, 30.

12. Ibid., 30–31.

13. Ibid., 33–34.

14. Ibid., 31–32.

15. Mary Murray Bosrock, *Put Your Best Foot Forward: South America* (St. Paul, MN: International Education Systems, 1997), 138.

16. Ibid., 34.

17. Ibid., 35–40.

18. Christina Binkley, "Where Yellow's a Faux Pas and White Is Death," *Wall Street Journal*, December 6, 2007, D4.

19. Letitia Baldrige, *Letitia Baldrige's New Complete Guide to Executive Manners* (New York: Rawson Associates, 1993), 219.

20. Hodge, *Global Smarts*, 182.

21. Axtell, Briggs, Corcoran, and Lamb, *Do's and Taboos Around the World for Women in Business*, 22–23.

22. Ivan Misner, "Networking Etiquette around the World: How Not to Embarrass Yourself When Networking in Another Country," *Business Credit*, September 2006, 43.

23. Wilen, *International Business: A Basic Guide for Women*, 92.

24. Ibid., 92–93 Lillian H. Chaney and Jeanette S. Martin, *Intercultural Business Communication*,

5th ed. (Upper Saddle River, New Jersey: Prentice Hall, 2011), 162-163.

25. Chaney and Martin, *Intercultural Business Communication*, 166–67.

26. Ibid., 169–71.

27. Ibid., 144–45.

28. Marlene L. Rossman, *The International Businesswoman of the 1990s* (New York: Praeger, 1990), 148.

29. Gary Althen, *American Ways*, 2nd ed. (Yarmouth, ME: Intercultural Press, 2003), 182.

30. Ibid., 181.

31. Axtell, Briggs, Corcoran, and Lamb, *Do's and Taboos Around the World for Women in Business*, 12–13.

32. Wilen, *International Business: A Basic Guide for Women*, 152–53.

33. Ibid., 150.

34. Axtell, Briggs, Corcoran, and Lamb, *Do's and Taboos Around the World for Women in Business*, 11.

35. Ibid., 162.

36. Ibid.

37. Robert T. Moran, Philip R. Harris, and Sarah V. Moran, *Managing Cultural Differences*, 8th ed. (Burlington, MA: Elsevier Butterworth-Heinemann, 2011), 310.

38. Ann Marie Sabath, *International Business Etiquette: Latin America* (Franklin Lakes, NJ: Career Press, 2000), 62.

39. Ibid., 53.

40. Ibid., 58.

41. Bosrock, *Put Your Best Foot Forward: Mexico/Canada*, 162–63.

42. Fred E. Jandt, *An Introduction to Intercultural Communication*, 4th ed. (Thousand Oaks, CA: Sage Publications, 2004), 269.

43. Ann Marie Sabath, *International Business Etiquette: Asia and the Pacific Rim* (New York: ASJA Press, 2002), 38, 40.

44. Ibid., 38.

45. Chaney and Martin, *Intercultural Business Communication*, 66.

46. Ann Marie Sabath, *International Business Etiquette: Europe* (Franklin Lakes, NJ: Career Press, 1999), 109.

47. Ibid., 112.

48. Jeanette S. Martin and Lillian H. Chaney, *Passport to Success: The Essential Guide to Business Culture and Customs in America's Largest Trading Partners* (Westport, CT: Praeger, 2009), 101.

49. Sabath, *International Business Etiquette: Europe*, 126.

50. Sabath, *International Business Etiquette: Asia and the Pacific Rim*, 89, 93.

51. Bosrock, *Put Your Best Foot Forward: Mexico/Canada*, 133–35.

52. Ibid., 101.

53. Sabath, *International Business Etiquette: Asia and the Pacific Rim*, 161, 164.

54. Ibid., 178, 180.

55. Sabath, *International Business Etiquette: Europe*, 85, 89.

56. Gregory Karp, "Female Managers Earn Less, Report Says," *The Commercial Appeal*, October 3, 2010, C1.

57. Alison R. Lanier, *Living in the U.S.A.*, 5th ed. (Yarmouth, ME: Intercultural Press, 1996), 72.

58. Mary Murray Bosrock, *Put Your Best Foot Forward: USA* (St. Paul, MN: International Education Systems, 1999), 244–45.

CHAPTER 11: INTERNATIONAL NEGOTIATION ETIQUETTE

1. Lillian H. Chaney and Jeanette S. Martin, *Intercultural Business Communication*, 5th ed. (Upper Saddle River, NJ: Prentice Hall, 2011), 205.

2. Sheida Hodge, *Global Smarts: The Art of Communicating and Deal Making Anywhere in the World* (New York: John Wiley & Sons, 2000), 189.

3. Chaney and Martin, *Intercultural Business Communication*, 93.

4. Raymond Cohen, *Negotiating across Cultures* (Washington, DC: United States Institute of Peace Press, 1991), 160–61.

5. Chaney and Martin, *Intercultural Business Communication*, 206.

6. Hodge, *Global Smarts*, 215–16.

7. Lillian H. Chaney and Jeanette S. Martin, *The Essential Guide to Business Etiquette* (Westport, CT: Praeger, 2007), 106.

8. Chaney and Martin, *Intercultural Business Communication*, 206–7.

9. David A. Ricks, *Blunders in International Business*, 3rd ed. (Malden, MA: Blackwell, 1999), 78.

10. Ibid.

11. Roger E. Axtell, Tami Briggs, Margaret Corcoran, and Mary Beth Lamb, *Do's and Taboos around the World for Women in Business* (New York: John Wiley & Sons, Inc., 1997), 67.

12. Cohen, *Negotiating across Cultures*, xi.

13. Ricks, *Blunders in International Business*, 78.

14. Nan Leaptrott, *Rules of the Game: Global Business Protocol* (Cincinnati, OH: Thomson Executive Press, 1996), 48.

15. David Altany, "Culture Clash," in *Culture, Communication and Conflict: Readings in Intercultural Relations*, edited by Gary R. Weaver, 2nd ed. (Needham Heights, MA: Simon & Schuster, 1998), 543.

16. Richard D. Lewis, *When Cultures Collide: Leading Across Cultures*, 3rd ed. (Boston: Nicholas Brealey International, 2006), 95.

17. Ibid., 153–54.

18. Ibid., 14–15.

19. Terri Morrison and Wayne A. Conaway, *Kiss, Bow, or Shake Hands*, 2nd ed. (Avon, MA: Adams Media, 2006), 24, 165, 283–84, 482–83; Chaney and Martin, *Intercultural Business Communication*, 207.

20. Chaney and Martin, *Intercultural Business Communication*, 208.

21. Morrison and Conaway, *Kiss, Bow, or Shake Hands*, 227.

22. Tracey Wilen, *International Business: A Basic Guide for Women* (n.p.: Xlibris Corporation, 2000), 109–10.

23. Joe Burris, "Overseas, We're Seen as Ugly Americans," *The Commercial Appeal*, October 22, 2006, M3.

24. C. Cellich, "Communication Skills for Negotiations," *International Trade Forum* 3: 22–28.

25. Marlene L. Rossman, *The International Businesswoman of the 1990s: A Guide to Success in the Global Marketplace* (New York: Praeger, 1990), 41.

26. Rossman, *The International Businesswoman of the 1990s*, xii.

27. Ibid., 140.

28. Axtell, Briggs, Corcoran, and Lamb, *Do's and Taboos Around the World for Women in Business*, 141–42.

29. Wilen, *International Business: A Basic Guide for Women*, 108–9.

30. Morrison and Conaway, *Kiss, Bow, or Shake Hands*, 68–69.

31. Robert T. Moran, Philip R. Harris, and Sarah V. Moran, *Managing Cultural Differences*, 7th ed. (Burlington, MA: Elsevier Butterworth-Heineman, 2007), 679–80.

32. Jeanette S. Martin and Lillian H. Chaney, *Passport to Success: The Essential Guide to Business Culture and Customs in America's Largest Trading Partners* (Westport, CT: Praeger, 2009), 60–61; Morrison and Conaway, *Kiss, Bow, or Shake Hands*, 76–77.

33. Chaney and Martin, *Intercultural Business Communication*, 173–74; Morrison and Conaway, *Kiss, Bow, or Shake Hands*, 94–99.

34. Morrison and Conaway, *Kiss, Bow, or Shake Hands*, 171–72.

35. Moran, Harris, and Moran, *Managing Cultural Differences*, 530–31.

36. Morrison and Conaway, *Kiss, Bow, or Shake Hands*, 174–76.

37. Leaptrott, *Rules of the Game: Global Business Protocol*, 26, 278–79.

38. Morrison and Conaway, *Kiss, Bow, or Shake Hands*, 183–85.

39. Martin and Chaney, *Passport to Success*, 158–60.

40. Morrison and Conaway, *Kiss, Bow, or Shake Hands*, 287.

41. Moran, Harris, and Moran, *Managing Cultural Differences*, 361.

42. Morrison and Conaway, *Kiss, Bow, or Shake Hands*, 318–19.

43. Ibid., 319.

44. Moran, Harris, and Moran, *Managing Cultural Differences*, 362.

45. Chaney and Martin, *Intercultural Business Communication*, 225; Morrison and Conaway, *Kiss, Bow, or Shake Hands*, 462–65.

46. Chaney and Martin, *Intercultural Business Communication*, 226; Morrison and Conaway, *Kiss, Bow, or Shake Hands*, 501–2.

47. Moran, Harris, and Moran, *Managing Cultural Differences*, 518–19; Morrison and Conaway, *Kiss, Bow, or Shake Hands*, 540–41.

48. Chaney and Martin, *Intercultural Business Communication*, 221; Morrison and Conaway, *Kiss, Bow, or Shake Hands*, 449–51.

INDEX

About the Authors

JEANETTE S. MARTIN is Professor at the University of Mississippi, School of Business. Having worked for such multinational corporations as Baxter International, Zenith, and Quaker Oats, she currently works with U.S. and foreign executives through International Professional Relations, Inc., to prepare them for foreign assignments. She has served as associate editor of the *Journal of Business Communication*, is the recipient of several national awards, and is the author of dozens of articles, book chapters, and conference presentations on intercultural business communication, education, emotional and cultural intelligence, and management information systems. She is coauthor, with Lillian H. Chaney, of *Passport to Success* (2008), *Global Business Etiquette* (2006), *The Essential Guide to Business Etiquette* (2007), and the textbook *Intercultural Business Communication*, 5th ed. (2011).

LILLIAN H. CHANEY is Professor of Management Emeritus at the University of Memphis. She has teaching experience at a South American university and has conducted training programs on communication, international and U.S. corporate etiquette, and business ethics for international companies, educational institutions, and government agencies. She is the author of over 100 articles and numerous conference presentations, with a specialty in intercultural business communication, and has received many teaching and research awards in the field. She is coauthor, with Jeanette S. Martin, of *Passport to Success* (2008), *Global Business Etiquette* (2006), *The Essential Guide to Business Etiquette* (2007), and the textbook, *Intercultural Business Communication*, 5th ed. (2011).